Portraits in Silicon

Portraits in Silicon

Robert Slater

The MIT Press
Cambridge, Massachusetts
London, England

This book was set in Bembo by Achorn Graphic Services and printed and bound by Halliday Lithograph in the United States of America.

Library of Congress Cataloging-in-Publication Data

Slater, Robert, 1943–
   Portraits in silicon.

   Bibliography: p.
   Includes index.
   1. Computer engineers—Biography. 2. Computers—History. 3. Computer industry—History. 4. Industrialists—Biography. I. Title.
TK7885.2.S57 1987   004′.092′2 [B]   87-2868
ISBN 0-262-19262-4

Contents

The Conceptualizers

The Early Inventors

The Early Entrepreneurs

Making the Computer Smaller and More Powerful

The Hardware Designers

The Software Specialists

Bringing the Computer to the Masses

Computer Science Pioneer

Preface

Computers were rare when I was growing up in the 1950s. My only contact with one occurred when my father, then a business executive, arranged for me to work part-time in his office. I was shown a large machine, perhaps four feet high and ten feet long, and told, "Your job is to feed the computer." I fed it with punch cards—for hours on end. My father's firm was one of the few to acquire these machines. Only a handful of businesses had been willing to take the leap into the world of computers that early in the game.

From that time—I was then thirteen or fourteen—until a few years ago I thought of using computers about as much as I did of flying a NASA rocket to the moon. As a professional writer for the past eighteen years, I knew of no other way to commit words to paper than by using a typewriter. My notion of progress was to discard my manual typewriter in favor of an electric one. Never once did it occur to me that there might be a different way to write news stories or books.

It was not until the spring of 1982 that I began to take an interest in computers. For only then were the once-distant, isolated "electronic brains" becoming cheap enough to seem accessible. Well, not exactly accessible, but within striking distance. To get one's hands on such a machine even then would have cost thousands of dollars.

As my acquaintance with computers grew, I naturally perused the growing number of books on the subject. It soon struck me that while literally thousands of books were being written about what type of computer to buy or how to use a certain computer, precious little had been written about the people behind the computers; it would be worthwhile, I thought, to know how they had become involved in their field, what were the special challenges that had led to their research, and how they went about their work. I wondered who all these people were, the designers, the entrepreneurs, the hardware people, and the software writers. It occurred to me that many new computer users and others too were probably as curious about them as I was. Hence, *Portraits in Silicon*.

As I got to know the subjects of this book, I began to sense that many of them had a strong desire to be understood better. After all, while they have explained their work to other scientists, researchers, insiders, to the world outside they remain hard to fathom, their work a mystery; their stories need telling. I knew that in limiting myself to thirty-four figures I would inevitably be asked why I had included this pioneer and left out that one. But by focusing on such a small number I felt that I could examine each person in depth: this, I believed, would be a contribution.

My goal was to interview as many as possible of the people I planned to profile. Here was a unique opportunity—a chance to talk to the founders of a field, to meet the people who were there in the earliest days and ask them what it was like. Of course, I wanted also to take a look at what the computer giants of the 1980s were doing. I decided to set out on a journey—for the most part around the United States, with one side trip to West Germany—to find the people I would write about, to see them in their homes and offices, to get to know them if I could. These were busy people, but they found a few hours for me. Almost every one I wanted to see, I did.

I began the journey in Silicon Valley, that array of buildings and brainpower located to the south of San Francisco. First I saw Gene Amdahl, in his office at Trilogy Limited, in Cupertino; then Adam Osborne, beginning all over at Paperback Software International in Berkeley. I saw William Shockley, at his home on the Stanford campus. This was followed by a visit to Intel, where I met Robert Noyce; I drove down to Monterey next to see Gary Kildall.

I then flew to Dallas, where Ross Perot ushered me into his magnificent office at Electronic Data Systems; the next morning I visited with Jack Kilby in the same city. Moving north to Minneapolis, I had a chance to talk with William Norris at Control Data

Corporation. A day or so later I was sitting in the home of John V. Atanasoff in Monrovia, Maryland, and later that day chatting with Grace Hopper in her Washington, D.C., apartment.

Dennis Ritchie and Ken Thompson invited me to meet with them at Bell Laboratories in Murray Hill, New Jersey, and so we talked as others around us kept right on inventing in front of their computer terminals. After a flight to Boston, I encountered Dan Bricklin at Software Arts (in a few months his company would be taken over by Lotus Development); the following day I headed for the snow-covered Dartmouth College campus to talk with John Kemeny and Tom Kurtz, as they were getting their new product, True BASIC, ready. Gordon Bell saw me at his home in Boston; and I caught up with Nolan Bushnell at a toy show in New York City. Konrad Zuse invited me to his home in Hunfeld, West Germany, not far from Frankfurt. I talked with Claude Shannon at his home in Winchester, Massachusetts, where after the interview he showed me some of his juggling and chess games. Finally, I visited with Jay Forrester in his office at MIT.

The perspective I have adopted in ordering the profiles is both historical and functional. The book begins with Charles Babbage, early in the nineteenth century, and carries forward to the 1980s, when the computer revolution was in full swing. It includes not only the key inventors of computer technology, but computer designers, builders of computer languages, software experts, and entrepreneurs as well. It would of course have been possible to cast a wider net, but these areas struck me as the most important to cover.

A word about the choice of people. Some have asked why I chose William Shockley, the co-inventor of the transistor, but omitted the inventor of the vacuum tube. Why did I select Apple founder Steve Jobs but cast aside his seeming entrepreneurial equal, Commodore's Jack Tramiel? Why did I give so much space to John V. Atanasoff? Or to Jack Kilby? Or to Dan Bricklin, but not to Lotus Development's Mitch Kapor? Why touch on Alan Turing and Claude Shannon, but leave out Marvin Minsky and John McCarthy? As I listened to the voices of the experts, I tried to understand their reasoning. Still the task was not easy. Those I consulted seemed to agree on twenty or twenty-five of the thirty-four figures on my list. The rest was open to debate.

I have also been asked what were the common elements I found in the people profiled. Perhaps the most significant strand running through their careers was a desire to expand the use of these machines, to place them in the public's hands rather than allow them to remain in isolated, secluded laboratories. In almost every case, too, there was a fascination with the unknown, a love of technology, science, gadgets, a great preoccupation with the future, and an eagerness to violate existing conventions. Above all else, however, I found a willingness to engage in just plain hard work, to put everything else aside, to focus on some far-off, elusive goal, and to persevere regardless of outside pressures or of how much time and energy it ultimately took. These were people who were willing to fail, who knew how to bounce back when they first missed the mark, only to miss the mark again and again.

If it contains a high degree of persistence, genius is also built in large measure on the work of those who came before. No honest man of research would pretend that his insights came out of thin air. So, too, in the inventions of these computer pioneers there was much standing on the shoulders of previous individuals. There are fascinating links between Grace Hopper and John Backus, and between Backus and John Kemeny and Tom Kurtz. As significant a breakthrough as the transistor was, it set off a new search for the integrated circuit, and thus there was a clear line of continuity in the work of William Shockley, Robert Noyce, and Jack Kilby. Many stood on the shoulders of Ted Hoff, including Nolan Bushnell and Steve Jobs. In a broader sense, all of these portraits are interrelated: their subjects all helped to build a revolution that is still far from over.

Acknowledgments

As I began my research on the pioneers and developers of the computer revolution, I wondered whether an outsider would be welcomed by this unique fraternity of genius and zeal. No one could possibly know as much as these wizards about their special areas of expertise. Anyone attempting to decipher their minds and their work would quickly reveal his own ignorance. To my surprise I found in my meetings with my subjects a willingness to share the excitement and joy of their work. I sensed that most of them thought that the public understands far too little about their achievements, that this book was an opportunity to open the window a little wider into their world.

Many people helped bring this book to its final form. First and foremost I want to thank the subjects of these portraits, who took the time for interviews and follow-up exchanges. They invited me into their offices, laboratories, and homes; they made available to me a wealth of literature about their work and showed patience and tolerance in handling my many questions. They are (in order of my interviews with them) Gene Amdahl, William Shockley, Adam Osborne, Ted Hoff, Donald Knuth, John Backus, Robert Noyce, Gary Kildall, H. Ross Perot, Jack Kilby, William Norris, John V. Atanasoff, Grace Hopper, Dennis Ritchie, Ken Thompson, Dan Bricklin, John Kemeny, Thomas Kurtz, Gordon Bell, Nolan Bushnell, Konrad Zuse, Claude Shannon, and Jay Forrester.

I also wish to express my gratitude to Mrs. John Mauchly, Gary Udine, Barbara Millard, Don McConnell, Al Alcorn, Sylvia

Gardner, Michael Moritz, Joseph T. Palmitessa, Dov Frohman, Harvey S. Gellman, Michael Jacobs, Senator Frank Lautenberg, Henry Taub, Robert Bouzon, Clark A. Elliott, Professor Bernard A. Galler, Tina Bonetti, Sharon Crowder, and Bruce Huie.

Special thanks are due to a number of others who took an interest in this project and through their expertise and friendship were a continuing source of aid and inspiration. Larry Pfeffer, a major figure in the computer field in Israel, first encouraged me to write this book and was there to answer frequent questions. Gwen Bell, the gracious and talented director of the Boston Computer Museum, made valuable contributions. Professor I. Bernard Cohen offered insights into the personality of Howard Aiken. And Arnold Goldman shared his knowledge of the computer industry from the 1950s and 1960s with me.

As in my previous book-writing endeavors, my editors and colleagues at *Time* magazine, both in New York and at the Jerusalem bureau, eased the path to publication. My thanks go to Jean Max, who contributed to this project in so many ways. Also to Gloria Olson for assisting in the crucial technical details of turning out a manuscript; to David Rubinger, *Time*'s photographer in Israel, for providing important technical assistance; and to Dorothy Resnik for organizing taped material used in this book.

A number of people agreed to read part or all of the manuscript, commenting upon and recommending ways of improving it. I wish to thank Dov Frohman, Marlin Levin, Dulcy Liebler, Zvi Ofer, and Larry Pfeffer for their time and advice.

M. R. Williams, Professor of Computer Science at the University of Calgary, Canada, must be singled out for his unique contribution. It was he who explained to me the complex technological details that are part of each profile. His patience and dedication have added immeasurably to this book. I cannot thank him enough.

Finally, a word about my family. They are by now used to my absorption in the writing of a book, but the demands on their patience were no less than in the past. I am grateful to them for making this project such a pleasant experience. My wife, Elinor, as with my previous books, critiqued my rough drafts with great care. Her editing and general suggestions had a great deal to do with the final shape of this book. She was a true partner in this endeavor. I thank her and dedicate the book to her.

The Conceptualizers

Charles Babbage

Grandfather of the Computer Pioneers

There is a tantalizing "if only" attached to the career of Charles Babbage. If only he had gone a bit farther, if only he had built the wonderful machines he envisioned. What might have been? Howard Aiken, who built some of the first computers, once remarked that had Babbage lived seventy-five years later, that nineteenth-century inventor might have stolen his thunder. Such speculation is always somewhat beside the point; yet there is something terribly incongruous about Charles Babbage—he was so far-sighted, so incredibly ahead of his time.

Mr. Babbage lived during a period whose existing technology made it difficult for a computer designer to implement his ideas. Hence, Babbage never built a computer. For that invention the world had to wait some seventy years after his death. Still, so precisely on target was his outline of a computer that Babbage is inextricably woven into the fabric of early computer history. He is justifiably called the first computer pioneer.

If it was true that nineteenth-century machinery was incapable of the precision required to build Babbage's machines, it was equally the case that he was obsessed by a sense of perfection that left him unable to finish one project before starting another. Hence, some blame Babbage himself as much as the lack of technology for his stopping at the water's edge of actually constructing a digital computer. Forgotten for decades after his death in 1871, Babbage achieved recognition for his work only with the dawn of the computer age in the 1940s.

Were he to visit our era, he would be startled to find computers so widely used. And yet, should he see the inside of any standard computer his shock would diminish. Though he might be taken aback by the use of electronic technology, the basic concepts of the central processing unit and memory would be strikingly familiar.

Babbage was a man possessed of one of the great inventive minds of the nineteenth century. He did so many things, and did them so exceedingly well. He was mathematician, engineer, and most of all, computer designer. It was as if there were ten different minds in that one body. In 1822 he designed his Difference Engine, regarded by some as the first automatic calculating device. Just over a decade later, in 1834, he began designing his Analytical Engine. Had something concrete emerged, it might well have been the first general-purpose computer. But no actual machine was built, and therefore his claim to fame rests largely on his elaborate drawings. Nevertheless, Charles Babbage has earned the distinction of being the first to conceptualize the computer. Nearly all of the principles on which today's computers rest derive from this long-overlooked nineteenth-century scientist. Babbage's Analytical Engine was meant to solve all mathematical problems, not only those using differences (as with the more limited Difference Engine). Most significantly, the Engine was also meant to have a number of features—such as the equivalents of branching, subroutines, and loops—that would have made it programmable. Punch cards, a medium that eventually found its way into computers, were to be used to transmit instructions.

Babbage was born on December 26, 1791, in what is now the borough of Southwark, London. He was a fragile, sickly child with an intense curiosity and an imaginative mind. Given a toy, he would break it apart to learn how it was constructed. He once built two hinged boards to enable him to walk on water. Babbage showed early an inclination toward mathematics, perhaps inherited from his banker father. Another childhood enthusiasm was for the supernatural. On one occasion he tried to contact the devil by pricking a finger to get a drop of blood and then reciting the Lord's Prayer backwards; he was disappointed to find that the devil didn't appear. His interest in the occult continued. He made an agreement with a childhood acquaintance that whoever died first would appear to the surviving member of the pact. When the friend died at age eighteen,

Babbage stayed up an entire night to await the apparition—only to discover that his friend had not lived up to his part of the deal. While at college Babbage formed a ghost club to gather information on supernatural phenomena.

In October 1810 Babbage entered Trinity College, Cambridge, where he studied mathematics and chemistry. His mathematics tutors proved a disappointment after Babbage decided that his knowledge surpassed theirs. The mathematics of Newton, two hundred years dead, still held sway at Cambridge, despite the new ideas circulating in Europe. Babbage and some friends founded a club called the Analytical Society, promising each other to do their best to leave the world wiser than they found it. The Society helped to revive the study of mathematics in England by stressing the abstract nature of algebra and by trying to import Continental developments.

Babbage considered entering the church, but rejected the option on discovering there was no money in it. He thought of mining as a potentially lucrative venture, but gave that up too. On July 2, 1814, he married Georgiana Whitmore. Between 1815 and 1820 Babbage involved himself largely in mathematics. He studied algebra and wrote papers on the theory of functions. Because he was a liberal during a period of Tory ascendancy, Babbage was unable to secure the patronage that would provide a paid position. Some professorships fell vacant, but his efforts to obtain one were unsuccessful. Georgiana Babbage gave birth to eight children in thirteen years; three sons survived into adulthood. Not close to his children, Babbage insisted that his wife care for them so that he could be free to pursue his interests.

Eclectic as he was dedicated, Babbage engaged in a continuing search to make life more efficient. He thought of a cheaper way for the post office to ship parcels. He plunged to the ocean depths in a diving bell to study submarine navigation. His inquisitive mind led him to test whether it was possible for man to walk on water—the answer was no; he also walked into an oven once to determine what the effect of brief exposure to a temperature 256 degrees Fahrenheit would be. Though he found the effect negligible, he left quickly.

He was a prolific author, publishing eighty books and papers in fields as diverse as mathematics and theology, astronomy and government. His *On the Economy of Machinery and Manufacturers,* written in 1832, has been called the pioneering effort in operations research. The book's main thesis is that industry requires a scientific approach. His gift for statistics encouraged him, perhaps only in jest, to calculate the odds on Biblical miracles: rising from the dead was put at no more than one in ten to the twelfth power! Apart from being the undeniable grandfather of the modern computer, Babbage was a major inventor. One invention was the "occulting" lighthouse, in which the light flashes on and off; the system is employed today around the world. Another was the ophthalmoscope, which physicians still use to examine the interior of the eye. Babbage devised instrumented railway cars used by British trainmen to measure stress while the train moved along the rails. It is owing to Babbage that British railroads have wide-gauge rails. He was also the outstanding cryptologist of his day, utilizing mathematical techniques to break ciphers—an activity that gave him much enjoyment.

If he had one dominant trait, it was a yearning for perfection. He moved from task to task with a persistence that produced flashes of brilliance. But he was too impatient to permit himself the time to translate those flashes into concrete reality. Always, however, he was exacting. After reading Tennyson's lines in *The Vision of Sin,* "Every minute dies a man / Every minute one is born," he wrote the poet, "It must be manifest that if this were true, the population would be at a standstill." He proposed this change: "Every moment dies a man / And one and a sixteenth is born." Tennyson appears to have taken the point, for he altered the lines to "Every moment dies a man / Every moment one is born."

Charles Babbage's most significant mark—though recognition of this came long after his death—was made in the field of mechanical calculating. The perfectionist Babbage placed great value on accuracy, and saw a need to improve the mechanical calculators of his day. Primitive and hand-operated, these were not only slow but also prone to error. Because of carelessness errors abounded in the astronomical charts and navigational tables, errors that led tragically to shipwrecks. Babbage tried to come up with a machine that could both compute and set type for a set of mathematical tables, thus avoiding the errors that emerged between the manuscript copy and the printed version.

One evening, while looking over a table of logarithms in the Analytical Society room at Cambridge, Babbage, half-asleep, was approached by another member who asked him what he was dreaming about. Looking up, Babbage replied that he had been thinking that it might be possible to find a way to calculate all the tables before him by machinery. This brief, rather undramatic conversation marked a turning point in early computer history.

Babbage resolved to work full-time toward his goal of automating the calculation of mathematical tables. By 1822 he had designed what he called the Difference Engine, a small device for calculating such tables—most importantly those for navigation, the prime need of the time—by using differences.

Babbage built a small working model. It could handle six-figure numbers and evaluate any function that had a constant second difference. Then on June 14, 1822, appearing before the Royal Astronomical Society, he proposed the construction of a large, full-scale Difference Engine, the first automatic calculating device. His paper to the Society, entitled "Observations on the Application of Machinery to the Computation of Mathematical Tables," was well received. "The whole of arithmetic now appeared within the grasp of mechanism," he later wrote. This paper was the very first on mechanical computing. Babbage conceived of a machine that could do numerous calculations automatically. Once the machine was started, the operator would be relegated to the sidelines as a mere observer. As Babbage proclaimed in a letter to Royal Society president Sir Humphry Davy, people might now be spared "the intolerable labor and fatiguing monotony" of repeated and similar mathematical calculations; instead, machines employing "gravity or any other moving power" could perform these "lowest occupations of the human intellect."

The Difference Engine would be powered by falling weights, elevated by a steam engine. One version of Babbage's Difference Engine would print numbers to eighteen figures and keep twenty figures internally. There would be no more typographical errors because the tables would be printed directly from the machine's metal plates.

By July 1823 Babbage had won the agreement of the chancellor of the exchequer to provide him with £1,500, substantially less than what he wanted but nonetheless a handsome sum. It was enough to encourage Babbage to believe that he had an official patron for as long as required, a mistaken impression on his part. The Difference

Engine was the largest government-financed project of its time, presumably because government officials were intrigued by the promise of more accurate navigational and artillery tables. Babbage eventually put up between £3,000 and £5,000 from his own pocket on the assumption that in time the government would reimburse him. He hired England's outstanding toolmaker, Joseph Clement, who in turn took on the country's best laborers.

Babbage hoped to have a full-scale working machine in two or three years, but he soon discovered that this was overly optimistic. It proved far more difficult than anticipated to put together the tools that would enable him to build the machine's parts. He spent the next few years designing parts for the Difference Engine, and then designing and trying to build the machinery that would make those parts. It was a tedious, frustrating procedure that, although it advanced British toolmaking, did not produce the desired results.

Babbage seemed at times his own greatest enemy. His obsession with perfection led him to order numerous changes in drawings. The laborers would then have to go back to the beginning and devise new tools, lengthening the project. His young son Charles died in June 1827, his wife in August of the same year. Babbage turned the care of his surviving children over to his mother. He never remarried. Within six months of his namesake's death, Babbage's father and another of his children died. Babbage spent the next year abroad.

Though he inherited £100,000 from his father and received an additional £1,500 from the government, finances continued to plague Babbage. He invested money of his own, and friends provided £6,000. Nevertheless, twenty years after he had conceived of the Difference Engine, the machine remained unfinished, and Babbage and the British government were bogged down in misunderstandings over who owned the invention.

At one point, progress in making the Difference Engine was slowed when Babbage and his toolmaker Joseph Clement could not get along. Clement had always found Babbage difficult to work with, but a further problem arose when Babbage decided to establish a workshop close to his home. (Clement's workshop was four miles away.) When Babbage asked Clement to move himself, his tools, and his drawings to the new workshop, the latter balked. He was not pleased at the prospect of having to divide his time and energy between two business addresses. Babbage was in a quandary. He had no wish to continue to pay Clement out of his own pocket, but he knew that to cut him loose would mean the project would come to a halt. Babbage turned frugal, and so all work on the Difference Engine stopped in 1833.

Around this time, a Swedish technical editor named George Scheutz, having read of the device in the *Edinburgh Review,* began to attempt the building of a Babbage-like Difference Engine. He was soon joined in the project by his engineer son Edvard. Failing to win support from the Swedish government, the two men proceeded on their own, by 1840 producing a small machine that could operate to the first order of difference. Over the next few years they expanded the machine to three orders of difference and included a printing feature. By 1853 they had their Tabulating Machine, as they called it. It could operate to the fourth order of difference, process fifteen-digit numbers, and print results out. It calculated far faster than any human being, and provided the first real evidence that machines could engage in number crunching.

In 1854 the Scheutzes showed their invention to the Royal Society of London, getting warm support from Charles Babbage himself. At the Great Exhibition in Paris the next year the Tabulating Machine won a gold medal, due partly to Babbage's lobbying efforts. Armed with the gold medal, the Scheutzes were able to sell the machine for $5,000 to Dr. Benjamin Gould, the director of the Dudley Observatory in Albany, New York. Dr. Gould used it to calculate a set of tables dealing with the orbit of the planet Mars. Few understood Dr. Gould or the machine. In 1859 he was fired! The Tabulating Machine was given to the Smithsonian Institution. A copy of the device was built in the late 1850s by the British Register General, the collector and publisher of vital statistics. The Register General used it to create a new set of lifetime, annuity, and premium tables for the insurance industry, and in general to make its own operations more efficient. Although the Scheutz device did not function properly at all times, and was far less ambitious than Babbage's proposed Difference Engine, the existence of this simpler version suggests that lack of technology might not have been the sole cause of Babbage's failure to build his machines.

Deprived of his tools and drawings—Clement had appropriated these after their dispute in 1833—Babbage decided to explore the design of a completely different machine, one that would be easier to build, far more versatile, and faster than the Difference Engine. He began in 1834, and during the next two years he conceived of the major features of the modern computer. Before the Difference Engine was even built, Babbage had realized its limitations. Fundamentally a special-purpose calculator, it simply whetted his appetite to reach the full potential of automatic calculating machinery. To be truly beneficial, a computer had to be general-purpose, capable of performing any arithmetical or logical operation. Babbage called this more sophisticated device the Analytical Engine. Had he succeeded in building one, it would have been the first general-purpose computer. Equally important, the Analytical Engine was meant to be programmable; that is, its operating instructions were alterable. Babbage wrote that he was astonished at the power he had been able to give to the machine, forgetting that he had yet to construct it. His biographer Anthony Hyman has called the Analytical Engine one of the most important intellectual achievements in history.

What has proved so astonishing about Babbage's concepts is their resemblance to those of modern computers. Instructions were to be entered into the Analytical Engine by punch cards, then kept in a store, essentially the memory of a modern computer. The idea of the punch card was adopted from the then-revolutionary Jacquard weaving loom, which used cards with holes to control automatically those threads that were to be passed over or under a moving shuttle. Babbage used the patterns of holes to represent mathematical commands rather than the position of threads. Though he came close, Babbage fell short of envisaging the entire nature of a modern computer. For one thing, he thought only of mechanical devices; electricity apparently never occurred to him. He also did not imagine instructions having both an operation and an address part.

Babbage considered a variety of scales of notation but decided upon the decimal for the Analytical Engine. There was a store (the memory) where the numbers were held. He planned to store the numbers on wheels with ten distinguishable positions. The numbers were then to be transferred by a system of racks to a central mill. The control of the entire process was to be handled via a number of punched cards that would specify the operation and provide the address of the operand in the store. Once the instructions were placed on operation cards, a device corresponding to the central processing unit of a modern computer would take the information and perform operations on it. One arithmetical operation would have been completed per second. The results would then be sent to the store. Final results would be either printed out or set in type— both steps being done automatically.

Babbage intended to have a storage capacity for one thousand numbers of fifty decimal digits. After researching many ideas for performing the four operations of arithmetic, he invented the notion of anticipatory carry. This was far faster than carrying successively from one stage to another. Babbage was also conscious of hoarding carry, by which whole series of additions could be performed with a single carrying operation at the end. The Analytical Engine would have required six steam engines to power, making a large racket.

Contemporaries of Charles Babbage might not have learned of the inventor's accomplishments had it not been for the efforts of Ada, Countess of Lovelace, the daughter of the poet Lord Byron. Babbage first met her at a party he gave on June 5, 1833. She was then seventeen years old. Nine years later in Italy, an Italian military engineer, Luigi Federico Menabrea, described the Analytical Engine's mathematical principles in a paper. In 1843 Ada Lovelace, by then an enthusiastic amateur mathematician, produced an English translation of Menabrea's paper, along with extensive notes, providing England with the first glimpse of Babbage's achievements in the computer field. These notes rank as one of the major documents in computer history. Ada wrote, "We may say most aptly that the Analytical Engine weaves algebraical patterns just as the Jacquard loom weaves flowers and leaves." For Babbage, Ada and her husband, the Earl of Lovelace, became lifelong friends, and Ada became Babbage's public advocate.

Only at the age of seventy-one was Babbage prepared to publicize any of his ideas. His first Difference Engine went on display at London's Science Museum, and Babbage was on hand to explain its workings. Visitors to his home in Babbage's later years found the inventor vigorous and eager to show off his workroom.

On the evening of October 18, 1871, two months before his eightieth birthday, Charles Babbage died. Only a few mourners attended his funeral, one sign of the lack of interest his contemporaries had shown his work.

Alan Turing

Can a Machine Be Made to Think?

2

The modern computer was built with the help of Alan Turing's pencil and paper. Not with metal or wiring, just an ordinary pencil and paper. When he wrote his famous paper in 1936, sixty-five years after the death of Charles Babbage, England's Turing could not have imagined that he would launch the computer age. But he did just that. He was no engineer, but worked only with his mind, a mathematician trying to solve complex, highly abstract problems.

Could someone build a machine that worked like the brain? Turing thought it shouldn't take more than fifty years to do so. By the 1980s, roughly the time Turing had predicted, the field of artificial intelligence was filled with researchers trying to find out more about learning and how the brain works. Their most useful tool has been the computer, the same device Alan Turing conjured up in the 1930s. He is rightly held to be one of the great early theoreticians in computer history.

In the 1940s Turing designed what are considered the first operational electronic digital computers. Special-purpose machines, they were soon eclipsed by Mauchly and Eckert's much faster ENIAC and Zuse's Z series of computers, a general-purpose device. Still, thanks to Turing, England took a giant step forward in computer development.

Alan Mathison Turing was born in Paddington, England, on June 23, 1912. His father's career in the Indian civil service kept parents and children apart during most of Turing's childhood. A retired military couple stood in loco parentis while young Alan and his elder brother attended elementary school. By the time Alan was three, his mother had spotted his brain power, first manifested in an impressive ability to remember new words. By age eight, he had developed an obvious interest in science; he was soon performing experiments in a basement laboratory. He wrote his mother, "I always seem to want to make things from the thing that is commonest in nature and with the least waste of energy."

Turing entered Sherborne School, sixty miles west of Southampton, at age thirteen. His teachers recalled that he was untidy, but they were also impressed with his interests in chemistry, astronomy, radio, and ciphers. From science he made the logical step into the world of mathematics. At fourteen he was able to conceive of terms in calculus without having studied the subject thoroughly. He also had an incredible ability to calculate in his head. It was during his early teens, too, that Turing developed a taste for competitive running.

After twice failing the scholarship exam for Trinity College, Cambridge, Turing won a scholarship to read mathematics at King's College, Cambridge. Schoolmates remembered him as most unconventional. One example: he rode his bicycle with an alarm clock tied to his waist so that he could time his own races. He had an active social life, pursued rowing, long-distance running, and playing the violin, though he never became proficient at the instrument.

Turing graduated in June 1934 and became a research student in mathematics. He spent the academic year 1936–1937 in the United States, studying at Princeton University. "The mathematics department here," he wrote home, "comes fully up to expectations. There is a great number of the most distinguished mathematicians here. J. v. Neumann, Weyl, Courant, Hardy, Einstein, Lefschetz, as well as hosts of smaller fry." In October of 1936 he became a research student at the Institute for Advanced Study in Princeton.

Turing made few friends, in part because he befriended only those his intellectual equal and in part because his mannerisms and eccentricities put people off. He had a stammer and a nervous laugh that made conversation with him nearly impossible. He was a sloppy dresser and often neglected to shave for fear of cutting himself—he would faint at the sight of blood. When he rode around on his bicycle he would put on a gas mask in an attempt to control his acute bouts of hay fever. Machines and gadgets entranced him.

When the chain of his bicycle developed a habit of falling off after a certain number of revolutions, he rigged up a mechanical counter that would keep count of the revolutions and so warn him in time to secure the chain.

It was at this time that Turing conceptualized the remarkable device called the Turing Machine, describing it in his landmark 1936 paper "On Computable Numbers, with an Application to the Entscheidungsproblem," published in the *Proceedings of the London Mathematical Society*. This ranks as one of computer science's most important early documents. Turing's place in the field of mathematical logic was now assured, as was his niche in computer history. He wrote the paper to refute David Hilbert, the well-known German mathematician, who believed that any mathematical problem could be solved. Hilbert sought a process for determining the truth of any mathematical theorem; in 1928 he defined this process as an activity that could be performed by an automatic machine.

Trying to prove Hilbert wrong, Turing put the question whether it was possible to prove any mathematical theorem true. He assumed that only a mechanical device would enable someone to carry out such an operation. But what kind of machine? Turing thought it would have to perform like all other machines once given the appropriate algorithm, the coded instructions—the program! Turing was in fact dreaming up a computer.

In his paper Turing concluded that some types of mathematical problems simply could not be solved by using automatic computers. Computing—so Turing argued—could be done only if the problem was restated in a proper algorithm. However, various types of mathematical and logical problems could not be converted to algorithms. For instance, some "real numbers" could not be computed by mechanical means. Furthermore, there was no method for indicating which of the numbers were or were not computable. Therefore, it was impossible to program them into an automatic computer, even if one had existed at the time. Thus, Turing had proved Hilbert wrong: not all mathematical theorems could be proven.

In the process Turing imagined what an automatic computer might be like, and herein lay a major contribution in computer history. He described a machine that would imitate the behavior of any other machine when supplied with the necessary instructions on punched paper tape. He imagined machines that would in some ways resemble typewriters. The paper would take the form of a tape, marked off into unit squares so that just one symbol could be written on any one square. The machine would be able to "read," or, as Turing put it, to "scan" the square of tape upon which it rested. Hence, the machine could not only write symbols but also erase them.

Turing spent the summer of 1937 in England and then returned to Princeton on a Proctor Fellowship, earning his doctorate there in May 1938, a month short of turning twenty-six. His thesis was entitled "System of Logic Based on Ordinals." John von Neumann, the mathematician and computer builder, invited him to be his assistant at the Institute for Advanced Study, but Turing decided to return to England in the summer of 1938 and take up a fellowship he had been offered at King's College, Cambridge. Though they did not work together, von Neumann took a strong interest in Turing's ideas and incorporated some of them in his own work.

After he returned to England, Turing found his talents soon put to use. In 1938 a young Polish engineer named Richard Lewinski came upon a secret signaling device while working in a German factory. After he was fired because he was Jewish, Lewinski contacted the English and offered to sell them information about this device—a modified version of the Enigma, a machine the Germans had been manufacturing and selling. This new version was being produced by the German military for its own use. Just back from Princeton, Turing was instructed to travel to Warsaw to interrogate Lewinski. Once he was smuggled to Paris, Lewinski reconstructed the machine from memory.

The Enigma, an electromechanical machine, using two electric typewriters, coded and decoded messages and enabled the Germans to communicate secretly between military headquarters and field units, on land and at sea. Convenient to use, the Enigma was portable—it could be set up on the battlefield. The Germans could not conceive of anyone breaking the cipher, so when the British did so, spies or traitors were blamed.

With the outbreak of war in the fall of 1939 Turing was dispatched to the Department of Communications in the Foreign Office. From then on his whereabouts became secret. One of the initial ten academics to be recruited for cryptoanalysis, Turing was assigned to the Government Code and Cypher School in Bletchley Park, an old manor house halfway between Cambridge and Oxford.

At first he was involved in the building of the so-called Bombes, the earliest machines to decipher Enigma. The loud clicking noise they made gave them their name. Turing's main accomplishment came thereafter, when he supervised the effort to build Colossus, the first operational electronic computer, as part of the ULTRA project. He hoped to use high-speed automatic transposition of ciphered characters and in this way to locate their underlying patterns. There would eventually be ten models in the Colossus series, the first of which became operational in December 1943— two years before ENIAC, the electronic digital computer built at the University of Pennsylvania. Decidedly limited, these special-purpose machines had the sole function of cracking ciphers. Still, they were the first major computers to employ vacuum tubes— 2,400 in each machine—as digital on-off switches.

Information could be entered into Colossus using paper tape at the remarkably fast rate of 5,000 characters per second. Colossus could count, compare, and do simple arithmetic. It had four electronic panels along with five optical punched-tape readers. Punched tape carrying messages was put into a reader. Colossus then compared the messages with Enigma codes, going through the tape over and over until it discovered a match. It would then print out the results. Like ENIAC, Colossus had no internal memory. Because the precise tasks that Colossus performed are still kept secret, its accomplishments remain the subject of conjecture. One story has it helping the British obtain advance information about German plans to bomb Coventry. Had this information been exploited, had civil defense measures been taken, many lives might have been saved. But, so the story goes, British Prime Minister Winston Churchill would not permit the civil defense measures to be implemented for fear that the Germans would learn that Colossus had broken their codes.

There is reason to believe that ten Colossus computers were performing by the end of the war; each one was an improvement over its predecessor. Again, a veil of secrecy hangs over what happened to these devices. The fact that some British RAF radio technicians were moved to northern Iran after the war, with the task of intercepting coded Russian radio messages, has led to the assumption that some Colossus computers were used in code-breaking efforts through the late 1940s.

At one stage during the fighting, Turing became convinced that the Germans would invade England, and he took precautions against such a prospect. He converted all of his money into silver bars, then transported those bars in a baby carriage to the woods near Bletchley Park, where he buried his treasure in two different places. The precaution proved ill-fated: not only did he hurt his back in trying to hide his financial reserves; after the war he could not remember the hiding places!

Following World War II, Turing wanted to find out if his 1936 theory could actually work. Could he build his own computer? An offer to develop the ACE—the Automatic Computing Engine—came in June 1945 from the newly formed Mathematics Division of the National Physical Laboratory (NPL), England's largest research agency, at Teddington. Turing's plan for the ACE appeared promising; later some compared it in importance to parallel American efforts. At first, Turing enjoyed Teddington. He renewed his interest in running. In 1947 he came in fifth in the Amateur Athletic Association Marathon Championship, and he thought of training for the Olympic trials. But he injured his hip and had to abandon competitive running, although continuing to run for recreation.

Work on the ACE went slowly, too slowly for Turing. The computer was meant to have a memory of 204,800 bits and to operate at a million pulses a second—that would have made it ten times faster than ENIAC. In February 1946 Turing came up with the entire design for an electronic stored-program computer. But facilities at NPL were too small to build a large machine. Other places were tried, among them the post office. When other computer specialists were asked for help, they turned the NPL down on the grounds that they liked neither Turing's machine nor Turing. He now wanted to leave Teddington and sought permission to take a year's sabbatical at King's College, Cambridge. In May 1948, furious that not even one component of the ACE had been assembled, Turing resigned from the NPL. The ACE took five years to complete, and when it was finished in May 1950, it was merely a scaled-down version of the original one planned. By that time Turing had gone his own way.

Only after the war did colleagues discover that Alan Turing was a homosexual. Some were relieved that the discovery was made so late. Turing's statistical clerk at Bletchley, I. J. Good, believed that had Turing's homosexuality been known, he might not have obtained his wartime clearance to uncover Enigma's mysteries—and that would have been a genuine loss for England. While it may be difficult to believe that England would have deprived its war effort of a leading scientist on these grounds alone, it can be imagined that the British government might have felt exceedingly uncomfortable in the knowledge that one of its cryptographers was a candidate for blackmail—for homosexuality was at that time a criminal offense.

In 1950 Turing produced another classic paper, "Computing Machinery and Intelligence." In that work, which appeared in the journal *Mind,* he posited an operative definition of intelligence and thinking. If someone could not distinguish between a computer and a human being on the basis of their answers to the same questions, then the computer could be said to be thinking.

Through his article Turing established the basis for the field of artificial intelligence. He began by asserting: "I propose to consider the question 'Can machines think?' " To attempt an answer, Turing described the "Imitation Game," which would in time be called the "Turing test." Three people play the game, a man, a woman, and an interrogator of either gender separated from the first two. The interrogator's task is to question the persons in the other room in order to find out which is the man and which is the woman—relying only upon the answers they give. The probe is done using a teletype, so that no clues to identity are given other than those revealed in the words of the answers themselves.

Turing then supplied a new object of the game, removing one of the players and replacing him or her with a machine. Now the interrogator was to discover which one was the human being and which one the machine. In effect, Turing put forth the imitation game as a way of deciding whether a machine is intelligent. Turing thought that within fifty years computers could be programmed to play the imitation game so effectively that after a five-minute question period the interrogator would have no more than a seventy-percent chance of making the proper identification. In other words, a machine would be capable of "thinking." One important step toward this goal came in the 1980s: the increasing application of "expert systems," computer programs that appear to permit a computer to "learn" proper responses on the basis of continuously updated information.

Turing's personal life deteriorated in the early 1950s. He became friendly with an unemployed youth on Christmas Day, 1951, and the two had an affair. Then early in 1952 Turing's home at Wilmslow, ten miles south of Manchester, was burgled by his lover's friend. Turing knew the name of the culprit but did not reveal it when he reported the break-in to the police; eventually they pieced together the whole story and charged Turing with gross indecency. Turing was tried and convicted, placed on probation for a year, and ordered to take the female hormone estrogen to reduce his sexual drive. The treatment was in lieu of serving a year in jail. That drug had the effect of making him impotent and enlarging his breasts.

Just over two years after the trial, on June 7, 1954, Turing killed himself by eating an apple that contained cyanide. Turing had made the chemical himself as part of his desert-island game: he would try to see how many chemicals he could manufacture from household substances by utilizing only homemade materials. His mother, Sara Turing, pointed out afterward that his work had been going well, that he had no special financial problems, and that his behavior prior to his death was normal. Believing his death to be accidental, she tried to have it officially regarded as such, but to no avail. Turing's life, so vital to computer history, thus ended in a cloud of mystery.

John von Neumann

A Name Synonymous with Computers

3

Before he turned his gifted mind to computers, John von Neumann had become one of the world's foremost mathematicians. Before he devoted his energies to machines that would eventually bear his name, von Neumann had hit upon the way to detonate the atomic bomb. Of all the computer pioneers and developers profiled in this book, none so singularly seems to warrant being called a genius as John von Neumann. In the 1940s he designed what remained the basic scheme of the computer four decades later. While there is debate over who invented the stored-program computer, von Neumann is generally credited with bringing the idea to the public's attention. More than anyone else, von Neumann stimulated public interest in the arcane, often frightening subject of computers. He sensed their potential for the sciences, and in speaking out enthusiastically about that potential, acquired a reputation as the leading force behind the dawning of the computer age.

John von Neumann was born in Budapest on December 28, 1903. He came out of an upper-class Hungarian background that produced other giants in mathematics and physics. His father, a Jewish banker named Max Neumann, earned sufficient Hapsburg respect to add the honorific "Margattai" to his family name (later changed, by John, to "von"). Janos, as the boy was named, was the eldest of three sons.

Even as a small child, Janos loved mathematics and constantly sought to adapt its logic to the world at large, Once, when he saw his mother look up from her crocheting to stare into space contemplatively, he asked her, "What are you calculating?" Long walks with childhood friend Eugene Wigner turned into discussions of set theory or number theory. His unusual intelligence was not limited to mathematics, however; from the age of six he joked with his father in classical Greek. A private tutor was hired for the boy when he was ten, after a teacher suggested to his father that Janos's special gifts be nurtured. The youngster made sure to mix with others his age, though, in order not to appear standoffish. He need not have been concerned. His superior intelligence was respected. From 1911 to 1916 he attended the Lutheran gymnasium in Budapest, becoming its best mathematician.

The turmoil of World War I had its impact on the von Neumanns. When the Communist regime of Bela Kun took power in 1919, banks were expropriated, leaving Max von Neumann little choice but to flee with his family to their home in Venice. They remained there four months, returning to Budapest in August 1919, two months after the fall of Kun. The episode turned Janos into a lifelong anti-Communist.

Though he enrolled in the University of Budapest in 1921, von Neumann acquired the bulk of his education at other institutions. Most of his time, especially from 1921 to 1923, was spent at the University of Berlin. There he could study with the mathematician Erhard Schmidt and listen to lectures by Albert Einstein. Von Neumann went on to the Swiss Federal Institute of Technology in Zurich, where he received a diploma in chemical engineering in 1925. A year later, on March 12, 1926, at age twenty-two, he obtained his doctorate summa cum laude in mathematics from the University of Budapest. He had minors in experimental physics and chemistry. Studying at the University of Göttingen in 1926 and 1927 as a Rockefeller Fellow, von Neumann mixed with some of the most superb minds in mathematics. There he became friendly with fellow student J. Robert Oppenheimer.

Between 1927 and 1930 von Neumann was a lecturer in mathematics at the University of Berlin. Rarely had one so young held that post. During his first year there he published five papers. Three of them, by setting out a mathematical framework for quantum theory, were of great importance for that field. A fourth paper was a pioneering effort in game theory. The fifth dealt with the link between formal logic systems and the limits of mathematics. By the

1930s von Neumann was recognized as one of the world's leading mathematicians. He spent the spring of 1929 in Hamburg, and it was then that he was invited to become a visiting lecturer at Princeton University—a turning point for his career.

Von Neumann arrived in the United States in 1930. After lecturing on quantum statistics for a year at Princeton, he was made a tenured professor in 1931. Mathematical hydrodynamics was the subject of his next year of lectures. In 1933, when the Institute for Advanced Study was founded at Princeton, von Neumann became one of the original six professors of its School of Mathematics. It was a post he would hold for the rest of his life. Von Neumann married Marietta Kovesi on January 1, 1930; they had one daughter, Marina, in 1935; the marriage ended in 1937. Von Neumann became a naturalized American citizen that year. On December 18, 1938, he married Klara Dan, who later became a programmer at the Los Alamos Scientific Laboratory.

Anecdotes about von Neumann often relate to his rare ability for instant recall. He could read a book, then years later quote it verbatim. Herman Goldstine, who worked closely with him at Princeton in the 1940s, once sought to test his memory by asking him to recall how Dickens's *Tale of Two Cities* began. Without pausing, von Neumann started to recite the first chapter, continuing for ten minutes or so until asked to stop. On another occasion Goldstine observed von Neumann give a lecture he had not given for twenty years—and, to Goldstine's shock, von Neumann used the same letters and symbols that he had used in the original lecture. But even more amazing was the speed with which he could perform complex calculations in his head. Once, a mathematician of some renown spent an all-night session trying to solve a problem with a desk calculator. The next morning von Neumann performed the same calculations in his head, in six minutes. It is no wonder that Eugene Wigner, the theoretical physicist and close acquaintance of von Neumann, compared his friend's brain to some kind of perfect instrument with gears that were machined to mesh accurately to a thousandth of an inch.

Von Neumann had a small, oval face with a large forehead. He was short and heavy-set. His English was clear, even elegant, though he retained a touch of a foreign accent. He spoke rapidly. Putting in endless hours, not stopping for a break until a problem was solved, he was the proverbial workaholic. Sometimes he would wake up at night to wrestle with a sudden insight. He was a careful dresser: vest, handkerchief in pocket, buttoned coat. He loved gadgets, and was among the first in the early 1940s to install a windshield sprayer on his car. Complex toys were a special delight of his. No ivory-tower recluse, von Neumann liked to be surrounded by people. He stood in awe of those with power, especially military men. When he himself acquired political power, as a member of the Atomic Energy Commission in the 1950s, he savored the trappings, particularly the helicopter that would touch down at Princeton to fly him to a Washington meeting. He hosted many parties while at Princeton, though at times he would drift away to his study to work and then return. Von Neumann loved to tell stories, and limericks were his specialty, the racier the better.

Acquaintances did find defects in von Neumann. He was a reckless driver sending one car a year to the junkpile in Princeton. He was no athlete, and indeed held all athletics in contempt. He overate, and when in Los Alamos thought nothing of driving 120 miles to a favorite Mexican restaurant. He was the archetypal absent-minded professor. Once, when his ailing wife Klara asked for a glass of water, he had to ask her where the glasses were kept, though they had lived in the same house for seventeen years.

A crucial moment in John von Neumann's career occurred when he began work on the building of the first atom bomb at Los Alamos in the early 1940s. As a result of that work he came to appreciate the great value of computers. J. Robert Oppenheimer, who knew von Neumann from Göttingen, persuaded him to become a mathematical consultant for the secret Manhattan Project late in 1943. To construct so powerful a weapon, much computation was needed. Hence the call to von Neumann. His background in mathematics and in shock and detonation waves was desperately needed. Von Neumann's key contribution had to do with the detonation of the atomic bomb. Others at the Manhattan Project had dismissed as useless the "implosion method"; but, relying upon his knowledge of the theory of explosions, von Neumann thought such a method could work. Oppenheimer was convinced, and so von Neumann worked out the details. Von Neumann, Edward Teller, and others on the Manhattan Project came up with the implosive lens, which generated a strong spherical shock wave that imploded or compressed a ball of plutonium or uranium isotope. When a critical point was reached, the chain reaction was set off. Proven correct at the Alamogordo test, von Neumann's technique was employed in the detonation of the Nagasaki bomb.

During the summer of 1944 von Neumann was eager to find speedier ways to compute. Oddly enough, his first real confrontation with computers occurred on a railroad platform. One day in June 1944, Herman Goldstine, a mathematician and army officer who was liaison between the Aberdeen, Maryland, Ballistics Research Laboratory and the secret computer project under way at the Moore School at the University of Pennsylvania, spotted von Neumann on the platform at Aberdeen. Goldstine was waiting for a train to Philadelphia. During the war years von Neumann's jobs took him back and forth between Los Alamos, Aberdeen (where he was a consultant at the Ballistics Research Laboratory), and Princeton. As Goldstine later related, "The conversation soon turned to my work." Goldstine may have had a case of hero worship for von Neumann. In the quiet of that railroad platform, the temptation to try to impress him must have been great. What better way to do so than by disclosing that he, Goldstine, was involved in building a computer at the University of Pennsylvania—a computer called the Electronic Numerical Integrator and Computer, or ENIAC. When Goldstine explained that the computer could perform 333 multiplications a second, von Neumann excitedly sought more details. "The whole atmosphere of our conversation," Goldstine recalled, "changed from one of relaxed good humor to one more like the oral examination for the doctor's degree in mathematics." Von Neumann obtained a clearance from the authorities to visit the project.

Arriving on September 7, 1944, at the Moore School of Electrical Engineering, where the computer was under construction, von Neumann gave the ENIAC program a respectability that it had hitherto not enjoyed. John Mauchly, ENIAC's co-inventor, regarded von Neumann as the most eminent mathematician in the world and was excited that such a figure was showing an interest in his work. Other scientists had dismissed ENIAC as a waste of time, diverting government funds that could have been put to better use on relay calculators and differential analyzers, then the state of the art. With John von Neumann as the scientific patron of ENIAC, however, criticism was neutralized. He was treated like visiting royalty, allowed to see everything, to ask about everything. What he saw was dazzling: the two accumulators calculated at a speed that was much faster than von Neumann could calculate in his head. But, sensing the vast potential within ENIAC, he already envisioned better-made computers that would dwarf even these abilities. In Mauchly's words, von Neumann was like a child with a new toy.

Utilizing vacuum tubes rather than electromechanical relays as its switches, ENIAC vastly improved computer speed. But it had one major flaw—it had virtually no memory. There were only twenty 10-decimal-digit numbers in ENIAC. Each time a new operation was performed, the machine would require replugging 6,000 switches covering three walls, and that could take days.

Von Neumann had become a permanent fixture in the ENIAC project as consultant, VIP visitor, and enthusiast. Yet ENIAC was, for von Neumann as well as for the others involved, a way station on the road to more sophisticated, more powerful devices. The main problem confronting the ENIAC team, as its members contemplated building something better, was how to build a stored, programmable memory. Their hope was to build EDVAC—the Electronic Discrete Variable Automatic Computer.

Few aspects of early computer history would spawn such controversy. A dispute has raged for decades over who precisely came up with the notion of a stored-memory computer, John von Neumann or others before him. The cause of the dispute was a 101-page document written by von Neumann and called *First Draft of a Report on the EDVAC*. The report arrived at the Moore School on June 30, 1945. Summing up the thinking of the Moore School team, von Neumann described the logic and makeup of the new computer, terming it "a very high speed automatic digital computing system," which would have a stored, programmable memory.

Herman Goldstine circulated copies of the *First Draft* not only to other Moore School members but to American and British scientists as well. The significance of this act was multilayered. For the first time outsiders, people not working on ENIAC, learned of the plans for a stored-program electronic computer. And John von Neumann was perceived by those outsiders as the prime mover behind the pioneering computer project, an inference he did little to discourage. Mauchly and Eckert were livid at Goldstine, for violating security regulations that kept them from spelling out their own highly important role in the EDVAC project and for jeopardizing their prospects of obtaining a patent. They were also infuriated at von Neumann, for permitting his name to go on the paper without giving proper credit to the Moore School research team.

Herman Goldstine, writing years later, helped to shape the myth of von Neumann's supremacy in the field. "It is obvious," he declared in his book *The Computer: From Pascal to von Neumann,* "that von Neumann, by writing his report, crystallized thinking in the field of computers as no other person ever did. He was, among all members of the group at the Moore School, the indispensable one . . . only von Neumann was essential to the entire task." If that was Goldstine's impression, it did not alter the fact that J. Presper Eckert had written a memo on the subject of a stored-program computer six months before von Neumann had ever been told of the work at the Moore School. It was inevitable that this dispute should linger.

The EDVAC, with its 4,000 tubes and 10,000 crystal diodes, was completed only in 1952. The computer remained in use until December 1962.

Von Neumann's talents were many-faceted. In 1944 he and Oskar Morgenstern published a classic work, *Theory of Games and Economic Behavior,* in which they analyzed certain simple games like poker and coin matching in order to demonstrate that a "best possible" method of play exists and is mathematically determinable. Their "game theory" could be applied to economic and sociological problems as well. Through this book von Neumann and Morgenstern made the first step toward a broad mathematical economics. Following World War II, von Neumann was overwhelmed with prestigious academic offers, none of which he accepted. MIT's Norbert Wiener suggested that he become chairman of the mathematics department. There was talk at the University of Chicago of establishing a new Institute of Applied Mathematics, which von Neumann would direct. But he was eager to build his own computer, and Princeton seemed the best place to do it. Not that the path was smooth. Members of the Institute for Advanced Study felt that their establishment was meant to be an idyllic ivory tower and not a place cluttered with unattractive pieces of machinery. Von Neumann, however, had the clout required to get his way. His plan was to build a fully automatic, digital, all-purpose electronic calculating machine, the fastest at the time. It was intended for scientific research, not the commercial market. The IAS computer, named for the Institute for Advanced Study, was started in 1946 and finished five years later.

Meanwhile, on March 22, 1946, von Neumann and Goldstine sought a patent for the EDVAC, basing their claim on the *First Draft*. They applied to the Pentagon's legal branch. On April 3, 1947, the army refused, arguing that although the *First Draft* qualified as published evidence, it was a year too late inasmuch as patents had to be filed within one year after published evidence appeared. EDVAC had to go into the public domain. Von Neumann, Mauchly, and Eckert were equally dismayed. All thought the patent rightfully belonged to them.

In 1948 von Neumann turned out more pathbreaking work. He and Norbert Wiener published their famous *Cybernetics: Or Control and Communication in the Animal and the Machine*. The book discussed the possibility that electronic brains would take over human tasks, both complicated and simple. In October 1954 von Neumann was appointed a member of the Atomic Energy Commission, which had as its main concern the stockpiling and development of nuclear weapons. He was confirmed by the United States Senate on March 15, 1955. In May he and his wife moved to the Washington suburb of Georgetown. In his last few years von Neumann was a major adviser on nuclear power, nuclear weapons, and intercontinental ballistic weapons. Owing perhaps to his background and early experiences in Hungary, von Neumann held decidedly right-wing political views. In an article in *Life* magazine published on February 25, 1957, soon after his death, he proved an avowed advocate of preventive warfare against the Soviets: "If you say why not bomb them tomorrow, I say, why not today. If you say today at five o'clock, I say why not one o'clock."

In the summer of 1954 von Neumann hurt his left shoulder in a fall. The pain persisted, and surgery revealed the presence of bone cancer. It has been suggested that von Neumann's cancer may have been caused by his attending nuclear weapons tests and staying at Los Alamos for long periods. As the disease progressed, attending the thrice-weekly AEC meetings required tremendous effort. Still, he remained an AEC member and member of the Scientific Advisory Board of the U.S. Air Force. When the end was near, the secretary of defense, his deputies, the secretaries of the army, navy, and air force, and all the military chiefs of staff gathered around von Neumann's bedside at Walter Reed Hospital in Washington, D.C., for a meeting; he was still that important to their deliberations. Only physicians and orderlies with security clearances could attend to von Neumann, so great was the concern that in his weakened and drugged state he might divulge secrets. John von Neumann died on February 8, 1957. He would never know the full extent of his influence on the computer field. But an indication of that influence is the name given to those devices in later years: they were called von Neumann machines.

Claude Shannon

Of Boolean Logic, Mice, Juggling, and Unicycles

4

When MIT students talk about Claude Shannon, they almost always mention first his fondness for unicycles. Anyone who has visited Shannon at his home will picture him surrounded by mechanical and electronic playthings. In the workroom a doll-like figure of W. C. Fields juggles metal balls, and a robot arm moves chess pieces stiffly around a board. The man who devised them has done his greatest work, however, simply by pondering, by sitting at a desk with paper and pencil and letting his mind wander. When he did so in the late 1930s, Shannon was the first to connect the procedures of symbolic logic to the switching circuits that are part and parcel of modern computers. With the discovery that symbolic logic— Boolean algebra—could be used as a way of organizing the internal operations of the computer, an incentive was created for scientists to begin building computers. So the computer industry owes a lot to this man, even though his interests have often strayed far from computers as such.

Claude E. Shannon was born on April 30, 1916, in the small Michigan town of Gaylord. His father was an atttorney and for some time a probate judge. His mother taught languages and became principal of Gaylord High School. Young Claude enjoyed the challenge of building things, especially mechanical things. He put together model planes, radio circuits, a radio-controlled model boat, and a telegraph system between his and a friend's house. He repaired radios for a local department store. Thomas Edison was both his childhood hero and a distant cousin, though the two never met. Later, Shannon would add Isaac Newton, Charles Darwin, Albert Einstein, and John von Neumann to his list of personal heroes. Enrolling at the University of Michigan in the fall of 1932, Shannon majored in electrical engineering. Mathematics intrigued him as well, and he tried to take as many courses as possible. One of those math courses, in symbolic logic, was to have a profound effect on his career. He received a bachelor's degree in both electrical engineering and mathematics. "That's the story of my life," says Shannon, "the interplay between mathematics and electrical engineering."

As he debated whether to find work as an electrical engineer or continue his studies, Shannon came upon a notice on a University of Michigan bulletin board advertising for a young engineering graduate to run the MIT differential analyzer. The most sophisticated of the analog computers of the 1930s, this machine had been built by Vannevar Bush, MIT vice-president and dean of students. It could solve differential equations of up to the sixth degree. Shannon won the job and while doing it worked also as a research assistant in the MIT Engineering Department in pursuit of a master's degree in electrical engineering.

When scientists brought him differential equations to be solved, Shannon would figure out how to put those equations on the differential analyzer. A large portion of his time was taken up with returning the machine to working order after mechanical failure. As he worked, Shannon became increasingly fascinated with the complex relay circuit: it comprised 100 relays and controlled the operation of the analyzer. He thought about the best way to design such a circuit. Shannon decided to do his master's thesis on the subject, hoping to find a mathematical procedure that would describe and analyze the behavior of relay circuits. He found that procedure in Boolean algebra, recalling the course in symbolic logic he had taken as a college senior: "I observed that this branch of mathematics, now called Boolean algebra, was very closely related to what happens in a switching circuit." Shannon's thesis, written in 1937, was called "A Symbolic Analysis of Relay and Switching Circuits." This was no ordinary master's thesis and would in time be recognized as one of the most significant in all of science: what Shannon had done was to pave the way for the development of digital computers.

The problem Shannon addressed was how to design arrays of relays so that they would switch on and off in the correct order and therefore be able to manipulate binary numbers. The first relays were used in telegraphy to extend the range of a signal by switching in additional batteries. A simple relay is made up of an electromagnet, a movable electrical contact, and a spring. Once the electromagnet draws the movable contact into the stationary contact, an electrical circuit is completed. Remove the energy from the electromagnet and the movable contact is pulled away from the stationary one by the spring, breaking the circuit. Relays therefore have only two states, on and off. Early relays could open or close only one circuit each, but modern ones can open and close many circuits simultaneously. The interconnection of these contacts among a number of relays allows complicated logical and control operations.

In Boole's system of logic, decisions are reduced to two possibilities, either yes or no, either true or false. Shannon observed that a switching circuit possesses the same logical duality, expressed as either closed or open; circuits can thus be assigned corresponding values of one and zero. Contacts in series correspond to a logical "and," contacts in parallel correspond to "or." And break contacts correspond to the logical "not." Shannon wrote, "It is possible to perform complex mathematical operations by means of relay circuits. Numbers may be represented by the positions of relays and stepping switches. Interconnections between sets of relays can be made to represent various mathematical operations." Thus, explained Shannon, relays could be so arranged as to carry out "and," "or," and "not" operations. Comparisons could also be made. For instance, is the number represented by x equal to the number represented by y? Formulas that follow the "if, then" pattern could be implemented via the circuits as well.

Shannon's conclusions had a major impact on early computer development, for he had shown that a machine was capable of handling all kinds of information—that not only could it add and subtract, multiply and divide, but it could also perform any operation involving logic. Boolean algebra, Shannon had demonstrated, was the key to making ideal use of computing machines.

On the advice of Vannevar Bush, Shannon pursued a doctorate in mathematics at MIT. The idea for his thesis was born during the summer of 1939 when Shannon worked at Cold Spring Harbor,

New York. Bush had been appointed president of the Carnegie Institution in Washington, D.C., and suggested to Shannon that he spend some time at the institution's branch in Cold Spring Harbor: the work that Barbara Burks was doing there on genetics, Bush thought, might be a subject on which Shannon could bring his algebraic theories to bear. If Shannon could organize switching circuits, might he not be able to do the same with genetics? Shannon's doctoral dissertation, entitled "An Algebra for Theoretical Genetics," was completed by the spring of 1940. After some struggles with the foreign-language requirement—he spent a few months working with a French and German tutor and stacks of flash cards, and he needed two tries to pass the German exam—Shannon received his doctorate in mathematics that year. At the same time he acquired a master's degree in electrical engineering.

T. C. Fry, director of the Mathematics Department at Bell Laboratories, was impressed with Shannon's work on symbolic logic in relays as well as his thinking on mathematics. So he invited him to work at Bell during the summer of 1940. There Shannon did research on switching circuits and came upon a new method of design that reduced the number of contacts needed to synthesize complex switching functions. He published a paper on his work entitled "The Synthesis of Two-Terminal Switching Circuits."

Shannon accepted a National Research Fellowship in the fall of 1940 that allowed him to work under the famous Herman Weyl at the Institute for Advanced Study at Princeton. In the spring of 1941 he was back at Bell Laboratories, now working full-time. With the war on, T. C. Fry was directing a program there on fire control systems for antiaircraft use. Shannon joined this group and worked on devices that observed enemy planes or missiles and computed the aiming of countermissiles. Without these devices England would have suffered far worse than it did.

AT&T, owner of Bell Laboratories, was the leading communications firm in the world. Research into communications had a natural place in the laboratories. In the decade after his initial breakthrough Shannon was encouraged by Bell to pursue research on communications wherever it might take him. By this time Shannon had become primarily interested in the electrical or electronic communication of messages. Little was understood about how messages were transmitted, and even less about how to improve the transmission. Shannon believed that mathematics held the key. But the right questions had to be asked. What precisely is delivered from one party to another when a message is passed on? When noise or encryption obscures a message, what is it that does not get communicated? How do you send information over a channel at the maximum rate?

Shannon's thinking would lead him to formulate a mathematical theory of what he preferred to call communication rather than information. "I wanted to understand if you could come up with a concept of information—what is going on when I'm talking to you." If he could come up with such a theory, then it might become possible to cut the cost of sending information. This all led to the publication in 1948 of his *Mathematical Theory of Communications,* which provided a set of theorems suggesting how to achieve the efficient transmission of messages over noisy media. Shannon demonstrated that any message could be transmitted with as great a reliability as one wished once the right codes were devised. His theorems would instruct systems engineers on how to eliminate noise by encoding signals. From those theorems came a major program to achieve reliable communications with a minimum of error.

In 1948 Shannon also published a monograph—the first on the subject—called *Programming a Computer for Playing Chess.* The design of computer games in subsequent years has been rooted in that paper. In 1953 he wrote a paper on computers and automata that was a pioneering effort in artificial intelligence. Invited in 1965 to the Soviet Union to lecture, while there he played chess with Mikhail Botvinnik, the world champion for many years. Shannon had the advantage of an exchange (a rook for a knight), but Botvinnik eventually won the game in forty-two moves.

As one of the founding fathers of the field of artificial intelligence, Shannon gave much thought to the learning process. To understand it better he built a maze-solving "mouse" in 1950, one of the first attempts at actually building a machine with some learning capabilities. The whole exercise began at Christmas, 1949, when his wife, Betty, bought him a large erector set. He and Betty would come home from their jobs at Bell Laboratories, eat supper, wash the dishes, and begin soldering on the living room floor. He had been contemplating machines that might "think" and solve problems.

The mouse was called Theseus, after the mythological Greek hero who, among many other feats, found his way through the Cretan labyrinth, slew the Minotaur, and then found his way out again by means of a ball of yarn supplied by Adriadne. Shannon's mouse was controlled by a relay circuit; it would move around a maze containing twenty-five squares. The maze could be changed. If it was, the mouse would search through the passageways until it found the arbitrarily placed goal. Theseus was apparently the first learning device of this level. The mouse appeared to be "learning," for it would search until it reached a known position and then proceed to the goal, adding that new knowledge to its memory.

Theseus's brain was a circuit of some 100 relays. The muscles were a pair of motors driving an electromagnet, which by magnetic action moved the mouse through the maze. Underneath the mouse were relays that were "remembering" which way Theseus had left a square the last time. In 1978 the Institute of Electrical and Electronic Engineers held an Amazing Micro-Mouse contest—and Theseus made a guest appearance.

Shannon spent the year 1956–1957 as visiting professor of electrical engineering and mathematics at MIT. During that year he helped put together the famous Dartmouth conference that proved to be the first major effort in organizing artificial intelligence research. After a year at the Center for Advanced Study in the Behavioral Sciences in Palo Alto, California, where he continued his research in communications theory, he became in 1958 a member of the MIT faculty as Donner Professor of Science, teaching mathematics and electrical engineering. Shannon remained a consultant to Bell Laboratories until 1972. In 1978 he retired from MIT as a professor emeritus. He is living in Winchester, Massachusetts, where he is usually to be found in a large ground-floor room at work on his juggling machines.

The Early Inventors

Konrad Zuse

A Little-Known Computer Builder

5

One of the myths about the pioneering period of computer history is that the principal founders of the field were entirely American. That myth was challenged in the mid-1960s, when information about Konrad Zuse's computers became accessible in the United States. It turned out that before and during World War II, a German engineer had developed a programmable, automatic, general-purpose digital computer. This machine, the Z3, predated Howard Aiken's Mark I, which Americans had believed until then was the first operational computer. It was also considered to be somewhat faster than the Mark I. Zuse contends that his Z3 was the first machine of its kind, and thus that it was he who built the first real working computer.

Most of his computers having been destroyed during the fighting, it is understandable that Zuse's accomplishments were largely overlooked for two decades after the war. Moreover, when he was building his computers few took him seriously—certainly not the German government, which appears to have been ambivalent at best about the contribution Zuse's machines might make to the war effort. It would take until 1965 for a description of his computers to be translated into English.

Zuse's inventions appear to have surpassed both John V. Atanasoff's ABC and the ENIAC, being both automatic and programmable. Had he received more official support, Zuse might have become the Howard Aiken or Alan Turing of the German military effort. Though he knew little or nothing of what was going on in the American computer field during the war, Zuse did get a look at Aiken's Mark I—the first programmable digital computer made in the U.S.—after German military intelligence had obtained a photo of it. In 1940 Zuse and his colleague Helmut Schreyer proposed to the German aircraft industry that they build a computer with 2,000 vacuum tubes. When asked how long it would take to build, Zuse said two years. By then, he was told, Germany would have won the war, making the computer unnecessary. Had he been given the go-ahead, Zuse feels he could have replicated Aiken's effort, using even fewer vacuum tubes.

Konrad Zuse was born on June 22, 1910, in Berlin. His father was a postal administrator who earned little but did what he could to support his son's interest in building calculating machines. The solving of technical problems became an early and abiding interest. At age eighteen Konrad studied architecture with the aim of becoming a designer. But he took up civil engineering at the University of Berlin's Technische Hochschule. If there was one type of work that civil engineers seemed to do more than anything else, it was solving equations—a tedious, time-consuming task that appealed to Zuse no more than it did to other students.

In 1934 Zuse had to learn the theory of static indeterminate structures, which was based on a part of algebra known as linear equations. But the task of studying the behavior of static structures such as buildings was terribly impractical given the limitations of existing calculators. An engineer had to solve a set of simultaneous linear equations in order to provide the correct structural support for a roof. But a student could practically do only six equations with six unknowns; increasing the number of equations dramatically increased the amount of calculation. Solving the equations for a large roof could take months. Like a number of other computer pioneers, Zuse began to sense that there had to be a more efficient way to perform such calculations than existing methods that required hours of drudgery with calculators. The solution lay in figuring out how to automate the machinery so that it required minimal human operation. Nothing that existed, even the desk calculators and punched-card machinery, was adequate. Zuse knew that building one more mechanical calculator would do no good. What he needed was a machine that would be dramatically faster than those mechanical models.

In the spring of 1935 he graduated from the Technische Hochschule with a degree in civil engineering. To finance his efforts he began working as a stress analyst for the Henschel aircraft company in Berlin. While there he did little else but perform extended calculations for the designing of aircraft, more of the same drudgery. In 1936, at twenty-six, he decided to build his own computers, having already put together the ideas for the type he wanted to build. That was a year before John V. Atanasoff's famous evening at the roadhouse and seven years before John Mauchly and Presper Eckert obtained approval to build ENIAC. Zuse decided to base his computer on the binary system—again, an idea that would not occur to Atanasoff until a year later in Iowa. Binary was selected to get speed from the computer; and the electromagnetic relay, he felt, was a good tool for expressing a binary digit. Though he would not discover Babbage until 1939, Zuse in effect recreated the inner workings of the Analytical Engine: he decided he must build a computer that could solve all equations. To do this his computer would need an arithmetic unit. He envisioned it doing floating-point mathematics. It would need a memory, a control unit to govern the movement of numbers and instructions, a device that would read the instructions and data from the punched tape (he used punched strips of old film), and finally an input and output unit in order to show the results.

Zuse called his first three computers the V1, V2, and V3—the V stood for Versuchsmodell, or "Experimental model." He later renamed them the Z1, Z2, and Z3 so they would not be confused with the German rocket bombs—the V1 and V2. Zuse's Z1 and Z2 computers were built before the war; the Z3 was constructed in 1941. All three computers were destroyed during the war. Only the Z4 would survive the German defeat. Zuse built the Z1 between 1936 and 1938 in the living room of his parents' home. It was 2 meters by 1.5 meters and was fully mechanical. The design was ingenious: the machine's memory comprised one thousand thin, slotted metal plates, substituting for the gears and axles that were found in traditional calculators. Punched tape controlled the machine. Although this part of the Z1 worked well, the arithmetic unit was problematic. Homemade parts did not allow computations longer than a few minutes. Connecting the storage unit with the arithmetic unit was not possible.

In 1938 Zuse filed a patent claim with the U.S. Patent Office for the computers he had built until then. He was refused. The reason: he was not precise enough in spelling out the nature of the hardware. The patent authorities believed—so Zuse thinks—that he had derived his work directly from Charles Babbage. That stung the German computer builder. He knew that he had done his work independently. Zuse also filed a patent claim with the German authorities at the same time, in 1938 for the early computers and in 1941 for the Z3.

When World War II broke out in 1939, Zuse, now age twenty-nine, was drafted as a simple soldier—in one of the great ironies of the time. For here was an inventor whose work held amazing promise. Yet those who could have supported his labors—perhaps to their own benefit—took no interest in him whatsoever. This was in great contrast to the British government, which from the start of the war made great use of Alan Turing; his computers are credited with playing a major role in the British victory. Zuse's computer efforts had been financed in part by a maker of calculators, who asked Zuse's superior officer whether he might be spared soldierly duties in order to work on an invention of major significance, one that would aid in the German air effort by accelerating calculations related to aircraft design. The officer replied that he considered the German air force infallible and in no need of further calculations. It would take another six months before Zuse was released from military service, and then he was not assigned to work on computers but to an engineering project with the Henschel aircraft factory in Berlin.

Zuse was not put off by the less-than–100 percent success of the Z1. He wanted to build yet another computer, this time a bigger and more complicated one. The Z2 would be electromechanical as opposed to the simply mechanical Z1. And so, while designing military aircraft for the Luftwaffe, he used his own money to work in his free time on an experimental model at his parents' home. On the advice of a telecommunications engineer named Helmut Schreyer, who collaborated with him, Zuse used secondhand telephone relays rather than the mechanical parts of the Z1's arithmetic unit. The relays had two great advantages: they permitted the arithmetic unit to carry and borrow property, and they enabled fast operation (a relay could turn on and off hundreds of times per minute). Zuse was also successful in connecting the arithmetic unit to the memory (still mechanical). For the most part the computer worked. As early as 1937 Schreyer urged Zuse to think of replacing the relays with vacuum tubes in order to attain even greater speed. But in the late 1930s vacuum tubes were expensive.

Though largely unreliable, the Z2 did work once. Fortunately it occurred when a leading aircraft design expert, Alfred Teichmann, was visiting Zuse's home. He was sufficiently impressed to find funds for Zuse so that he could continue developing his computers. Teichmann believed that the next model of Zuse's computer could help solve wing fluttering, an aircraft design problem. As a result Zuse became the only German permitted to develop computers during the war. That hardly meant that his work was appreciated. He led a lonely existence. He had few friends or colleagues who really understood what his computer efforts were all about.

The Henschel aircraft factory, though it showed no interest in computers themselves, was nevertheless eager for Zuse to help it with a computational problem of some urgency connected with the calculation of airplane wing accuracy. Although there had been no delays in production, the calculations were performed by conventional means—desk calculators—and were thus expensive. Zuse informed the factory that he could solve the problem by designing a special-purpose computer. He sought approval to build a prototype. If the factory said yes, he promised himself he would use the occasion to build a general-purpose computer that could solve other problems besides wing flutter equations. The factory commissioned him to set up a fifteen-man firm, which led to the building in late 1941 of the Z3, the first fully functional, program-controlled, general-purpose digital computer. That was two years before ENIAC was started, and two years before the British, led by Alan Turing, began cracking German codes with Colossus, the electronic deciphering device. Zuse was later astonished to find that ENIAC had been built with 17,468 vacuum tubes. That was far more expensive than anything he had tried to build. Even the Z3 did not contain vacuum tubes but was electromechanical.

The Z3 contained nearly all the main characteristics of the conventional computer, chief of which were a memory and a type of program control. As Zuse was completing his Z3, John V.

The Z3 computer

Atanasoff was putting together most of the elements of what some consider to have been the first American computer, the ABC. Atanasoff's work differed from Zuse's in that his ABC was not fully functional whereas the Z3 was. Moreover, the ABC could handle only certain kinds of calculations, while the Z3 was a general-purpose machine. An operator had to control the ABC at almost every step, pressing buttons and turning knobs, putting in and taking out punch cards. Zuse's machines were far more intricate. They were both automatic and programmable.

The Z3 cost Zuse only $6,500 to build: the only one of the early Z machines to abandon the mechanical memory, the Z3 used a relay-based memory. It was built from 2,600 relays and comprised the operator's console, a tape reader, and three cabinets. Its small memory could store only sixty-four 22-bit numbers. The machine's speed, while impressive, was not that of ENIAC. The Z3, a bit faster than the Mark I, could multiply in three to five seconds, while the Mark I could multiply in six seconds; ENIAC could multiply in 2.8 milliseconds. The Z3 could add, subtract, multiply, divide, find square roots, and do other sophisticated jobs. The computer was used largely to evaluate the determinant of a complex matrix, a method for solving equations with several unknown variables. An operator would enter the initial values by hand into the memory. Then the machine's operations would be controlled by the punched tape.

In 1941 Zuse wanted to build an electronic computer using 2,000 vacuum tubes. He thought such a computer could be used effectively for work on ballistics. Unlike the British, he had not thought of performing work in decryption: "I wasn't a magician. I didn't understand enough of those problems."

The factory still needed special-purpose computers, and so in 1942 and 1943 Zuse built two that calculated wing and rudder surfaces, figuring the proper adjustment for each weapon's wings. The computers were called the S1 and S2.

Now that the Z3 had been successful, Zuse wanted to build an even larger, faster, more powerful computer. He envisioned one with a bigger memory—five hundred and twelve 32-bit numbers as opposed to sixty-four 22-bit ones. The Z4 was Zuse's most sophisticated computer. It could add, multiply, divide, or find a square root in three seconds. This time he had the support of the German military for a general-purpose computer, although the aircraft ministry, which ordered the computer, was interested in it only for calculations in aircraft design.

By 1942 Zuse had founded a firm called Zuse Apparatebau. For most of the war he had worked alone, but by war's end he had twenty employees. After the Germans were soundly defeated in February 1943 at Stalingrad, Zuse became convinced the war was lost. His computers, he then reasoned, could be of value to the postwar world. But life was uncertain, and he could not be sure he or his machines would survive the fighting. The Allied move on Germany had a serious effect on Zuse's computer building. Allied bombers were striking at Berlin almost every day. The Z3 was destroyed in 1943. Before fleeing from Berlin in March 1945 Zuse had to move his Z4 three times around the city to avoid bombing raids, some of which damaged his workshop.

As far as Zuse knew, he was one of only a handful of people building computers. It was wartime, and learning what the rest of the scientific community was doing was virtually impossible. Yet at one stage Zuse did come upon news of non-German efforts. It so happened that a clerk who worked in Zuse's firm had a daughter working for German intelligence. One day the clerk, violating the

The Z4 computer

firm's secrecy code, divulged to his daughter what Zuse's company was working on. That information rang a bell in the daughter's mind; she recalled coming across a photograph in intelligence archives of something similar. Word got back to Zuse himself that a photo existed in German intelligence files of a non-German machine. He wanted to look at it. But how could he? The existence of the picture was highly secret information, and neither the clerk nor his daughter should have been discussing it with anyone. Still, Zuse approached the German authorities and somehow convinced them to let him talk to the intelligence people. When he did, Zuse did not let on that he knew about the photograph. He merely expressed an interest in seeing anything that intelligence might have on non-German computers. The answer came back that there was nothing in intelligence. Zuse knew this not to be the case. He approached the same people again, urging them to look in a certain box. Zuse cannot account for their failure to take him to task for knowing precisely where the photo was. At any rate, the picture was produced—and there was Howard Aiken's Mark I! It revealed little to Zuse, however, beyond the fact that the Americans had been working on something similar to his machines; he later insisted that the Mark I in no way influenced his work.

Zuse was allowed to leave Berlin during the final months of the war. He and an assistant carried the dismantled Z4 by wagon to Göttingen, 100 miles to the west, in March 1945. He had been ordered by the government to take his equipment into underground factories near Northeim, but after visiting there, and seeing concentration camps for the first time, Zuse decided he could not stay. He headed for the mountains, settling in Hinterstein, a peaceful village in the Bavarian Alps. Aiding him in getting equipment and papers out of Göttingen at one point was Lieutenant General Walter Robert Dornberger, boss of rocket expert Werner Von Braun at Peenemunde. In flight, Zuse, like most other German inventors, wanted to avoid capture by the Russians. He preferred being taken by the Americans or the British. Zuse has always felt that had certain British officials who knew of his computer work discovered him, he would have been immediately taken to Britain. There he might have gone on to build computers for the British during the postwar years. Instead he remained in Germany. He lived in Hinterstein until 1946, his equipment hidden in the basement of a farm building. Upon their entry into the region, American army officers questioned him and looked at his machine, but decided quite properly that the Z4 held no security risk. Zuse was permitted to go free.

While in Hinterstein in 1946 he asked the help of a German filmmaker who was able to travel to the United States because he had an American wife. The filmmaker contacted IBM chief Thomas Watson, who had his German office contact Zuse. A preliminary negotiation actually occurred between IBM and Zuse over his Z series computers, but IBM eventually lost interest. Whereas Zuse had hoped IBM would sponsor his work in computer technology, IBM wanted merely to purchase his patents for existing technology.

Zuse moved to another Alpine village, Hopferau, near the Austrian border, in 1946 and remained there for three years. In this peaceful setting he had time to think. Hardware development had come to a standstill after the war, and so Zuse turned to programming. In 1945 he had developed what he called the first programming language for computers, Plankalkul, contending that it was the only universal language for calculating. Plankalkul was a prototype programming language that anticipated latter-day structured programming. The language included some unusual constructs, among them the idea of variables representing rather large and small numbers. Zuse believed that his new language could be employed for solving more than mathematical problems. He had studied chess in order to test the language so that he could further one long-standing project, the formulating of rules of universal calculating. To Zuse's regret, no one showed any interest in his language.

In 1949 Remington Rand expressed interest in Zuse's work, not fully trusting their own electronic developments. They asked Zuse to develop a fully mechanical computer based on his Pipeline Principle, which made the repeated additions needed to do multiplication more efficient. Remington Rand Switzerland also ordered a series of forty electromechanical Z9 computers. Sadly for Zuse, he could not fully commercialize his invention, though he had perhaps the only working computer in all of Europe.

The Z4 was leased in the Technische Hochschule in Zurich, where Zuse was then living, in 1950. For a number of years it stood alone as the one computer of any significance on the Continent, solving complex mathematical and engineering problems. Visitors came from around the world to see the marvel. As the machine's inventor, Zuse felt proprietary about the Z4, so much so that on nights when he had nothing else to do he would wander over to the building where the computer was located. By the time he entered the building he could already hear the Z4's sounds, though the machine was on the top floor. From those sounds he could actually tell whether his computer was performing its tasks on schedule.

Zuse built a small company in 1949 named Zuse KG, which developed into a leading manufacturer of small scientific computers, employing a thousand people. He stayed with the firm until 1966. In recent years he has been engaged in part-time consulting for the firm, as well as in painting, a lifelong hobby to which he can now give more attention. He lives in the Hessian village of Hunfeld, a few hours' drive from Frankfurt. Some of Zuse's earlier paintings are signed "Kone See." When asked why, he explains that he had good reason for using the pseudonym. "If there were delays in getting computers to customers, as sometimes happened, I didn't want anyone to say, 'Stop painting and get those machines ready.' "

John V. Atanasoff

The Inventor of the Digital Computer— According to the Law!

6

Who invented the computer? It's not an easy question to answer. But John V. Atanasoff believes he is the inventor, and a court of law has supported his contention. Ironically, Atanasoff, a physicist who conceived of a computer while an academic in Iowa in the 1930s, is better known in Europe than in the United States. Even the Americans who were building computers in the late 1940s and early 1950s didn't know who he was. And yet, thanks to a lengthy court battle in the early 1970s, Atanasoff has won the legal right to be called the inventor of the digital computer. He is convinced that he deserves that credit: "After Babbage, I was the one who turned computing into its present channels." Those who lost the case—the inventors of ENIAC, John Mauchly and J. Presper Eckert—contended that the court was wrong and that they were the inventors of the computer. Although the question is still debated by some, most computer historians consider it unresolvable and ultimately of little interest. What can be said with certainty is that each of the three— Atanasoff, Mauchly, and Eckert—made essential contributions to the evolution of the digital computer.

Mathematics was the center of John Vincent Atanasoff's interest from childhood. Born in Hamilton, New York, on October 4, 1903, he came of mathematical-minded parents. His father, a Bulgarian immigrant, was an electrical engineer, and his American-born mother was a teacher who enjoyed doing algebra into her nineties. When John was a youngster the family moved to Florida after his father obtained engineering work there. John was precocious. With help from his mother he learned to read early and loved what he could absorb from books. He believed that by reading he could understand anything. Spelling was a problem—one that would move him later in life to try to improve the written English language.

In 1913, when he was nine years old, John Atanasoff began his march in the computer world. His father, who was in charge of the electrical system of a phosphate mine, installed electrical wiring in his home, making it one of the first in the area to have electric lights. From the elder Atanasoff John learned the fundamentals of electricity. That same year his father had made a purchase that would have a deep impact on John's life: a new slide rule to replace an older one. Finding he had no real need for the new slide rule, Atanasoff gave it to his son, who within two weeks could use it proficiently. From February until August of 1913 John Atanasoff worked on logarithms, using J. M. Taylor's 1895 college algebra text, obtained from his father's library. He could not forego baseball, however, and so he divided his days between the baseball diamond and the slide rule.

By age ten he was studying physics and chemistry as well as pursuing mathematics. His mother gave him a book that explained how to calculate numbers to bases other than the ten digits used in the decimal system. (Later, in deciding to use base-2 numbers in digital computing, Atanasoff thought back to that early book: "When I got to work on computers, one of the things that revolved in my mind was that maybe computers would work better to bases other than ten.") When the math became too hard for his mother, he taught himself.

During high school Atanasoff decided to become a theoretical physicist. "The teachers found the easiest way to keep me entertained was to get good books in science and put them in front of me." He entered the University of Florida in 1921. With no other theoretical subjects available, he opted for electrical engineering. He received an engineering degree in 1925. In September of that year he went north to Iowa State College to teach mathematics and do graduate work in physics and mathematics. He received a master's degree in mathematics in 1926.

Atanasoff moved to the University of Wisconsin to complete his doctoral work in and teach mathematics. His thesis, completed in July 1930, was entitled "The Dialectic Constant of Helium." Returning to Iowa State College, he became an assistant professor in the mathematics department. He studied electronics on the side, concentrating on improving his knowledge of vacuum tubes. Eventually he became an associate professor of both mathematics and physics at Iowa State.

Although he had inherited some mechanical ability from his parents, inventing a computer was far from Atanasoff's mind during his early adult years. In 1935, however, he grew frustrated at the difficulty his graduate students had in finding the solutions of large systems of simultaneous algebraic equations for solving partial differential equations. He considered employing existing analog devices, but these were inaccurate and hard to use. (Atanasoff coined the word "analog" for this type of computer.) He thought of using an IBM calculator, but after he had modified it with extra equipment, IBM reprimanded him for tinkering with their machine. At any rate, the calculator was not sufficiently powerful. Vannevar Bush's differential analyzer, though it could solve ordinary differential equations, was still too limited.

Over the next two years Atanasoff spent many long evenings in his office in the physics building at Iowa State College, contemplating how to ease the burden of his graduate students, who, he felt, were spending too much of their time on certain problems. Atanasoff had his students test Monroe calculators, but they simply weren't powerful enough for his needs. Once he considered taking thirty similar Monroe calculators and driving them with a common shaft. But the machines were too slow. Even with the deft use of Marchant desk calculators it would take at least eight hours to solve eight unknowns. Twenty-nine equations with twenty-nine unknowns would take 381 hours, or forty-seven work days, with no margin for error.

Atanasoff thought that a device using a digital approach would prove valuable, but such machines didn't exist. He would have to invent one himself—although his research left him little time for such an undertaking. He had little information on which to rely. For example, his knowledge of Charles Babbage, the nineteenth-century computer visionary, was limited to encyclopedias.

It was then that he got into his automobile!

Most inventors cannot point to one moment when that sudden

insight came to them, when lightning struck. John Atanasoff can. "I remember it perfectly, as if it were yesterday. Everything came together in that one night." It happened one winter evening in 1937 after he had spent a half hour in his office. He got into his car and drove over eighty miles an hour from Ames, Iowa, across the Mississippi River into Illinois, 189 miles. "I went to assuage my internal torment on computing," he recalls. The length of the journey didn't bother him. "I was very frustrated. . . . By driving fast I could force myself to give attention to driving and not thinking." As he crossed the Mississippi he thought of getting a drink. He wanted rest and warmth against the cold—it was twenty degrees below zero. Stopping at a roadhouse, he took a table for himself, and for the next three hours nursed two drinks of bourbon and water while he let his mind wander. Something about the solitude afforded by the isolated roadhouse, and the indifference of those nearby, served to nourish Atanasoff's mind. He sensed that his brain was working to full capacity. "All of a sudden I realized that I had a power that I hadn't had before. How I felt that so strongly in my soul, I don't know. I had a power—I mean I could do things, I could move, and move with assurance."

He came upon four new ideas that evening, and based on those ideas he was able to set about the task of conceptualizing an electronic digital computer. The first was to use electronics as the computer's medium, challenging the conventional wisdom that electronic components were unreliable. He had tested vacuum tubes and, as had others, found them to have reliability problems. But now he reasoned that vacuum tubes were no more unreliable than the relays used in the large electromechanical calculating devices of the day, and that their use would offer a great advantage. While relays could turn on and off hundreds of times a minute, vacuum tubes could switch on and off thousands of times a second.

Next, Atanasoff thought of using base-2 numbers (binary) in memory and computing. In those days memory was called data retention. Atanasoff applied the term memory and it stuck. By using binary, in which the on and off of an electrical circuit would be represented by ones and zeroes, one could put much more information on the punched cards that recorded instructions. But learning binary could be difficult, and so Atanasoff had wavered until he got to the tavern. His third idea was serial calculation, which enabled the computer to handle large numbers, making it that much easier to learn binary.

Atanasoff's fourth idea concerned the memory device. The circuit that he wanted to use could hold an electrical charge for only a short period. Now Atanasoff hit upon a new technique that would permit the computer to detect and regenerate the charge before it leaked away. He would use condensers for memory that would regenerate their own plus or minus state so the state would not change in time. He called this regenerating process "jogging."

Atanasoff felt no urgent need to write these ideas down. They were there in his head, and that was enough. "If an idea ever occurred to me, it was engraved perpetually, forever." Nearly half a century later Atanasoff was pleased to note that all four of those ideas thought up at the tavern had found their way into contemporary computers.

He spent more than a year working on jogging and logic circuits. In the spring of 1939 Atanasoff and Clifford Berry, a graduate student whom he had hired, began work on a prototype of a computer; Atanasoff boasted that he planned to invent the most powerful one yet made. For all his confidence Atanasoff remained uncertain where his project was heading. The entire idea of creating an electronic digital computer filled him with awe. He was treading on new ground.

The prototype was completed by November 1939. The two men thought of using a magnetic memory but instead used a binary card punch/reader: although the concept of wire recorders had been devised, the magnetic components for it were not good. On March 1, 1941, they won a grant from Research Corporation for $5,330, a large sum in those days. The grant led Atanasoff's employer to conclude that he might be on to something significant. According to Atanasoff, he had to sign a patent agreement in which Iowa State College would apply for a patent and he would split his royalties from the computer with the school. Oddly enough, the school never applied for a patent, and all Atanasoff could do, tied by the agreement not to apply for the patent himself, was to keep up the pressure on the school to change its mind. In December 1940 Atanasoff and Berry visited the U.S. Patent Office in Washington, D.C., for a few days, looked through many documents, and found nothing to threaten a possible patent. But Iowa State wouldn't

The ABC computer

budge: the school authorities were apparently convinced that the device had become obsolete.

Atanasoff and Berry sought simplicity. The ABC (for Atanasoff-Berry Computer, as Atanasoff later insisted it be called) used 300 vacuum tubes for the logic circuitry and capacitors for the automatic jogging or regeneration of memory. It was the first machine to perform arithmetic electronically. Atanasoff believed the ABC was superior to the Harvard University Mark I built by Howard Aiken, in that it could solve systems of linear algebraic equations, which the Mark I could not do, and in that it was electronic rather than mechanical.

The ABC stored numbers by mounting them on two Bakelite drums, eight inches in diameter and eleven inches long, using electrical capacitors. Each drum could store thirty binary numbers of fifty binary digits (or bits); the numbers were stored in condensers that were set into the skins of the drums. Charges stored in the condensers were maintained by thirty tubes so they would not drain away. The drum would rotate and the number could then be read off. There were thirty add–subtract units. Base-10 punch cards, with fifteen digits and a sign, were used for input. Arithmetic could be performed after the numbers were converted to binary. An operator pushed a button to indicate where numbers should go.

Atanasoff regarded the machine as a great success. "Every damn thing worked. We didn't have much to deal with, but everything worked." The machine did work—save for the binary card punch/reader. Even though the card puncher failed only once every 100,000 times, that was sufficient to keep the ABC from solving large sets of linear equations. If the puncher malfunctioned, the ABC would spew out or take in incorrect numbers. Atanasoff and Berry experimented with cards made of various materials, but in vain. The ABC was limited, accordingly, to solving no more than a few simultaneous equations. Still, the ABC settled many doubts about how an electronic computer might be built. Not only that. Atanasoff believed he had demonstrated that an electronic digital computer was indeed feasible.

The first of Atanasoff's controversial encounters with John Mauchly, a physicist from Ursinus College, in Collegeville, Pennsylvania, took place in December 1940, when Atanasoff was still laboring to perfect the ABC. Both men were attending the meetings of the American Association for the Advancement of Science on the University of Pennsylvania campus. Mauchly gave a lecture on the potential use of analog computers in handling problems in meteorology; he discussed the use of a harmonic analyzer, which he had built, in dealing with some weather phenomena. Atanasoff was in the audience. Waiting until all others had talked with Mauchly following the lecture, Atanasoff introduced himself as someone with an interest in computers, especially digital computers. He then told Mauchly of his machine-in-progress, a computer using vacuum tubes that was likely to have a great impact on digital computing. Atanasoff invited Mauchly to come to Iowa to see the ABC.

Mauchly took up the offer on June 14, 1941. He and his son were Atanasoff's house guests for the next five days, during which time the two men talked endlessly of computers. Mauchly examined documentation, and Berry ran through a small demonstration of the ABC. The machine could solve twenty-nine simultaneous equations with twenty-nine variables. Berry was still working on the binary card punch and reader that would have allowed input-output and slow memory. Mauchly asked to take a copy of the documentation home, but Atanasoff balked. Three months later, in late September 1941, Mauchly wrote Atanasoff to ask whether it might be possible to build an "Atanasoff Calculator" at the Moore School of Engineering at the University of Pennsylvania. Replying on October 7, Atanasoff said that he wanted the ABC to remain a secret at least until a patent application could be filed.

World War II caused Atanasoff to drift away from the building of computers. In 1942 he became chief of the Acoustics Division at the Naval Ordnance Laboratory (NOL) in Washington, D.C., where he supervised the acoustical testing of mines. The key part of the ABC, the arithmetic unit, was successfully tested in 1942, giving Atanasoff the feeling that the computer project had been largely finished. But the ABC was never actually used. With the war on, the building of electronic computers had far less priority than other more defense-related projects.

John Mauchly, working as a part-time statistician in the same section, informed Atanasoff in 1943 that he and J. Presper Eckert had come up with a new way to compute that was different from Atanasoff's. Atanasoff asked Mauchly to explain what he was doing but got the terse reply, "I cannot. The subject is classified." The "new way" had to do with ENIAC, the first fully operational electronic digital computer, which was being put together under strict secrecy for the military at the University of Pennsylvania.

In 1945 Atanasoff was awarded the Navy Civilian Service Award. It was about that time that the Bureau of Ordnance asked him to help in building a computer at the Naval Ordnance Laboratory. Though the navy gave him much support ($100,000 at the outset), Atanasoff contended that he could not both do the computer project and complete work in the NOL Acoustics Division. The navy finally scrubbed the computer effort. One reason may have been a report submitted by project consultant John von Neumann, who wrote that Atanasoff was not competent to manage a project of this size. Atanasoff did not return to computers after the war's end. "I'd worked on computers for twelve years or so and under very hard circumstances. I wanted a change of life." Years later he regretted abandoning his computer efforts, but that was when it had become apparent to him that his machine was indeed revolutionary. In the early 1980s he acknowledged that had he understood the potential of the ABC he would have kept working on it.

Robert Stewart had been at Iowa State and worked with Atanasoff in the famous Helgoland Big Blast experiment on April 18, 1947, for which Atanasoff had invented equipment to detect and record underground seismic and sonic waves. Stewart later made this appraisal of his colleague: "J.V. was a most unusual individual. The sparks just flew. It was the most exhilarating and yet frustrating period of my life. I was a grad student. I was looking for a hero and found one. I was trying to put his ideas into practice. The frustration came from the fact that he kept coming up with better ideas. You came out of a conversation with him and your head would be aching—kind of like getting a drink from a fire hose."

Atanasoff remained head of the Acoustics Division at NOL until 1949 and then became chief scientist for the Army Field Forces in Fort Monroe, Virginia. During 1950–1951 he was director of the Navy Fuze Program at NOL. In 1952 he founded a firm called Ordnance Engineering Corporation in Frederick, Maryland, and after four years sold it to Aerojet General Corporation, also in Frederick. He became vice-president of the latter firm as well as manager of its Atlantic Division, but left in 1961, no longer interested in being a corporation man.

Atanasoff next became a consultant in the automation of package handling. He started a company called Cybernetics, Incorporated, also in Frederick, which supplied advice or material of a semiscientific nature. His son, John II, eventually took over the business. Atanasoff and his wife have two other children, Elsie and Joanne.

Although he eventually became a vigorous campaigner on his own behalf, Atanasoff took up the cudgel to prove that he was the inventor of the first electronic digital computer only after being urged to do so by others. On June 15, 1954, a patent attorney representing IBM, A. J. Etienne, visited Atanasoff, telling him, "If you will help us, we will break the Mauchly-Eckert computer patent. It was derived from you." Hesitating at first, Atanasoff recalled what Mauchly had said to him in that brief conversation in 1943, namely, that he and Eckert had invented a new method of computing, different from Atanasoff's. He had believed Mauchly at the time, but the IBM lawyer put things in quite a different light.

In fact, it was in the interests of the large computer firms not only to break the Mauchly-Eckert patent but also to debunk Atanasoff's ABC, in order to ensure the validity of patents filed for their computer projects. The death of Clifford Berry in 1963 removed from the scene the person best qualified to corroborate Atanasoff's claims. Nonetheless, Atanasoff became increasingly convinced that ENIAC had indeed been derived from his ABC and that it was worth pursuing the matter. Moreover, he was encouraged by the recognition being given him, even though sometimes it was in far-away places. In 1970 Bulgaria gave him its highest scientific achievement award, the Bulgarian Order of Cyril and Methodius, First Class. He was also honored by the Bulgarian parliament for inventing the computer.

The issue came to trial in the early 1970s. In 1971 Sperry Rand, the company that had acquired Mauchly and Eckert's ENIAC patent, sued Honeywell for nonpayment of royalties. Honeywell countersued, alleging that ENIAC had been derived from the earlier ABC and that the patent was therefore invalid. To prepare his evidence in the case, Atanasoff and his lawyers located Atanasoff's former colleagues and asked them to help reconstruct the ABC. At the trial Atanasoff explained precisely how the ABC worked, pushing buttons, causing lights to light. It was enough to impress Judge Earl R. Larson, who decided in favor of Atanasoff. The decision was announced on October 19, 1973, the day before the "Saturday Night Massacre" in the Watergate scandal, and accordingly was lost in the media shuffle. Though it may not have made him world famous, the verdict did describe Atanasoff as the inventor of the electronic computer, ENIAC having been based largely on his idea. "Eckert and Mauchly," wrote Judge Larson, "did not themselves first invent the automatic electronic digital computer . . . but instead derived that broad subject matter from Dr. John V. Atanasoff, and the ENIAC patent is thereby invalid." (Furthermore, Larson asserted, ENIAC had been used in H-bomb development over a year before the patent was sought, and a patent is valid only if the invention has existed less than a year before the application is filed.)

The verdict outside the courtroom, however, has been decidedly mixed. Atanasoff remains bitter at not receiving the credit he believes he deserves. He had a stroke in 1975, but recovered and still lives on his 200-acre farm near Monrovia, Maryland—in a house for which he designed the air-conditioning system, the kitchen cabinets, the rain gauge, an 800-pound rotating front door, and a heating conservation system that recirculates hot air from the top of the house to the bottom. To those who contend that the ABC didn't work, Atanasoff replies: "With me the accomplishment is getting the ideas. As soon as you got the ideas, anybody can build it."

During and after World War II Atanasoff developed an interest outside computers that he has called his "avocation"—trying to do something about the troubles youngsters have in learning to read English. War and violence spurred him to think of a way to help people: "When I worked for the army, I spent every day trying to kill people, and in some ways I was fairly successful." In 1943 he made a study of written languages and concluded that English needed the most improvement of all. Spelling, in his view, was at the root of the problem: English was an extremely nonphonetic language. So he designed a binary, phonetic alphabet that furnished enough letters to make reading and spelling simpler. Although he believes it would allow people to learn how to read English two to three times more quickly, Atanasoff has little faith that his new language will catch on quickly. If it should be adopted, he considers it would be his greatest accomplishment—greater than the invention of the computer.

John V. Mauchly   J. Presper Eckert

John V. Mauchly and J. Presper Eckert

The Men Who Built ENIAC

7

Legend has it that when ENIAC—that 30-ton monster with its 17,468 vacuum tubes and 6,000 switches—was turned on for the first time, the lights of Philadelphia dimmed. Did they dim out of respect for the ushering in of a new age? As a sign of the immense power suddenly at mankind's disposal? Those who created the legend—for it apparently has no basis in fact—and passed it on were among the awestruck. And their awe tells us a great deal about how the world greeted the coming of the computer age.

ENIAC was truly an electronic whiz kid. It provided the break-through in speed that scientists and mathematicians were searching for. Completed two years after the Harvard Mark I, it was a thousand times faster than Howard Aiken's invention. Indeed, it was more than a thousand times faster than any computer to date. ENIAC could multiply in 2.8 milliseconds, divide in 24 milliseconds. Until ENIAC appeared, a skilled operator of a desk calculator took around twenty hours to produce acceptable results for a trajectory calculation. The same calculation took twenty minutes on the differential analyzer, an early electromechanical analog calculating machine and the most sophisticated computer of its day. ENIAC could perform a trajectory calculation in just thirty seconds.

Awkward and, by the standards of later computers, embarrassingly primitive, this ENIAC was. To give the computer new instructions, someone had to change the external wiring manually, in much the way a telephone operator rearranged the plugs on a switchboard. Yet for all its crudeness, ENIAC did indeed herald the dawning of the computer age. The two men who built it, and in doing so stand out as two of the major pioneers in computing, are John V. Mauchly and J. Presper Eckert.

To their great chagrin Mauchly and Eckert will forever be associated with the controversy over who in fact invented the first computer. Because they worked for the military and were sworn to secrecy, they could not tell their story at the time. But others, feeling less constrained, exposed the mysteries of the wartime laboratories, speaking excitedly of creating an electronic brain that could take over much of mankind's work, doing it better, faster.

Mauchly had revealed his inventive genius during childhood. He had a special fascination with electricity and a deep curiosity about calculating machines. Born August 30, 1907, in Cincinnati, he was nine when his family moved to Chevy Chase, Maryland, outside Washington, D.C., where his father had been made chief of the Section of Terrestrial Electricity and Magnetism at the Carnegie Institution. At age five John had put together a flashlight so he could search through a dark attic with a friend. During elementary school he installed electric doorbells to make some pocket money from neighbors. He devised a trigger on the stairs so that when his mother came to check if he was sleeping, his reading light automatically went off. Her descent turned the light back on! On April Fool's Day he wired the front door so that anyone ringing it would get a slight shock.

Dismantling an adding machine at an early age spurred an interest in all things that calculated. In 1925 Mauchly entered Johns Hopkins University in Baltimore and studied electrical engineering. An outstanding student, he became bored and didn't think much of engineering. And so in September 1927, after only two years of college, he was given a scholarship to attend the Hopkins graduate school of physics—he never obtained an undergraduate degree. He worked summers doing computation at the wind tunnel of the Bureau of Standards. His specialty at Hopkins was molecular spectroscopy. Always he was seeking ways to do calculations faster than was possible with existing equipment. He obtained his doctorate in physics in 1932. A year later he became head of the physics department at Ursinus College in Collegeville, Pennsylvania, near Philadelphia. Mauchly had married Mary Walzl in December 1930.

He began doing research on calculating energy levels and then switched to meteorology. Hoping to improve weather prediction, he wanted to show that the sun was a primary influence on climate. He wanted to prove statistically that if one saw a flare on the sun, some climatic phenomenon would then occur on earth within a specific number of days. Having hired a group of mathematics graduate students at fifty cents an hour, Mauchly had them calculate their data on office adding machines; the enormous amount of weather data he accumulated made it clear that a computer was needed. Mauchly saw electronics as the key to faster computing. Vacuum tubes, however unreliable, were far speedier than the existing punch-card equipment or desk calculators. However, the prohibitive cost of vacuum tubes diverted him to a consideration of gas tubes as a substitute.

Mauchly was forever experimenting with different technologies to build a fast counting device. He made visits to the labs of Johns Hopkins graduates and began experimenting with neon tubes, buying a hundred of them from General Electric; he borrowed vacuum tubes from students' radios. The circuits Mauchly built between 1936 and 1940, using neon and other gas tubes and vacuum tubes, were meant to move him toward electronic digital computing. He could not afford to build a computer using electronic elements, though he might well have tried had he had the cash. Students soon understood the risk involved in giving Mauchly a radio to fix: he would cannibalize the parts. Neon tubes were slow. He built a gas-tube counter that could count 500 times a second, but he had no way of knowing if it would be reliable at higher rates. He also built an analog device, a harmonic analyzer.

On December 4, 1940, Mauchly wrote to John de Wire, a student of his, that within a year or so he hoped to be the first to build an electronic computing device "which will have the answer as fast as the buttons can be depressed. The secret lies in 'scaling circuits,' of course." (Scaling circuits were used to count pulses electronically.) It was at this point that Mauchly presented his paper on the use of computers for handling weather statistics at a conference at the University of Pennsylvania; immediately following the lecture he met John V. Atanasoff. In June 1941 Mauchly traveled to Ames, Iowa, to see Atanasoff's ABC computer. He came away from his visit feeling largely disillusioned. He had at first been impressed with Atanasoff's methods, which struck him as ingenious. But he was dismayed that the ABC was not automatic, that each step had to be controlled by an operator pushing buttons, that it could not be programmed. He had hoped to find a computer that was a vast improvement over existing technology, but he felt that Atanasoff had not exploited the main features of vacuum tubes, their versatility and their speed. Nor had Atanasoff made provision for the unreliability of vacuum tubes. While in Iowa Mauchly learned that he had been accepted into the Moore School of Engineering's Emergency Science and Management Defense Training Course. The course, which admitted twenty specialists in mathematics and the sciences, was designed to train them to become electronic engineers. It was here that the paths of John Mauchly and J. Presper Eckert crossed for the first time.

Like Mauchly, Eckert had been a most talented youngster, with an engineer's mind and a willingness to design the strangest devices. An only child, he was born in Philadelphia on April 9, 1919, into a family of real estate developers and builders. At age eight, he built a crystal radio set on a pencil. At twelve, he designed a small boat that could be moved by a magnet underneath it, winning first prize in a hobby fair. At fifteen, he designed a remote-controlled bomb that exploded on the school stage when activated by means of a push-button box in the audience. Near graduation from the William Penn Charter School in Philadelphia he designed his most bizarre and, so far, perhaps most practical device: a sound system at the Laurel Hill Cemetery to drown out the noise of the nearby crematorium so mourners would be undisturbed. By the time he had completed secondary school in 1937, Eckert had also completed the first year of engineering mathematics. Though he had been admitted to MIT and wanted to go there, Eckert's mother wanted him close to home. His father wanted him to study at the Wharton School of Finance at the University of Pennsylvania. Following his parents' wishes, he enrolled at Wharton but remained only briefly, hating business studies. He wanted to switch to the physics department. Because the enrollment was full, he entered the Moore School of Electrical Engineering. Still annoyed at having to forego MIT, Eckert at first achieved poor grades but graduated in 1941.

Always he was inventing. During one college summer he constructed a device that could measure the concentration of naphthalene vapor using ultraviolet light. He later perfected circuits for using strain gauges. Then he developed instruments that would measure fatigue limits in metals. During World War II he built a device to test ways of setting off enemy magnetic sea mines. The device could record rapid changes in tiny magnetic fields. He worked on problems dealing with radar, including timing devices that measured radar targets. While a lab instructor for the Moore School's wartime electronic engineering course in the summer of 1941, he struck up a friendship with one of the twenty students— John Mauchly. Eckert was twenty-two, a master's student, twelve years younger than Mauchly; but they hit it off immediately. While others thought Mauchly's plans were unrealistic, Eckert convinced him that his dream of building an electronic vacuum-tube computer was possible.

As already noted, in June 1941 Mauchly had examined John Atanasoff's ABC. In September he wrote to Atanasoff, noting that he had ideas "which are nothing like your machine" and that he wished to "make exploratory tests of some of my different ideas with the hope of getting something very speedy, not too costly, etc." He asked Atanasoff for his approval to incorporate some of the ABC's features into a computer. According to his second wife, Kathleen Mauchly, he merely wanted to encourage Atanasoff to join him at the Moore School, where the two men would work together building the computer. Nevertheless, Atanasoff's reply was negative.

Pressure was mounting on the American military establishment. The allies had invaded North Africa in November 1942 but had discovered to their dismay that because the ground was softer in North Africa than in Maryland, their firing tables were off. Without the table an artilleryman could not function. Maryland's Aberdeen Proving Ground, part of the U.S. Army Ordnance Department, was receiving requests for new ballistic tables that required the calculation of hundreds of trajectories for each table—at a rate of six tables per day. The Aberdeen scientists, specialists in ballistics research, were engaged in work with the Moore School to compute these tables. The differential analyzer, their best machine at the time, was not accurate enough, and Eckert, for one, felt that the analyzer had reached its limits. Mauchly exploited the moment to suggest that the Moore School build an electronic high-speed vacuum-tube computer. Numbers would travel from one column to another by moving electrical pulses through wire circuits, which could count those pulses faster than 100,000 per second.

The Moore School was less than excited about the idea, but Mauchly had Eckert on his side. Mauchly and Eckert had a hard time convincing others to put their trust in electronics, especially in vacuum tubes. Critics argued that the tubes burned out and differed in quality. Enrico Fermi, the great statistician and physicist, informed John von Neumann that with the number of tubes in ENIAC it would probably run only five minutes without stopping. But Mauchly and Eckert weren't worried; they knew that the computer was a thousand times speedier than any other device, and if it worked only five minutes of every hour it would still be a hundred times faster than any other machine. Eckert also knew that theater organs used vacuum tubes successfully. What was more, the organs' tubes had not even been used with full current or voltages. So he was convinced that large vacuum-tube-operated devices could work.

In August 1942 Mauchly drafted a five-page memo, "The Use of High-Speed Vacuum Tube Devices for Calculating," urging electronic circuits as a way of increasing calculating speed. The machine that he envisioned would perform a thousand multiplications per second, trajectories in one to two minutes—fifteen to thirty times faster than the analyzer! But the real dawning of ENIAC occurred in September, when Aberdeen ordered its liaison with the university, Lieutenant Herman Goldstine, to check if work on the differential analyzer could be accelerated. By March 1943 Mauchly found Goldstine willing to listen to his ideas about electronic computing. When Goldstine asked Mauchly to put those ideas on paper, Mauchly happily said that he already had, thinking of his August 1942 memo. But to Mauchly's great distress, he was told by Dr. John Grist Brainerd, a Moore School administrator who would become project superviser for ENIAC, that the memo was missing. To rescue matters Mauchly's secretary, Dorothy Shisler, managed to reconstruct the memo from her shorthand notes.

There was some resistance from several government and development managers who thought a computer wasn't feasible given the current technology. Still, Aberdeen approved the project on April 9, 1943, Eckert's twenty-fourth birthday. Army Ordnance provided $400,000 for the highly secret building of the first electronic all-purpose computer, the fastest yet—it would be called the Electronic Numerical Integrator and Computer, or ENIAC. At first the name stopped with Integrator, inasmuch as the plan called for using the machine only for equations relating to the calculation of general tables and the flight of a shell. But after others came to believe that ENIAC should be used for other problems, "and Computer" was added to the name. The plan to build ENIAC was so hush-hush that the Moore School people referred to it only as the PX Project.

At times the secrecy made life difficult for the participants. That same year Eckert reported to his draft board, comprising a French teacher and two men in the textile business. The latter two could not imagine that anyone at a university could be doing anything for the war effort—and Eckert couldn't describe his work. Except for the French teacher, who for some reason sympathized with him, the board thought of him as a draft dodger. Eckert was called before the board a number of times, and when the French teacher went on vacation he appeared likely to be drafted. By this time, however, the university had realized the importance of ENIAC and contacted the Ordnance Department, which provided Eckert with a letter, as did the head of the Selective Service. After that Eckert wasn't bothered by his local draft board.

Mauchly and Eckert's dream was to build a computer that could do in just a day or so what had previously taken a year. But between the dream and the reality much hard work was necessary. The largest electronic equipment built until then—electronic radar devices—contained only 200 vacuum tubes, while ENIAC would require about 17,000. In fact, had Mauchly not had subroutines in the machine, ENIAC might well have required a million tubes, a number so large that probably no one would have seriously considered building such a device.

Fifty people worked on the project, all full-time except Mauchly, who carried a full teaching load as well. The construction site was prosaic enough, a converted Moore School classroom. Special clearance was needed to enter the inner sanctum behind locked doors. Mauchly, the principal consultant to the project, and Eckert, the chief engineer, strove for simplicity. ENIAC would not use the binary system, making it easier on operators, who would read the results right away without converting to binary digits. The longest number ENIAC could handle would be twenty digits long. The master programmer had memory for all branching and discrimination. Each accumulator stored a ten-digit number. However, the memory for operations was not stored digitally along with the data and could not be altered.

Few would forget the work habits of Eckert and Mauchly. Eckert liked to work things out orally in the presence of someone; it didn't matter whether it was a technician or a night watchman. He was highly nervous and would rarely sit in a chair or stand still while thinking. Often he would crouch on top of a desk or pace back and forth. Mauchly was a workaholic who would sometimes be at the office several days in a row without stopping for sleep.

Getting supplies wasn't easy. Eckert had to plead with the Signal Corps to let him have thousands of electronic vacuum tubes. A major problem was the reliabiliy of those tubes. But Eckert solved it by running the tubes a great deal under the graded voltages, making them last longer. A key part of the machine was the accumulator, the adding unit. Two were needed to perform an addition. A number had to be transferred from one accumulator to another. The accumulator then served as a storage for ten digits. ENIAC's read-only storage was three function tables that could hold up to 300 numbers, the equivalent of a modern computer's read-only memory. Numbers would be fed into ENIAC on IBM card readers at a rate of 125 per minute. The output was 100 IBM cards a minute.

Mauchly and Eckert had immersed themselves in ENIAC. It took until the latter part of April 1944 before they felt they were on the threshold of success. Only two accumulators and the cycling unit, which supplied the pulses, had been built thus far. But if two accumulators could collect data, interact with one another, and follow orders, the two inventors would consider the idea successful. One day, satisfied that the accumulators had indeed worked, Eckert and Mauchly went to the basement of the Moore School, where Kathleen McNulty (whom Mauchly later married) and Alyse Snyder were working on the differential analyzer. Would the two women like to see what they had accomplished thus far?

Eckert and Mauchly set up the two accumulators, each with 500 tubes, with a cage around it. Mauchly had a wire with a small button on the end of it. Pressing the button, he generated pulses to go into one accumulator. The fifth neon bulb lit up. "Watch this," said one of the two men. Immediately into the second accumulator went the number 5 to the fourth place—so the number was 5,000. "We looked at this in amazement," Kathleen Mauchly later recalled, "because we thought, 'All of this equipment to transfer that 5 over there.' Then they explained to us that the 5 had gone over there a thousand times in that second and become 5,000." They had multiplied 5 times 1,000 and obtained the number 5,000! After this achievement Mauchly and Eckert built the other eighteen accumulators. It would be another twenty months before the entire ENIAC would work for the first time.

As early as December 1943 Mauchly and Eckert began thinking about building an improved ENIAC that would provide better storage. Their three-month progress report, written that month, included a suggestion for another computer. Then in January 1944 Eckert wrote a patent disclosure (witnessed by Mauchly), purely for their own use at the time—in order to establish the date and content of the stored-program idea. The idea took on concrete form when in the fall of 1944 the army's Ballistics Research Laboratory agreed to fund the Electronic Discrete Variable Automatic Computer, or EDVAC. Also top secret, it was called Project PY.

During the fall of 1944 the project took on a new complexion. John von Neumann, the eminent mathematician, lent prestige to ENIAC and EDVAC merely by taking an interest in them. However, von Neumann's visit to the Moore School created a new rivalry for the claim of authorship. Acting as sole publicist for the secret computer work in Philadelphia, von Neumann threatened to steal Mauchly and Eckert's thunder as prime movers of ENIAC and EDVAC. Sensing that computers would have large commercial value, Mauchly and Eckert wrote to the Moore School administration on September 27, 1944, that they intended to take out a patent on the ENIAC. The university did not have a patent policy at the time, and the dean of the Moore School advised Mauchly and Eckert to hire their own patent attorney: neither the Moore School nor the university would do so. The pair thus consulted some government lawyers to help them write their patents.

Through EDVAC, the two inventors now proceeded to develop their stored-program idea. Indeed, their main contribution to the EDVAC project—the machine was not actually built until 1952, after both Mauchly and Eckert had left the Moore School—was the invention of the circulating mercury delay line store. Bits circulated as ultrasonic pulses in a column of mercury. Once each bit got to the end of the column, it became an electrical signal that could be read. This provided sufficient capacity to store program information and data. ENIAC had a capacity of only twenty words of memory, much too little to store programs or data. But each delay line in EDVAC could hold hundreds of words.

In June 1945 von Neumann sent his *First Draft* on EDVAC to the Moore School. Herman Goldstine, the army-university liaison officer, distributed copies inside and outside the Moore School, infuriating Mauchly and Eckert, who were concerned lest they lose all patent rights to von Neumann. ENIAC had been funded to speed up trajectory calculations, but the computer was simply not ready before war's end in May 1945. A decision was taken that spring to complete the ENIAC, and a staff of five women (among them Kathleen McNulty) was recruited for an intensive summer course. By early November the computer was virtually finished. Some preliminary tests were still advisable but von Neumann's urgent interest in using ENIAC to resolve problems connected with H-bomb development took precedence. On December 10 the first full test of ENIAC was performed, in the presence of two scientists from Los Alamos. The test worked, and in the sense that ENIAC confirmed the mathematics used by the Los Alamos scientists, ENIAC contributed to the development of the H bomb.

On February 16, 1946, ENIAC was unveiled in formal dedication ceremonies. Flawlessly, it completed its first problem: a highly secret numerical simulation for the yet-untested hydrogen bomb. The exercise which would have taken existing calculating machines forty hours, took ENIAC twenty seconds. Mauchly and Eckert had given birth to a new age, and the proof lay in this 80-foot-long, 8-foot-high, 3-foot-deep monster weighing thirty tons. How complicated it all seemed, with its forty panels, 10,000 capacitors, 6,000 switches, and those 17,468 vacuum tubes. Some 4,000 red neon tubes were on the front of the machine, showing the functioning of various parts of ENIAC. If an error occurred, the calculation could be rerun at a very slow speed so the operator could use the lights to find the flaw. "Every science fiction machine since then," Eckert has noted, "has had flashing lights all over it."

At the outset every time the machine came up with a wrong answer, machine failure was blamed. In time the staff looked for programming errors and discovered that these were usually the source of the breakdown. Eckert would take a slide rule and recheck every circuit. He realized he had to do this or else the rules the staff had set would not be followed. The 4,000 knobs on ENIAC were a problem as well: when the staff wiggled a few they found that they could easily come loose. Someone proposed that they use hardened set screws with a hole in the switch shaft. That kept the knobs from falling off. Then there was the potential problem of mice eating the wire. As a test, some mice were put in a cage, starved for some time, and then offered different kinds of wire. When it was discovered that the mice loved the type of wiring that had been planned for ENIAC, other wiring, which passed the mouse test, was chosen. The total cost of the machine: $486,804.22.

Hindsight reveals ENIAC's flaw—it had no internal stored memory. To reprogram ENIAC, operators had to walk around the room, throw switches, and turn, plug, and replug dials. Still, at the dedication the machine computed the trajectory of a 16-inch naval shell in less than real time. The true significance of ENIAC was lost on most of the reporters who came that Saturday to watch the test. Some didn't even file stories, others ran short items. Only the *New York Times* saw something for the future. It ran a front-page story headlined "Electronic Computer Flashes Answers, May Speed Engineering." Mauchly and Eckert, their photos running on an inside page, were touted as ENIAC's inventors. Later, Mauchly would regret one omission in the explanatory lectures he and Eckert gave that day. Neither mentioned that computers might help put man into space.

In the spring of 1946 the University of Pennsylvania, sensing what potentially lucrative options ENIAC offered, insisted that Mauchly and Eckert relinquish the right to patents on their computers. Both, however, believed the university had promised them ENIAC and EDVAC patents. Disagreeing, the university gave them an ultimatum. If they were to continue working at Pennsylvania on EDVAC, they would have to assign all future patents to the university. The two men resigned on March 22, 1946, contending they had been fired.

Meanwhile, ENIAC, the only fast computer in the world, was a big attraction. It was kept at the Moore School for a year before being moved to Aberdeen in 1947. Used mainly to create firing tables for new weapons, the computer was also involved in the design of wind tunnels, the study of cosmic rays, random number studies, thermal ignition, and weather prediction. ENIAC remained operational until October 22, 1955. By then faster computers existed, and maintaining the 17,468 tubes had proved too expensive.

Spurning an offer to start IBM's computer lab, Mauchly and Eckert founded their own firm, Electronic Control Corporation (ECC), in an office over a clothing store in Philadelphia in the spring of 1946. Financing came from a $25,000 loan given by Eckert's father. The computer builders went into business specifically to design an EDVAC-type machine for the federal Bureau of the Census. They began work, however, with a contract from the government to do a feasibility study on a magnetic tape drive and mercury delay line memory. Though formally they no longer worked at the University of Pennsylvania, that summer Mauchly and Eckert taught a six-week course at the Moore School entitled "Theory and Techniques for Design of Electronic Digital Computers." It was the first real opportunity for people to exchange ideas on electronic computing. The Moore School Lectures, as they came to be called, marked a major event in early computer history.

It was at the end of that summer that tragedy struck John Mauchly. He and his wife, Mary, went swimming on Labor Day weekend at the New Jersey shore. Mary drowned. Two years later Mauchly married Kathleen McNulty.

In the fall of 1947, needing money, Mauchly and Eckert entered into a contract with Northrop Corporation in California to build the BINAC—Binary Automatic Computer. Engaged in a project to develop a long-range guided missile for the Air Force, Northrop had fastened onto the idea of using computers for airborne navigation. In October 1947 it gave Mauchly and Eckert a $100,000 contract to build a small numeric computer that, while not meant to work during a flight, would perhaps spur progress toward that goal. Only when miniature solid-state components were invented did airborne computers become feasible. BINAC was completed in August 1949, $178,000 over budget—the two inventors absorbing the loss themselves. Preoccupied with their Census Bureau project—the future UNIVAC—Eckert and Mauchly gave little attention to BINAC. As a result, the machine, though it was the first electronic stored-program computer (EDVAC would not be completed until 1952), did not run well.

Built with two serial processors, BINAC functioned more like two computers than one, providing a safety back-up for airplanes that would eventually be critical. Each part of the device was built as a pair of systems that would check each step. All instructions were carried out once by each unit, and then the result would be compared between the units. If they matched, the next instruction would be carried out; but if there was a discrepancy between the two parts of the machine, it stopped. The processors were only 5 feet tall, 4 feet long, and a foot wide, tiny for those days. Each one had 700 tubes. While ENIAC could perform 5,000 additions a second, BINAC did only 3,500, but the latter computer could do 1,000 multiplications a second, more than three times as many as ENIAC (333). With a large mercury delay line memory, each of the two BINAC processors could store 512 thirty-one-bit words.

BINAC was never more to Mauchly and Eckert than a stepping stone to UNIVAC. The two men believed in the commercial potential of computers, and the computer they would build wound up a highly marketable product: some forty-six were sold, indicating that there were customers for computers even if they cost hundreds of thousands of dollars. All those firms, among them IBM, that had dismissed the commercial opportunities of computers were forced to sit up and take notice with the success of Mauchly and Eckert's UNIVAC. Even Mark I inventor Howard Aiken had suggested that the two men were on the wrong track, that there would never be enough work for more than one or two computers.

By the fall of 1949 the Eckert-Mauchly firm was in financial difficulties, raising uncertainty over whether it would be able to build UNIVAC. That fall, the firm's main investor, Henry Straus, who had a 40-percent interest in Eckert-Mauchly, died in a plane crash. Without money to pay the bills, Eckert and Mauchly took the first reasonable offer—from Remington Rand. The two inventors received $70,000 for their patents plus guaranteed salaries of $18,000 a year over the next eight years. So it was that Remington Rand completed UNIVAC and delivered it to the Bureau of the Census on June 14, 1951.

UNIVAC was the fastest computer built up to that time. In 1951 it was the only commercial general-purpose electronic computer in the world. Its key feature was the stored-program aspect, with both data and instructions stored side by side; programmed instructions were put on magnetic tape rather than the more primitive punch cards. One magnetic tape reel could hold one million characters—an amount that would have required tens of thousands of punch cards. UNIVAC contained only 5,000 vacuum tubes (compared to ENIAC's 17,468) and was more compact than its predecessors. The main processor measured only 14.5 feet by 7.5 feet by 9 feet. While ENIAC operated at a clock rate of 100,000 pulses per second, UNIVAC's rate was 2.5 million pulses per second. UNIVAC required no set-up time: information was fed in on magnetic tape. In contrast with ENIAC's twenty 10-digit number storage, UNIVAC had a 1,000-word internal high-speed storage available.

Enthusiasm over UNIVAC—and computers in general—was small. A 1950 *Business Week* story noted: "Salesmen will find the market limited. The UNIVAC is not the kind of machine that every office could use." But this was before UNIVAC had been put through its paces and truly shown off to the public. UNIVAC passed its first major test on election eve of 1952. With only seven percent of the presidential vote in, forty-five minutes after the polls closed, it predicted that Dwight Eisenhower would defeat Adlai Stevenson by garnering 438 electoral votes. When Eisenhower actually won 442 electoral votes, UNIVAC was acclaimed.

Both Mauchly and Eckert had become employees of the Remington Rand—soon the Sperry Rand—Corporation. Mauchly was director of UNIVAC applications research for the UNIVAC Division of Sperry Rand until 1959. He and Eckert then parted company. Mauchly formed his own computer consulting firm, Mauchly Associates, which developed computers for scheduling tasks and introduced the critical path method, CPM, by which computers were used to help schedule jobs and resources as part of the planning for the construction of large facilities such as hospitals and hotels.

In 1968 Mauchly formed Dynatrend, a systems consulting company. He began forecasting the weather but moved over to predicting stock market trends. In 1974 he acquired an infection that led to various complications from which he never fully recovered. He died in 1980.

Eckert became director of engineering for Remington Rand's UNIVAC Division. He was given the title Vice-President and Director of Research in 1955, and since 1963 has been Vice-President and Technical Adviser for Computer Systems for the Sperry (now UNISYS) Corporation. In 1969 he was awarded the National Medal of Science.

The patent controversy over ENIAC had a long history that culminated in the legal battle with John Atanasoff. Mauchly and Eckert had applied for the patent on June 26, 1947, and in 1950 had assigned their ENIAC patent rights to Remington Rand. The patent was issued only on February 4, 1964, after which Sperry began receiving royalties from firms building computers. Mauchly and Eckert received $300,000 each. Sperry sued Honeywell in 1971, charging patent infringement after Honeywell failed to pay royalties. Honeywell then countersued. It contended that ENIAC had been based on Atanasoff's prior invention, the ABC.

The trial lasted almost a year, ending on March 13, 1972. Finally, on October 19, 1973, Judge Earl R. Larson decided against Sperry, hence against Mauchly and Eckert. The judge ruled that the original patent was invalid for two reasons: First, because ENIAC had been used for H-bomb work over a year before the patent was sought, whereas a patent is valid only when the invention has existed less than a year before the application is filed; and second, because Eckert and Mauchly had derived the essential concepts of the electonic digital computer from Atanasoff.

Mauchly was outraged. He contended that he had been building electronic and digital equipment five years before he had even heard of the Iowa inventor. Long after the trial the issue of who built the first digital computer remained. It will probably never be resolved. But that cannot detract from the major attainments of Mauchly and Eckert—builders of ENIAC and UNIVAC.

Howard Aiken

Builder of the First American Electronic Brain

8

His invention, the Mark I, is remembered fondly as the first American electronic brain. Actually it was electromechanical, not electronic; and its creator believed strongly that no machine should ever be credited with thinking. At any rate, Howard Aiken and the Mark I are of great importance to the computer story. For this was the first computer unveiled for the American public—years before Mauchly and Eckert's ENIAC, which was kept from view for military reasons. For a long time the Mark I was thought to be the world's first operational program-controlled computer; but when details of the German Konrad Zuse's World War II computers became known, the Harvard machine moved ever so slightly from center stage in computing history. Aiken once called his invention merely the idea of a lazy man—and it is clear that he did not fathom the impact this lazy man's idea would have on society. But it was through the Mark I that a great many people learned about computers; indeed, it is fair to call the dedication of the Aiken machine in August 1944 the inauguration of the modern computer. Aiken hoped that in building a computer he would somehow benefit society. Yet after the machine was built, he knew it had the potential to harm as well as to benefit. Aiken always understood the limitations of a computer: it would not be able to do the thinking for a business executive, but its speed would make work easier and more efficient.

Aiken showed that it was indeed possible to build a large-scale automatic computer capable of performing according to a program and, most significantly, capable of producing reliable results. And the Mark I was not his only major achievement; Aiken is equally known and admired for having set up the first school of advanced computer science and for having created international interest in the subject.

Howard Hathaway Aiken was born on March 8, 1900, in Hoboken, New Jersey. He spent most of his childhood in Indianapolis, where he attended Arsenal Technical High School. While in high school he also worked twelve hours a night at the Indianapolis Light and Heat Company. In 1919 he entered the University of Wisconsin, in Madison, supporting himself throughout his four years there by working as an operating engineer at the Madison Gas and Electric Company. Aiken received a degree in electrical engineering in 1923; he continued to work for Madison Gas, now as chief engineer, responsible for the design and reconstruction of the company's electric generating station. He remained with Madison Gas until 1928.

The knowledge Aiken acquired in the course of designing and operating electric power generating stations would later help him devise his plan for automatic computing machinery. Between 1928 and 1931 he worked for the Westinghouse Electrical and Manufacturing Company as a general engineer, applying the firm's products to the design of electric generating stations. He worked for the Line Material Company in Milwaukee in 1931 and 1932.

After spending ten years as an electrical engineer, Aiken felt he had chosen the wrong field. He decided to study mathematics and physics, and enrolled for a year at the University of Chicago for that purpose. He continued his studies at Harvard, where he obtained a master's degree in physics in 1937 and a doctorate in physics in 1939. Between 1937 and 1939 he also worked as an instructor in physics and communications engineering at Harvard.

Aiken saw himself as a spiritual descendant of Charles Babbage. Few of the other computer pioneers would delve into Babbage's writings with equal intensity. By the mid-1930s he had begun to contemplate building a large-sized calculator, and he noticed, in poring over Babbage's *Passages from the Life of a Philosopher,* that the nineteenth-century inventor had written of building one too. The calculators in use in the 1930s could carry out only one arithmetical operation at a time. Babbage had conceived in his Analytical Engine of a giant-sized calculator that would perform a series of arithmetical operations automatically, and Aiken hoped to replicate the Babbage device.

In a 1937 memo entitled "Proposed Automatic Calculating Machine," which he distributed privately, Aiken described the calculator he envisioned as "a switchboard on which are mounted various pieces of calculating machine apparatus. Each panel of the switchboard is given over to definite mathematical operations." Aiken wanted to take the available punch-card tabulators and sorters, put them together, and make some modifications. But it was clear from his memo that his calculating machinery would be an improvement over the old punched-card accounting kind: it would handle most mathematical functions, and it would be automatic.

Aiken did his doctoral thesis on the theory of space charge conduction. The work involved tedious calculations of nonlinear differential equations. In the thesis he expressed frustration over the time required by these equations: to get a numerical solution for even a small number of interesting cases would have meant an amount of calculation beyond human capabilities. And so, like other computer pioneers, he drew the conclusion that the best solution was to build his own machine! From 1939 until 1941 Aiken taught mathematics at Harvard as a faculty instructor. Beginning his research on a large-scale calculator in 1939, he worked in conjunction with engineers at the IBM engineering laboratory in Endicott, New York, In 1941 he became an associate professor of applied mathematics at the Harvard Graduate School of Engineering. In 1946 he became a full professor.

One of the influences on Aiken's design for the Mark I—also known as the ASCC, for Automatic Sequence Controlled Calculator—was a conversation he had with Harvard physicist H. R. Mimmo, in which the latter told Aiken about the problems encountered in designing electrical pulses for radio propagation experiments that would not interfere with ongoing radio services. Mimmo and Aiken talked about some of the devices that could be used to generate pulse functions. "Rather suddenly," Mimmo later recalled, "we were discussing, across my office desk, the possibility of directing the activities of scores of computing units, initially talking in terms of racks of interrelated machines, each roughly equivalent to the Marchant or Monroe desk computers of that day and age. . . . The point of greatest interest, of course, was Howard's eager proposal of a band of paper tape, centrally governing the program of the individual units."

Once Aiken's ideas had crystallized, he approached a number of firms, among them Marchant, Monroe, and National Cash Register. He was congratulated for having come up with an interesting idea, but no one suggested it was worth pursuing. Harvard president James Bryant Conant made it clear to Aiken that he was jeopardizing his chances of getting tenure by working on such improbable notions. It was only when Aiken got in touch with IBM's Thomas Watson, Sr., that the Mark I got off the ground. On learning that Aiken wanted to build a general-purpose computer for scientific calculations, two of his Harvard colleagues, Theodore H. Brown of the Business School and astronomer Harlow Shapley, had suggested that he talk with astronomer Wallace Eckert at the Watson Computing Bureau at Columbia University. IBM had been sponsoring research at Columbia during the 1930s that would lead to Eckert's mechanical calculator for astronomers. Aiken became convinced, however, that his thinking was more advanced than that of the Columbia group, and in 1937 he approached Thomas Watson. Watson had no great faith that the scientific market would bear fruit for IBM, but he liked Aiken's proposal. So he gave his backing to a project that would involve adapting the components and techniques of IBM statistical devices to Aiken's planned automatic scientific calculator.

If World War I was the chemist's war, World War II was surely the mathematician's. Aiken took a leading position among the mathematicians called into service during the years 1939–1945. He began as school officer of the Naval Warfare School at Yorktown; but at one point an influential navy man asked him why he wasn't running the Mark I. He had his orders, was Aiken's terse reply. Within hours the orders were changed. Aiken was instructed to leave for Harvard immediately, to become the officer in charge of the U.S. Navy Computing Project. Aiken joked that he was the only man in the world to be commanding officer of a computer.

The Mark I differed from Vannevar Bush's differential analyzer, in that Aiken's computer could handle nearly all mathematical problems whereas Bush's device solved only differential equations. The Mark I was electromechanical and thus anticipated the electronic computer revolution. Electronic devices, having no moving

The Mark I

parts and thus requiring almost no maintenance, as well as being faster and increasingly cheaper than electromechanical devices, would soon represent the clear choice.

The Mark I was an impressively large piece of machinery, 51 feet long, 8 feet high, and 2 feet thick, and weighing 5 tons. It had three-quarters of a million parts, five hundred miles of wiring, and three million wire connections. It made no more noise, however, than several typewriters working side by side. Its staff affectionately called it "Bessie," because of its labors in computing Bessel functions—solutions to a type of differential equation. To those who worked on it and became familiar with computers of later years, Mark I seemed somehow a far cry from a computer. "No one looking at it today," said Grace Hopper in 1983 (as Lieutenant Hopper during the war, she was one of the first to program the machine), "would really believe it was a computer. You'd hardly believe it was a calculator. . . . It would be hard to recognize Mark in today's world."

Mark I had a set of 72 standard IBM mechanical rotating registers, which formed the essence of the machine. These registers whirled around, carrying out operations on numbers. Each one of them could store a single 23-digit number plus sign indication. The numbers went from one register to another by electrical signal.

In a 1946 article in the journal *Electrical Engineering,* Aiken and his coauthor Grace Hopper wrote: "The development of numerical analysis . . . and methods for solving ordinary and partial differential equations have reduced, in effect, the processes of mathematical analysis to selected sequences of the five fundamental operations of arithmetic: addition, subtraction, multiplication, division, and reference to tables of previously computed results. The Automatic Sequence Controlled Calculator was designed to carry out any selected sequence of these operations under completely automatic control." The Mark I had four paper-tape readers, one a control tape for instructions, the other three for data input. Data was fed into the machine via two IBM card readers and a card punch. Two electric typewriters printed its output. In order to work the Mark I it was necessary to adjust 1,400 rotary knoblike switches on an external panel, which set the values for the 60 constant registers.

Why did Aiken choose to make the Mark I electromechanical rather than electronic? For one thing, he had, in common with most of his contemporaries in the 1940s, little faith in vacuum tube technology. But in truth he held few preconceived views about the type of components to use in building a computer. The important thing, he felt, was to get the machine built. A pragmatist, Aiken sensed that the interior of the computer would depend a great deal on who was financing the project. Monroe would have wanted mechanical parts, whereas RCA would have gone for electronic components. IBM, who did pay, wanted tabulating parts—so that was what the Mark I was made up of.

Final construction of the machine was delayed by American entry into World War II. At last in January 1943 the Mark I was demonstrated at Endicott, and a year later Aiken was able to perform astronomical calculations with it. The Mark I was dismantled and shipped to Harvard for its official unveiling in May 1944. The big machine had cost $500,000—two-thirds borne by IBM, the other one-third by the navy. It used many of the components that could be found in IBM equipment: cam contacts, typewriters, card feeds and punches, relays, counters. Thomas Watson, Sr., traveled to Harvard for the unveiling ceremony in the belief that he and IBM would be accorded much credit for their contribution to the new machine. He was in for a shock. Aiken took full credit. Watson angrily observed that IBM could not be simply tacked on as a postscript. He was as loyal to IBM as Harvard people were to Harvard.

Watson had a final word with Harvard president Conant: the Mark I, he said, belonged to IBM, not Harvard—and IBM would no longer fund research at Harvard. Later generations of IBM leadership never forgot or forgave Aiken. Thomas Watson, Jr., in recalling the incident, has remarked that he believes his father and Aiken might have killed each other had they been armed.

Aiken had managed to build the first program-controlled computer, and though it was obsolete at birth (because ENIAC was five hundred times faster), it was nevertheless quite powerful. One problem that took four specialists three weeks to solve was completed by the Mark I in only nineteen hours. Most significantly, it was available to people outside the secret preserve of the military. Immediately after the Mark I's unveiling, the navy assigned both it and its inventor to war work specifically dealing with gunnery and ballistics problems and naval design. Throughout most of the sixteen years it was in operation its principal task was to calculate mathematical tables, for which it was quite well suited.

Though the Mark I was heralded as a machine that could solve almost any known problem in applied mathematics, Aiken naively boasted that six Mark I's would be sufficient for all the computer needs of American scientists. Yet Howard Aiken's invention would have little long-range impact on the world of computing. It was electromechanical—and already the magic word was electronics. By the time the Mark I was on the scene, ENIAC was virtually complete and vacuum tubes were gaining acceptability.

Not until late in 1946 was Aiken permitted to return to full-time work at Harvard. In January 1947 he was made director of Harvard's new Computation Laboratory, holding that post until 1961. Some believe that Aiken's greatest achievement—greater even than building the Mark I—was the environment he created at Harvard, helping the university to become one of the first real training grounds in computer science. Aiken's laboratory did pioneering work in such new fields as mathematical linguistics, the automatic translation of languages, switching theory, and the use of magnetic cores and magnetic drums as computer components. Aiken was the general editor of the *Annals of the Computation Laboratory,* and was the coauthor or editor of numerous volumes of mathematical tables and books on switching theory.

Work on the Mark II was begun in November 1945; it was

constructed by Aiken for the Dahlgren Proving Ground of the Navy's Bureau of Ordnance. Whereas the Mark I used electromechanical parts, the Mark II was built with electromagnetic relays. It could handle ten-decimal-digit numbers, storing some 100 of them. The Mark II was three times as large as the Mark I and twelve times faster. One of its most intriguing characteristics was that it could be operated as either one or two separate computers. The Mark III, completed in March 1950, was also built for the navy and was known as the Aiken Dahlgren Electronic Calculator, or ADEC. It had magnetic drum storage and could multiply at eighty operations per second. The Mark IV was completed in 1952 for the U.S. Air Force. It incorporated 200 magnetic-core shift registers.

In 1961 Aiken retired from Harvard and moved to Fort Lauderdale, Florida. He became Distinguished Professor of Information Technology at the University of Miami, helping the school set up a computer science program and a computing center. He also founded Howard Aiken Industries Incorporated, a New York consulting concern. He had always told friends that a good professor with half a mind should be able to run circles around people in industry. Now he would prove it. He said he would spend the remainder of his life trying to make money, and he did just that.

Aiken was the recipient of numerous awards, but the ceremonies associated with them bored him. What he liked were occasions when he could take paper and pencil and, as he once put it, explain how "computin' machines" actually functioned. At times he found himself explaining such matters to a head of state.

A colleague of Aiken's, Jacquelin Sanborn Sill, described him in a speech given in 1973 as "human, humane, and patriotic." He drove his students hard. A favorite line of his was, "I am a simple man and I want simple answers." On putting a particularly difficult task to a student, his parting shot would always be, "Have fun!" In return students affectionately referred to him as the boss or the old man—among themselves, of course. Once a student approached him with the concern that someone might steal his (the student's) ideas before the publication of his thesis. "Don't worry about people stealing an idea," replied Aiken. "If it's original, you will have to ram it down their throats."

Aiken was never impressed with what came to be called artificial intelligence. He did not believe that such a thing could exist. One simply could not invent a thinking machine. The connection between thought processes and the activities of mechanical calculators was not a proper subject for discussion in his lab. Aiken disliked the notion of patents; the idea of proving who invented something was distasteful to him. He openly shared his work with others. Lecture fees were surreptitiously given over to staffers, sometimes as wedding gifts or as loans between paychecks.

Howard Aiken died on March 14, 1973. Those who worked with him remember him as a personality of great presence and force. Fred Brooks, who was at the Harvard Computation Laboratory from 1953 to 1956 as a graduate student and went on to design the IBM System/360 computer, described the Aiken he knew in 1953: "[He was] at the height of his powers, alert, energetic, forceful, self-assured. About six feet two and formidable. He dominated any room he entered. And you can see from the Spockian ears and the raised eyebrows, he had a positive Mephistophelian look."

Jay W. Forrester

The Core Memory Man

9

Back in the late 1940s the small group of scientists who were concerned with computers held widely varying views as to what these machines might actually do for mankind. It was the military that produced the first real need for computers. But even it was not sure just how the machines would help it—only that they were the coming thing and should be built.

It took some brilliant innovators to turn computers into equipment that was workable and useful. One of the most important was Jay Forrester, a man whose contribution to early computer history ranges from his leadership in the vast enterprise known as Project Whirlwind to the discovery that using coincident-current, random-access core memory could greatly expand information storage in computers. It is impossible to imagine a conversation about the early days of computing in which the name Jay Forrester would not pop up. He left his mark in so many different places. Some of his work has been superseded, but none of the new technology could have been developed without his coming first.

Forrester emerged as a major figure in computers in the late 1940s and early 1950s. He sensed early that they could be useful in solving a variety of problems, and he became one of the great advocates of digital computing, pushing MIT in that direction, pushing the military, and ultimately pushing his country. He was the organizer of one of the most significant computer projects in history, Project Whirlwind. Even Forrester's zeal and persistence, however, might not have prevented that enterprise's death from lack of interest and lack of cash, had outside events not played their part in revitalizing it. Forrester had the U.S.S.R. to thank. In exploding an atomic weapon and then supporting the invasion of South Korea, the Soviets forced the United States to take a sober look at its air defenses. These defenses were found wanting. A need arose for a firm, dedicated hand to guide the building of computers to modernize America's air protection. Chosen for the task was Jay Forrester. He handled the design and construction of the SAGE system. The SAGE computers, modifications of the Whirlwind machine, were designed and built by IBM and MIT scientists in a collaborative effort; they were known as the AN/FSQ7 computers.

Forrester's innovations stood the test of time. The SAGE program, relying upon Whirlwind computers, lasted into the early 1980s. By that time Jay Forrester had long been involved in computer studies of a very different complexion. He had joined the faculty at MIT's Sloan School of Management, where he used his background in computer technology to create a new discipline called system dynamics.

He gave the field Whirlwind and SAGE, improved methods for keeping vacuum tubes operating, and perhaps most significantly, his version of core memory. Talking to him, one quickly perceives a razor-sharp mind. He listens to a question, appears abstracted for a moment, and then enunciates an answer in which there is not one superfluous word. He seems the essence of a scientist. One is surprised to learn, therefore, that he traces his roots back to a cattle ranch near a Nebraska town called Climax whose population numbered only ten when he was born there on July 14, 1918. Cattle ranching did not appeal to him. He attended a one-room country school and began doing simple electrical experiments. In his senior year of high school he took old automobile parts and built a wind-driven, 12-volt electrical system that supplied the first electricity to his family's ranch. He had planned to enter the agricultural college at the University of Nebraska but a few months before enrollment in the fall of 1935 changed his mind and decided upon electrical engineering as a major. When he graduated in 1939, Forrester had the best record of the seventy electrical engineering graduates.

He began graduate studies at MIT in July 1939, working at first as a research assistant in the High-Voltage Laboratory. In the middle of the 1940–1941 school year Forrester started work in Gordon

Brown's new Servomechanisms Laboratory, part of the MIT Electrical Engineering Department. His work for the master's degree in electrical engineering, put aside during the war in favor of military research, was completed in 1945. Brown supervised Forrester's thesis, entitled "Hydraulic Servomechanisms Developments."

In December 1944 the navy's Special Devices Center had sought out MIT to build an aircraft stability and control analyzer (ASCA) to be used in the testing of new aerodynamic designs. Forrester had been thinking of pulling out of the Servomechanisms Laboratory at that time; maybe he would start his own business in automatic control. But Gordon Brown wanted him there, and so he showed Forrester a list of a dozen projects and told him to pick whichever he liked. Forrester looked the list over, and suddenly the idea of starting his own business seemed much less attractive than getting involved in some new research. Especially appealing was the ASCA project. He told Brown he would take it on.

Forrester was supposed to build an analog computer that would simulate an airplane's performance with the pilot as a part of the system. Aircraft controls would be available to a pilot, and responses from the simulated plane would be in real time. The purpose of the simulator was to anticipate the effects of engineering changes on performance and thus to save money. Soon after taking on the project—it was now the spring of 1945—Forrester realized he had serious problems. If he were going to include the pilot's control reactions and provide simulated responses by the airplane in the time these would actually take, he would need extremely high-speed servos with quite short response times. But they were lacking. By the summer Forrester had become convinced that analog devices would simply not be fast enough to achieve the real-time computing that was required.

At this stage a major turning point in Forrester's thinking occurred. It happened because of a man named Perry Crawford, formerly of the MIT Center of Analysis, and at that time working at the navy's Special Devices Center. After hearing of Forrester's doubts, Crawford suggested that he look into digital computing. He offered to put him in touch with the people at Harvard and the University of Pennsylvania, and as a result Forrester had a meeting in Philadelphia with John von Neumann, J. Presper Eckert, and others. That visit made Forrester a digital-computer enthusiast.

Next he had to persuade Gordon Brown. That proved easy; and in January 1946 a digital computer development program was started at the Servo Lab.

No one seemed interested in analog computers any more. That April the contract specifications for ASCA were modified to take into account that Forrester and his team would be using digital computers rather than analog ones. The project became known as Whirlwind. Forrester was now director of the Digital Computer Laboratory, a successor to the digital Computer Division of the Servomechanisms Laboratory.

In early 1947 he thought of building an EDVAC-type serial machine but gave that up after realizing that it would be too slow for calculations in real time. Later in that year Forrester and Robert R. Everett, associate director of the project, shifted to a general-purpose parallel computer. In November Forrester grew impatient at the fact that deteriorating vacuum tubes and crystal diodes would shut down the Whirlwind computer several times a day. No one knew much at that stage about the life of vacuum tubes, except that after 500 hours most of them stopped operating. Any machine with several thousand vacuum tubes, each with a life of only 500 hours, was not going to run very long between failures. Forrester came up with two ideas that he felt were almost as dramatic as his core memory.

First, he increased the life of vacuum tubes from 500 to 500,000 hours by using a silicon-free cathode material that eliminated the previous loss of cathode emissions. Next, he multiplied that life span by ten—to five million hours—by putting a marginal checking system into the Whirlwind that automatically detected any electronic component that was beginning to operate improperly. It could be repaired before it might cause an error. In time, Forrester and his staff designed a high-speed electronic digital stored-program computer that ran in real time. It became possible to monitor air traffic or even a military campaign. His computer handled not only flight simulation calculations but general engineering and scientific needs as well.

Whirlwind was the largest computer project of the late 1940s and early 1950s, with 175 people working on it at a $1 million annual budget. Project employees found Forrester somewhat formal and distant, but they had great respect for his know-how. Whirlwind's frame was erected in August 1948. It occupied 2,500 square feet of floor space. Working on the Whirlwind, people had the feeling of being inside the computer: one walked down a corridor with four banks each of components to the left and right. It had only 4,000 vacuum tubes (compared to ENIAC's 17,468). Building Whirlwind took three years; it was virtually operational in early 1950. Whirlwind was the fastest computer of the early 1950s. It could add two 16-bit words in two microseconds and could multiply in twenty microseconds. The Harvard Mark I took six seconds to multiply. Whirlwind was superior to the Mauchly-Eckert computer as well, for ENIAC was not a general-purpose machine.

Whirlwind was not entirely reliable. Inside it were thirty-two electrostatic tubes which stored 2,048 16-bit words. The computer was out of order a few hours each day. It also could not run programs that required a great deal of read/write memory. Its memory was problematic in another way, too: each storage tube would last no more than a month and cost $1,000 to replace. The monthly cost for memory therefore ran $32,000.

Having improved electrostatic storage tubes as much as he could, Forrester turned to another idea that had the potential of creating much larger computer storage. This was the notion of magnetic-core memory. So far, every approach to computer memory had revealed serious flaws. The one-dimensional mercury delay line, while probably reliable enough, was quite expensive and slow; the two-dimensional Williams Tube (which used a cathode-ray tube) was too unreliable. At one point Forrester developed a cathode-ray tube memory (called the MIT Storage Tube) that would permit random access to the stored digits; unlike the Williams Tube, it was continuously replenished by a flood of electrons from a second gun in the tube; a deflected beam could be used to alter the nature of the charge and read it. The MIT Storage Tube could store 1,024 binary digits. But there was a drawback. Each one cost $1,000 to make and would last only a month, yielding a storage cost of $1 per binary digit per month.

"There it is," Forrester summed up nearly four decades later, "the motivation for something better in economic terms: $1 per binary digit per month was not feasible computer storage. There was simply nothing that was suitable, and I had a project and a reputation that rested on our solving the problem. So it was very much a case of necessity being the mother of invention." The answer seemed to lie in creating three-dimensional storage, because it would potentially be more compact, have larger amounts of storage, and be less expensive than the one- or two-dimensional kind.

At first, in 1947, Forrester tried to devise a logic for a three-dimensional cube where the intersections would be the storage elements. He planned to use small neon cells as the elements of those intersections but worried about the unreliability and slowness of secondary emission devices. After some time he laid that project aside, but he kept in mind building a three-dimensional array: "I was more or less alert to the possibility that some other kind of element might function in such a concept."

One evening in the spring of 1949 he was looking through the magazine *Electrical Engineering* and came upon an advertisement for a material called Deltamax, developed by the Germans in World War II for magnetic amplifiers in tanks. It was now being sold in the United States as a core material for magnetic amplifiers. Deltamax used direct current to saturate the core to vary the current being controlled. Forrester asked himself whether there was any way to make this nonlinear element work in the three-dimensional array he had worked on earlier.

For several evenings thereafter he strolled the streets near his suburban home, thinking about the problem. "It was a challenge, a turning over of ideas, trying to see how to fit that particular kind of device into a structure that would permit selection and switching of individual elements. Actually, storage is not a matter of just getting a memory. It is primarily the matter of getting switching so you can access the memory. The question is how to get it at a reasonable cost."

Within a week or two he had come up with an idea for a two-dimensional array. He then spent a few more weeks searching for a way to extend two-dimensional storage to three dimensions. It was while horseback-riding during a vacation on his father's ranch in Nebraska that Forrester saw the solution.

Back at MIT, he ordered some Deltamax. Experiments began. He ran a current through rings made of the material, magnetizing them in the north or south direction. The north direction represented a one, the south a zero. It worked: his small Deltamax rings did the right kind of reversing from one binary state to another.

After the power was turned off they retained the states they were in. There was only one trouble: Deltamax did not in fact have the needed performance. It was too slow and sensitive to physical pressures.

Then, aided by a graduate student named William Papian and other engineers, Forrester turned to another alternative. He strung magnetic ferrite cores shaped like doughnuts on a grid of wires. Each core on the grid possessed its own coordinates—or address— in much the same way that a place on a map does. To read or write a binary digit into a magnetic-core memory, one energized the correct pair of row and column wires on a certain grid. A 16-bit computer would have every bit in the word located at the same address on every grid.

The magnetic ferrite cores were faster, less expensive, and easier to handle than Deltamax, but Forrester saw no reason to exude confidence that the magnetic materials would function the way he theorized. A special computer was built to run the necessary tests, under the direction of graduate student Kenneth Olsen, later president of the Digital Equipment Corporation. The new cores performed admirably: their magnetic characteristics seemed to be permanent and reliable.

Core memory was moved to the Whirlwind computer in the summer of 1953, after the tests were completed. As a result Whirlwind, now with an access time of six microseconds, was twice as fast as when it relied upon the MIT Storage Tubes. But it would be another three or four years before the industry accepted the notion that this was a superior form of computer memory. "Then," Forrester recalls with a smile, "it took the next seven years after that to convince them that they hadn't all thought of it first." Forrester's invention permitted high reliability and high speed at a lower cost. From the early 1960s the price of core memory dropped steeply. Core storage provided access to data and instructions in a few millionths of a second. It could be kept for as long as needed. Maintenance time on storage was cut to a small fraction of the former effort. Random-access coincident-current core memory doubled operating speed and paved the way for many more computers than would otherwise have been economically justifiable. With the arrival of core memory serial-type memory disappeared; everyone eventually went over to Forrester's approach.

With the memory problem solved, Whirlwind was still not over its troubles. There were still people who wondered whether it was worth the effort. And when a solution was needed for the problems involved in the manual plotting of aircraft, a left-over dilemma from World War II, Whirlwind was not immediately looked upon as the source for that solution. Though existing methods for finding enemy aircraft were far from adequate for any major battle, incredibly no improvement had yet been sought. "We came along," says Forrester, "and suggested that this was a place where digital computers might be applied. This was a very radical idea at a time when no high-speed general-purpose digital computer had yet functioned—to suggest that they could be built for continental air defense."

It was so radical that few in the military wanted to take the risk of engaging in such speculative research. The navy was thinking of scrapping the Whirlwind project and putting its funds to better use. Then the Russians stepped in. It was in August 1949 that American intelligence informed President Harry Truman that an atomic weapon had been exploded in the U.S.S.R. What was more, the Soviets, according to these intelligence reports, now had the capability of carrying that device over the North Pole and right into the heart of the United States! Suddenly there was tremendous interest in Whirlwind. Could it indeed become the center of an air defense system? Could computers operating in real time protect American citizens from a nuclear attack? Wrapped in the American flag, Whirlwind would survive.

What would a Whirlwind computer do? It would run aircraft simulators and aim missiles. Most importantly, it would be able to identify unfriendly aircraft automatically and then predict the course of those planes and direct interceptor fighters. A Whirlwind computer would have information about friendly planes stored in its memory. To identify hostile aircraft, it would compare the information picked up on radar with the information about the friendly planes. If the information didn't match, Whirlwind would go to work. The Whirlwind program now had a purpose. Its computers became the prototype for the sophisticated air defense system that was set up in 1958 to provide defense against a Soviet attack. This arrangement was called SAGE, for Semi-Automatic Ground Environment System. Jay Forrester became its director.

In its first test, on April 20, 1951, SAGE was put through a simulated run directing an interceptor plane to its target. The results were highly satisfactory. Within two years it could handle forty-eight aircraft at the same time. By July 1958 the whole system was being implemented. SAGE would perform its mission for another twenty-five years. In 1983 when it was phased out, SAGE was using some of the oldest operational computers in the world.

In 1956, after he felt SAGE was going smoothly and no longer needed his attention, Forrester began to think of what to do next. MIT president James Killian suggested that he might be interested in working at the new MIT Sloan School of Management. Forrester agreed. He began to use computers to model and analyze human social systems, creating a discipline that is now called system dynamics. It involves the use of computer simulations to examine how the policies of corporations and social systems determine successes and difficulties. The method has been applied to studies of energy, unemployment, human mobility, foreign exchange rates, tax policies, and the economic forces that underly inflation. In 1956 Forrester was named Professor of Management at the Sloan School; he became Germeshausen Professor in 1972. He currently heads the System Dynamics program.

Forrester has written a number of influential texts in his new field. *Industrial Dynamics* appeared in 1961, *Principles of Systems* in 1968. *Urban Dynamics,* published in 1969, dealt with the growth and stagnation of cities. His 1971 *World Dynamics* presented a global model of economics and the utilization of resources, analyzing the interrelationships among population, capital investment, natural resources, pollution, food production, and the quality of life.

The Early Entrepreneurs

Thomas J. Watson, Sr.

Founder of IBM

10

During the 1940s computer people built machines for each other. But once World War II was over, the next step was clear—putting the magical devices into the hands of the public. That was where Thomas J. Watson, Sr., found his niche. Though he himself seemed unconvinced of the commercial possibilities of electronic computers, the calculating- and tabulating-machine company that he had already built into a giant would quickly take its place as the leading computer enterprise of the twentieth century.

Watson's was a classic success story of the American free enterprise system. In founding and developing IBM—International Business Machines—he presided over one of the nation's most intriguing and influential corporations. During the 1920s and 1930s it established itself as a leading manufacturer of automatically operated electromechanical business machines. By the end of the 1950s it led the industry in the manufacturing of electronic computers and business machines. In 1985 IBM was doing $50 billion worth of business, had 400,200 employees, was the fifth largest American firm, and was the largest computer maker in the world.

The computers IBM built in the 1940s offered no significant technological breakthroughs. But had there been no Tom Watson the calculator might have remained just that—a calculator—without graduating into the computer with all of its information-processing capabilities.

Thomas John Watson was born on February 17, 1874, in Campbell, New York, a rural area southwest of the Finger Lakes.

As a child he helped his father run the small farm and lumber business by which the family was supported—and neither trade appealed to him. He did, however, cherish throughout his life the values his parents taught. All manner of work should be done well, people were to be treated respectfully, and neatness in dress was important. The supreme virtue, however, was loyalty—Watson called it "family spirit." He liked to say that one should put one's heart in the business and the business in one's heart.

Although his father would have preferred his taking up the law, Watson spent a year studying business and accounting at the Miller School of Commerce in Elmira, New York, and then in May 1892 found work as a bookkeeper in Clarence Risley's Market in Painted Post, New York. His salary was a relatively high $6 a week. Bookkeeping, however, was not to his taste. The people he really admired were traveling salesmen—their lives seemed thoroughly romantic. So, at age eighteen, he hit the road, peddling sewing machines, pianos, and organs. Another salesman, named George Cornwell, made Watson his assistant, and the young man moved about his native upstate New York, making $10 a week. He had no winning smile, no big handshake, but people apparently liked his reticence. Having accumulated some cash, Watson bought a butcher shop in Buffalo, hiring a few people to run it. He himself went back on the road with a more established salesman named C. B. Barron, who had become his mentor. Barron had convinced the Buffalo Building and Loan Association to let him and Watson sell its stock. Barron set great value on making a positive first impression; accordingly, the young Watson bought a new wardrobe and made sure to employ a happy, smiling approach.

Unfortunately, Watson's luck turned sour. Barron absconded with the money they had earned after a few weeks, and the irate bank fired Watson. What is more, the butcher shop failed. Watson was unemployed, In October 1895, in Buffalo, he was hired as a salesman for John Henry Patterson's National Cash Register Company (NCR). Although he would one day be called the world's greatest salesman, those first ten days of pounding the turf were not easy for Watson. He did not make one sale. Things brightened when he was taken under the wing of John J. Range, the NCR district manager for upper New York, who must have been a better teacher than Watson's first two. Watson was soon outearning everyone in the Buffalo NCR office.

In 1899, when he was twenty-five, Watson was promoted to branch manager of NCR's Rochester office, a territory no one wanted. Casting about for ways to improve the spirit of his sales force, he hit upon the motto "THINK": the phrase "I didn't think," he would tell his salesmen, cost companies millions of dollars. Framed placards with that one word appeared in the company's offices. Years later at IBM he would reintroduce the motto.

Watson was clearly a star on the rise. Four years later, in 1903, he was chosen over four hundred other NCR salesmen to direct a new secret operation aimed at undermining the increasingly profitable business of selling second-hand NCR machines, which was cutting into NCR's new-business trade. Watson established stores near competitors who were doing well, undersold them, and hired away their salesmen. Some called his methods ruthless; others were more generous. Whatever the case, Watson never liked to talk about that period—as if he knew there was not much there of which he could be proud. Still, so successful was he that NCR asked him to duplicate his feat in Chicago and Philadelphia. In 1907 Watson was transferred to NCR's headquarters in Dayton, Ohio. Three years later, at the age of thirty-six, he was promoted to sales manager, a top executive job at NCR. So pleased was John Patterson with Tom Watson that he bought his prize employee a house and a Pierce-Arrow car.

Disaster struck in 1912. Though he had little or nothing to do with the activities alleged, Watson was one of thirty NCR executives accused by its main competitor, American Cash Register Company, of, among other unfair business practices, seeking to eliminate the second-hand trade. At that time Watson had become engaged to Jeannette Kittredge. He offered to end their engagement because of his legal troubles, but Jeannette refused. They were married on April 17, 1913. He was thirty-nine, she was thirty. (They had four children: Thomas, Jr., Jane, Helen, and Arthur.)

The trial received considerable publicity, as NCR was a major enterprise. On February 12, 1913, the verdict was handed down: Watson received a one-year jail sentence and a $5,000 fine. The court's decision was appealed, and the case remained pending for some time. Watson's career went into a tailspin. In November 1913 he had the bad sense to disagree with Patterson over company sales strategy—in front of other NCR executives. Three months short of his fortieth birthday, Watson was dismissed.

He landed on his feet. A number of firms offered him large salaries; rather surprisingly, he chose to go with the Computing-Tabulating-Recording Company (CTR), a firm deep in financial problems. But Watson knew what he was doing. He sensed the need for machinery that could perform the many accounting tasks that were too time-consuming to be done manually. Tabulating machines had proved their value during the 1890 American census: they had reduced the period of tabulation from seven years to three. In 1911 Hollerith's Tabulating Machine Company, manufacturer of a punched-card machine that did quick and varied tabulations, had merged with three other firms to form CTR. Watson's goal, to be achieved by building up a sales force and developing sophisticated business machinery, was to overwhelm the competition, NCR. Some have suggested that the spark of revenge burned brightly in him. Yet there was a less emotional reason for Watson's choice of CTR: he wanted a company that could exploit the growing need for speedier tabulation, and CTR looked ideal to him.

On May 1, 1914, Watson became general manager of CTR. The company was then producing time clocks, butcher scales, and simple accounting machines; Watson planned to concentrate his time and energy on the tabulating-machine part of the business. He was given a salary of $25,000 a year and an option on 1,220 shares of stock. The understanding was that once the criminal charges against him were cleared up, he would be named president. Finally in 1915 the Court of Appeals set the verdict aside. A new trial was granted. However, the government agreed to drop the case, and the suit was settled by a consent decree. Watson refused to sign the decree, believing that to do so would be to admit his guilt. His promotion to the presidency of CTR came soon thereafter.

Watson's influence on CTR was apparent. The tabulating-machine division led the growth in the company's sales from $4.2 million in 1914 to $8.3 million three years later. Watson constantly sought the most from his engineers. He prodded them to invent a machine that would be an improvement over the rival Powers firm's statistical printer, which rented for $100 a month. In 1919 he showed a sales meeting of CTR a printer-lister superior to the Powers machines. Once a switch was flicked, cards flowed through it and the machine printed results. Salesmen, some standing on their chairs, cheered. By 1920 CTR's gross income had risen to nearly $14 million.

It was in 1924, at the age of fifty, that Watson became chief executive officer. That year, he changed CTR's name to International Business Machines Corporation—a title conveying the broadness of scope he envisioned for his company. Though he had long known that the potential market for sophisticated business machines was great, Watson was still astonished to learn from a 1929 report that only two percent of the nation's accounting needs were being handled by machines. By the early 1930s he was thinking in terms of data processing, of handling information on a scale that only a very swift, complex piece of machinery could manage.

But these were the years of the Depression. Watson's efforts to push tabulating machines and time clocks during the 1930s met with little success. By 1938 IBM had sales of only $35 million a year. Two events occurred, however—events with which Watson had nothing to do—that suddenly provided new direction. One was the Social Security Act of 1935. The other was the Wages-Hours Act of 1937. Now businesses had to record wages paid, hours worked, overtime earned. The market for tabulating machines and time clocks sprang to life almost overnight. Existing machines worked far too slowly, but electronic equipment was still years away.

Looking for a way to make a dramatic breakthrough, Watson backed Howard Aiken in 1937 in his proposed plan to build a faster calculator. Aiken received $100,000 at this point; eventually IBM would contribute $500,000, the total cost of the project. Aiken wanted his machine to be a general-purpose device, capable of storing data. The project took not a few months, as at first expected, but six years. While he was sponsoring what would become the first programmable digital computer made in the United States, Watson was also building IBM. He was an astonishingly enlightened business tycoon, a man who sensed the real potential of technology, who had a genius for business organization, who shrewdly perceived the value of cooperating with others, especially the government. Watson was serious about the business, serious about himself, a sixteen-hour-a-day man who eschewed vacations. There was compensation: as early as 1940 he was making $546,294 a year, a salary exceeded by only one man in the country, movie mogul Louis B. Mayer.

Loyalty to the firm was a virtue above all others. That was the Watson theme. The business was like a football team, with Tom Watson—a strikingly handsome man, with a penetrating gaze—as both coach and cheerleader. Techniques were developed to reinforce the employee's devotion to IBM and to Tom Watson. There was the emphasis on dark suits and white shirts; THINK signs hung on office walls; employees sang company songs (one lyric went: "Our voices swell in admiration; Of T. J. Watson proudly sing; He'll ever be our inspiration; To him our voices loudly ring"), received benefits, went to company training programs, attended rallies. Watson would never fire anyone—that would undermine others' loyalty to IBM. He would simply train the person more, supervise him more, or perhaps put him in a less demanding job.

He hated excuses. On one occasion a market executive began to explain why some IBM salesmen had been unable to land accounts, blaming the machine for not working properly. Listening impatiently, Watson finally broke in. "I wonder if I might say a few words. This is a meaningless exercise. There is only one reason for losing an account: neglect." Watson offered his employees the promise of employment for life with no worry about layoffs. Workers were allowed to complain—and to do so directly to Tom Watson. A foreman was supposed to help the worker, not push him about to get a day's work out of him. This work style became fashionable in later years—in the egalitarianism that prevails in Silicon Valley, and in the sense of family instilled by Japanese management. Tom Watson was way ahead of his time. The results proved him right: in the 1950s and 1960s IBM would grow, and grow, and grow.

Watson had strong views as to how a patriot should act. In peacetime going after the big buck was acceptable; in wartime it was not. During World War II IBM produced Browning automatic rifles, bombsights, and other military items. The company took only a 1.5-percent net profit on war production and used the money to set up a fund for the widows and children of employees killed in action. IBM tabulators helped break the Japanese code before the Battle of Midway.

Watson could have given up his business career during the war to take a cabinet or diplomatic post. President Franklin Roosevelt asked him to be secretary of commerce, but Watson declined. Roosevelt then offered to appoint him ambassador to Great Britain, but again he refused. Joseph Kennedy, Sr., got the job. If IBM was good to the United States during World War II, the war was good for IBM as well. The company's revenues went from $62.9 million before the war to $141.7 million after; IBM's data-processing production efforts received a definite boost.

The Aiken project, IBM's first step into the computer age, got started in earnest only in 1940. Aiken wanted to build the machine at Harvard's laboratories, but Watson insisted that he do the work at IBM's Endicott, New York, facilities so that he, Watson, could keep careful watch over progress. Aiken's machine, the Mark I, was believed to be the first general-purpose automatic digital computer, a notion that was later dispelled when Konrad Zuse's pioneering efforts in Germany became known in the United States. Its official unveiling came in May 1944 at a press conference at Harvard. Watson and Aiken fell out over the question of credit for creating the Mark I. As a result of the disagreement Watson demanded that his engineers come up with a new machine that would outdo the Mark I. It was somewhat reminiscent of Watson's earlier eagerness to demolish NCR after feeling mistreated.

The new IBM machine was the Selective Sequence Electronic Calculator—the SSEC. When completed in 1947, it was far more powerful and flexible than anything previously built. Thanks to its 12,500 vacuum tubes and 21,400 relays, it could solve partial differential equations. For several years the SSEC was the only publicly accessible device that could do electronic computation. Its tubes could store eight 20-digit decimal numbers; its relays could hold 150 numbers; 20,000 numbers were also stored on sixty-six reels of punched tape. The size of its memory made it far more powerful than the ENIAC.

The SSEC was first demonstrated on January 27, 1948, at an IBM showroom in New York City, where it calculated all past, present, and future positions of the moon. For the next four years it did calculations for a number of important firms on a variety of problems ranging from the design of turbine buckets to oil field exploration. IBM's actual entry into electronics had come with the building of the IBM 603 electronic calculating machine, which reached the market in 1946. Then in 1948 it produced the 604, one of its big marketing successes: over fifty-six hundred 604s were manufactured in the next decade.

Following the Korean War the pace of the design work quickened, leading to the 701, IBM's first production computer, designed primarily for scientific calculations. One-fourth the size of the SSEC, the 701 was twenty-five times as fast, performing 21,000 calculations a second. Nevertheless, the 701, unveiled in 1952, lagged behind Sperry Rand's UNIVAC. The IBM needed an operator to feed punched cards into it, while UNIVAC could deal with a complex sequence of commands recorded on magnetic tape without an opertor. To its credit the 701 was considered the most complex piece of machinery ever put together. Called also the Defense Calculator, it launched IBM as a real computer firm. Twenty 701s were produced, leased at the high price of $24,000 a month. At first, IBM was going to charge $12,000 a month, but it soon became apparent that the price would have to be doubled. Not one order was lost, suggesting to IBM executives that, as Thomas Watson, Jr., put it, "We've got our hands on something with this electronics."

Thomas Watson, Jr., had become president of the company in 1952. The popularity of UNIVAC was making IBM nervous; it had nothing to match Sperry's machine. IBM now committed itself wholeheartedly to computers, and the upward trend began. The 650, a medium-sized computer that rented for $3,000 to $4,000 a month, reached the market in December 1954. It was a great success, known as the first mass-produced computer, with 120 machines in place in its first year. Some 1,500 were made in its fifteen years of existence. Also in 1954, the 704 computer, successor to the 701, was introduced.

Two new IBM computers followed in 1955 and 1956: the 702, a combination of the 701 and a machine designed by IBM for the Social Security Administration; and the 705, the first commercial computer with magnetic memory, and successor to the 702. Some one hundred 704s and 705s were sold.

IBM would continue to build computers—the System/360 in 1964 and the PC in 1981 among them—and dominate the industry. But Tom Watson would no longer be around to watch. To the end of his days, he retained the title of chairman of IBM. In May 1956, a month before his death, he turned over the international side of IBM to his younger son, Arthur, and passed on executive power to Thomas, Jr. The founder of IBM died of a heart attack on June 19, 1956, at age eighty-two.

William Norris

Founder of Control Data Corporation

11

It was a daring stroke, approaching your friends, asking them to invest in a new, nebulous company with no product. Wall Street was aghast. Bill Norris was crazy. Nobody tried to undertake a computer start-up through public financing. It was simply not done. But the unconventional Mr. Norris hadn't been stopped in the past and wouldn't be now. He showed a UNIVAC computer to a physician friend, who asked, "You mean that's what you're manufacturing?" "Not exactly," replied Norris, "but that's the field we're in." The doctor invested $25,000. Norris minced no words with prospective investors. They would be taking a risk, and if it didn't work out, they shouldn't come running to him with complaints. He would feel bad enough having lost his own money.

But Bill Norris didn't lose any money. Nor did his three hundred risk-taking friends. The company he founded in 1957, Control Data Corporation, became in time one of the leaders of the computer industry, its computers among the best made, and Bill Norris irritated the Watsons and IBM no end. With annual revenues of over $4 billion and $7 billion worth of assets, CDC had become by the early 1980s the leading company in large-scale scientific and engineering computers and computer services. It was also a world leader in peripherals and services. Norris himself did not fare badly: by the early 1980s he and his family were worth $25 million. CDC would fall on hard times in the mid-1980s, and Norris would be blamed for the downturn; but when this slide occurred it was only after years of great business success.

Norris was born on July 14, 1911, on a farm in Red Cloud, Nebraska. Like other computer pioneers in their youth, he was fascinated with radio equipment. He built his own receiving and sending set and became a ham radio operator. His room was filled with copies of *Popular Mechanics*, copper wire, and vacuum tubes, as well as Zane Grey's tales of the Wild West. On his walls were lists of the call letters of fellow radio amateurs. He sent away to electronics magazines for radio parts and gadgets, funded in part by parents who were impressed with his intelligence; they were even convinced he knew more than his physics teacher.

Getting an education was not simple for Norris and his twin sister Willa. They had to walk or ride a pony, no matter what the weather, to a one-room schoolhouse a mile from home. While in high school Norris developed a strong interest in physics. He studied electrical engineering at the University of Nebraska. When his father died in 1932 of a heart attack, he left the university a month early and went home to help on the farm. He was still given his degree. With few jobs around, Norris ran the family farm for the next two years, taking a civil engineering job that involved laying out terraces and dams once the farm improved.

Notified in 1934 by the university dean that the Westinghouse Company was hiring, Norris applied and immediately faced a dilemma. He could work part-time as an engineer or full-time as a salesman. Choosing the full-time job, he sold X-ray machines and other equipment. Timid at first, he eventually learned the ropes and stayed on until 1941 before taking a job as an electrical engineer for the U.S. Navy in Washington. After Pearl Harbor Norris was commissioned in the Naval Reserve, assigned to Communications Supplementary Activity. He joined mathematicians, physicists, and engineers from corporations and universities in highly secret intelligence work, trying to break Japanese and German codes. At first they worked with paper and pencil, but when that proved too slow they turned to the most recent electronic devices—still highly inadequate. Norris rose to the rank of commander.

At the war's end, navy officials were distressed at having to disband their prized intelligence unit, realizing that code breaking would be just as important in peacetime. Norris and a few colleagues suggested forming a private firm that would continue to work for the navy. Finding investors was not easy, largely because

Norris and his partners could not reveal the nature of their products. Still, they found one, John E. Parker, a successful investment banker. His one stipulation was that the navy agree in advance to buy the firm's product—which it did. So in September 1946 Engineering Research Associates (ERA) was established, starting off in a former glider plant in St. Paul, Minnesota, making electronic digital machines. Norris was one of three vice-presidents under Parker, who served as president. At first Norris was in charge of marketing, but he became involved in operations as well. ERA quickly acquired a good reputation as an efficient supplier of high-speed digital data-handling equipment, as well as large-scale memories. In its first year ERA had revenues of $1.5 million, with a $34,000 profit.

Parker now decided to sell the firm—"the dumbest thing he ever did in his life," in Norris's view. It may well have cost the investor $100 million in future losses. But Parker thought he had received a good price from James Rand, the head of Remington Rand, who paid him $1 million, eighty-five times ERA's original worth. Norris, then vice-president and general manager, balked but could do little. The firm was so rich in personal talent and technology that Norris believed it had the potential to reach the status IBM would eventually acquire. After all, by 1952 ERA had built over eighty percent of all American-built electronic computers. For the firm to remain an industry leader, Norris was convinced that he and the others at ERA had to retain their creative freedom and attract large sums of cash, neither of which could happen once the sale had taken place.

Remington Rand kept Norris and his colleagues in St. Paul. Now merely one of three computer units within Remington Rand, ERA still built the fastest and most reliable hardware in the computer industry. Yet the firm was in trouble. Remington Rand failed to provide sufficient support, in Norris's view. ERA itself was hampered because it could not disclose much of its still-classified work; beyond that there were the jealousies and fierce competition between ERA and another Remington Rand computer unit, the Eckert-Mauchly firm.

After Remington Rand and Sperry Corporation merged in 1955 (becoming Sperry Rand), Norris became vice-president and general manager of the new St. Paul–based electronic computer division called UNIVAC. One of the few bright spots for Norris was his relationship with General Douglas MacArthur, board chairman of Sperry Rand from 1955 until his death in 1964. MacArthur showed up at Sperry Rand headquarters in Norwalk, Connecticut, each Thursday and would invite Norris (who also made frequent trips to headquarters) to accompany him on the two-hour drive back to New York. Once, Norris told the general that he had never forgotten something he had heard him say in a speech: "There is no such thing as security in this world. There is only opportunity." MacArthur could not recall saying it but remarked that it certainly sounded like something he would say.

For Norris, his days at Sperry Rand were one of those great might-have-beens. Had the company, with its large financial resources and sales force, thought in bold strokes, had it invested wisely and generously, it might well have attained IBM's stature. At that time, the mid-1950s, IBM had still not made a major commitment to building computers. Norris tried to push Sperry Rand in this direction, but his appeals fell on deaf ears. IBM moved ahead in the late 1950s to become the dominant player in the computer industry, to Norris's great regret. Highly frustrated, he and eight other important figures in Sperry Rand left the company in June 1957 to try to do on their own what they had failed to convince Sperry Rand to do. As the senior member of the group, and the one with the most skill and experience in marketing and obtaining government contracts, Norris was understood to be the leader.

Still, he needed some help from his friends. And he got it. He decided to put in $75,000 of his own; with $25,000 from his physician friend, he had $100,000 speedily. Eventually there was enough, as 615,000 shares were scooped up at $1 per share. None of the three hundred stockholders had a controlling interest. Mindful of Parker's ploy, Norris did not want anyone, including himself, to be able to sell CDC over the objections of other senior executives. At first CDC planned only to do research and development on electronic equipment. Building computers came later. To Norris, the computer field appeared one big opportunity, yet he had no specific game plan. Certainly he had no great yearning to take on the existing computer firms, including the giant, IBM.

There was a difficult settling-in period. For one thing, headquarters were rather modest, a rented office in an old warehouse, with chipboard partitions dividing the floor space. Breaking with Sperry Rand proved troublesome. Norris and other former UNIVAC people were accused in a lawsuit of stealing trade secrets. The legal entanglements took a few years, but a settlement was arranged without money changing hands. CDC signed a consent order promising not to use some information they had acquired while at UNIVAC. CDC was young enough, flexible enough, to move in any of a number of directions. One of Bill Norris's shrewdest early moves—acquiring computer designer Seymour Cray of UNIVAC and giving him free rein—was the key factor in determining what type of firm CDC would be at the start and assuring its initial success. At the time CDC had neither the inclination nor the infrastructure to enter the computer field; yet Cray convinced Norris that there was money to be made in building an inexpensive, powerful solid-state computer using printed circuit modules. The computers would have to be designed specifically for scientific and engineering applications; then, so long as they were the best computers in the field, the big institutions—aircraft firms, universities, the Department of Defense—would gladly buy them. Such an institution would be far less concerned, said Cray, about the computer builder's ability to hold its hand, furnishing software support after the computer was in place.

The question was what type of computer to build. The current crop of IBM competitors had been trying to dent the computer giant's dominance of the business data processing market. For Norris to have joined in this struggle would have made no sense. He chose to play in a different ballpark entirely, sensing that engineers and scientists would want powerful computers that could perform large, complex computations. Previously those computations had not been attempted or even considered. Norris could exploit the fact that engineers like Seymour Cray, who would actually build the machines, would be the best salesmen possible. They would know their product inside and out, they would be able to answer clients' question on the spot. IBM's sales force couldn't possibly compete with the boys at CDC.

The computer that pulled CDC out of its birth pangs was the 1604, built by Seymour Cray. It was compact, versatile, and—at $1.5 million, half the cost of the competitive IBM computer—quite a buy. When it reached the market in 1958, it was one of the first

The 1604 computer

fully transistorized computers and the largest scientific computer at the time. Debuting just eight months after the founding of CDC, the 1604 was first purchased by the navy's Bureau of Ships.

Norris knew that CDC needed more than just brains. If it was to survive it would need manufacturing facilities to reach what he called "critical mass." So in 1958 he initiated a program to acquire new companies, beginning with Cedar Engineering Incorporated, a Minneapolis manufacturer of electronic instruments and control devices. Cedar nearly flattened CDC: it cost $500,000 to make it profitable, and in the process CDC workers had to agree to a fifty-percent salary cut. CDC employees often told manufacturers' representatives who sold electronic parts to arrive at 11:30 a.m., in the hope that the salesmen would buy them lunch.

The 1604's early success was phenomenal. CDC couldn't make them fast enough to keep up with the demand. Total sales in CDC's first, unprofitable year were around $780,000. But within two years CDC had turned a profit, something none of the other IBM competitors had managed to do. Among the stories of how the 1604 came to be named is this one: By adding CDC's 501 Park Avenue address to the name of the computer Norris had built at ERA—the 1103—one got 1604! But the most likely version focuses on the fact that the 1604 had 16,384 words of memory and four tape units. In trying to find a model number that did not conflict with another manufacturer's the engineers chose to use the 16 (K'S) and the 4 (tape units) and then to add 0—hence, 1604.

The customers were pleased with CDC's sophisticated electronic technology, transistors and all. But Norris knew there was risk in concentrating on the building of large computers, given the rapidly changing computer technology; beyond that, the market for these machines was quite limited. Unlike the other major computer manufacturers, CDC did not have other product lines on which to fall back if its luck soured.

Seymour Cray has been credited with CDC's initial gains—but it was Bill Norris who enabled the master computer designer to function so freely and effectively. Norris and Cray had a most unusual employer-employee relationship. By the force of his stunning record, Cray obtained from Norris a continuing hands-off attitude that permitted him to work without managerial supervision, second-guessing, or interference. Norris, in turn, sensed that this was the best way to exploit Cray's obvious skills. Norris arranged for Cray to work in a laboratory far from CDC—near Cray's rustic home at Chippewa Falls, Wisconsin. Norris would go visit him there, but only infrequently.

By 1959 CDC had sales of $4.5 million. That year Cray produced the Model 160 desk-sized computer, which sold for $90,000. A year later, when CDC sales had grown to $28 million, Cray began working on the 6600; when it appeared in August 1963, it was twenty times faster than any other computer. Norris liked to point out that CDC would not have to sell very many 6600s to make a profit: each one cost $7 million.

The 6600 was universally recognized as a first. It had a unique packaging design that resulted in more components per cubic inch than in earlier designs. It could execute an average of over 3 million instructions per second, and it had 131,072 words of magnetic-core storage. CDC had always tried to build the fastest scientific computers; the next step was the 7600, followed by the Star 100 in November 1974. Then came the CYBER 205, one of the first supercomputers to introduce vector processing. CYBER 205 is capable of

The 6600 computer

up to 800 million operations a second and is regarded by CDC executives as the fastest computer under a variety of applications, including aerodynamic simulations.

In 1961 there were only two computer companies operating in the black, IBM, which had locked up 82 percent of the computer market, and CDC, with 1.6 percent. Early in 1961, with the 1604 making an important impact on the market, IBM modified its Model 7090 and sold it more cheaply than a 1604. The following year CDC couldn't get one order. Later in 1961 CDC came out with an enhanced version of the 1604—the 1604-A. The battle continued: IBM produced the 7094—an upgraded 7090—and CDC retaliated with the more powerful 3600. Then IBM produced the 7090 II in response. In December 1968 Norris took IBM to court.

Norris was hardly popular at CDC for taking on IBM. It was too expensive, too risky, many felt. But Norris was insistent. He charged that IBM's new 360/80 computer was a paper machine, a phantom computer that would never see the light of day but was aimed merely at stopping the sale of CDC's 6600. IBM's selling techniques, he declared, were unethical. He demanded triple damages for CDC's losses and called for IBM's dismemberment. CDC was helped in its case by possessing powerful computers and sophisticated software that could index, sort, retrieve, and summarize the millions of pages of required documents. This was one of the first times high-speed computer technology was put into service in a major legal case. It helped CDC to win (eventually—the case dragged on until 1973), and it also opened a new revenue producer: Norris would later sell this data service for a fee to others involved in big, complex legal actions.

By the mid-1960s Norris had become convinced that total dependence on mainframe computers was unwise. It was obvious to him that IBM had a position in the hardware field that made competition brutal. He looked for other business. Observes Norris, "You can build the greatest instrument in the world, but it's what you do with it that's most important; and that's the reason why I got more interested in applying it than in creating the tool." The acquisition of Commercial Credit Company put CDC on a solid footing. It meant that CDC could handle the leasing of its computers more easily.

Around this time also, in a controversial move, Norris took the company into the peripheral products business. He had decided on

The CYBER 205

the bold step of developing and making peripherals for other computer firms besides CDC. Some colleagues objected to giving competitors the benefit of CDC's own technical know-how, but Norris prevailed and ultimately was proved correct. Indeed, between 1969 and 1971, when the large-computer market suffered a setback, CDC was able to fall back on peripherals business.

The 1970s brought some very good news for Norris. In 1973 the IBM case was resolved when IBM paid a handsome price to have CDC abandon its fight. The settlement included $101 million in cash. Norris was also permitted to buy the Service Bureau Company, IBM's data services subsidiary, on favorable terms. IBM had to remain out of the data service field for six years, aiding CDC's growth. This acquisition more than tripled CDC's service business, adding a large data-processing orientation to its previous engineering and scientific data service base. Norris built CDC by joint ventures as well. An important one was finalized in 1972, when Norris signed with National Cash Register to begin a cooperative project called Computer Peripherals Incorporated (CPI), to manufacture high-speed printers, magnetic systems, and disk memories.

Norris's entry into the data service business met considerable resistance within CDC. Norris argued that there were many clients who could not afford CDC's computers but would be eager to buy a little piece—a few minutes or an hour—of a computer at a time. He first offered simply "raw time" on one of his computers; CDC's first data service center was opened in Minneapolis in 1962. A computer used for test purposes at CDC was initially put at the disposal of the center. Then more centers were opened, linked together nationally and internationally by means of a network known as CYBERNET. By 1982, CDC had assets of $6.9 billion and 56,000 employees, with $4.3 billion in revenues; its net profits were $155 million, and revenues from computer systems were $705 million; the peripherals and service branches, neither highly popular at their inception, earned $1 billion in revenues.

Influenced by the race riots of 1967, Norris sought to help American blacks by creating jobs for them. He began by locating a CDC plant in the inner-city area where most Minneapolis blacks lived. That approach was copied successfully in other parts of the country. Norris insisted he was not being philanthropic; he was using good, prudent business sense. Still, he could not conceal his social consciousness. Another example was his PLATO project, a computer-based education and training system that diagnosed, drilled, tested, and graded someone in a self-paced routine. Even during his days in the navy and later at ERA Norris had wondered about the possibility of digital computers being used to improve the quality of educational methods, though their high cost made such ideas appear impractical. PLATO was first offered commercially in 1976 and met a certain indifference. Norris would spend over $900 million on the project. He remains convinced twenty years after beginning PLATO that it will one day become CDC's largest revenue earner. The world needs better, less costly education and training.

Norris is a great believer in cooperative projects. Apart from Computer Peripherals and the PLATO system, CDC embarked on a different kind of cooperative venture in 1978, setting up City Venture Corporation, a consortium of business, professional, and religious organizations, to revitalize and renew run-down urban areas. In addition, Norris founded Rural Ventures to improve small-scale farming.

In 1982 he helped set up one of the boldest cooperative computer ventures, Microelectronics and Computer Technology Corporation (MCC). Major American firms would donate their brightest researchers and provide financial support for a joint think tank to keep the American computer industry competitive with Japan's. Based in Austin, Texas, MCC was predicated on Norris's belief that American electronics firms have to band together or buckle under the Japanese threat—not a very popular notion in free-enterprise America. By the winter of 1986 some 330 scientists from twenty-one firms, including CDC, Digital Equipment Corporation, Boeing, 3M, RCA, Honeywell, and Motorola, were working on seven projects from computer architecture to semiconductor technology. Among the projects under way: increasing the computing power of microchips by increasing the number of wires that can be attached to one from 32 to 1,000; computer-aided design of powerful microprocessor chips; the development of faster and more efficient software; and the designing of advanced computer architecture. The first project has had some success: MCC's researchers have managed to boost the number of microchip connections to 328. As for the advanced computer project, the best guess is that it will take another ten years.

Picked to run MCC was Bobby Ray Imman, former director of the National Security Agency. At first the MCC companies didn't send their best people, but later they did. Norris has expressed optimism that MCC will succeed: "Our culture doesn't contain a lot of incentive for cooperation as in the case of the Japanese. But that has to change, because we can't afford to have everyone keep reinventing the wheel." He is frank in saying that while big firms are better at production and marketing, small companies can do things faster and for less money and are often more creative than their large competitors. That is why he has been so much in favor of cooperation. Noting that his own CDC is the most cooperative company he knows, Norris has said that he would be happy if on his tombstone was written, "He worked like hell to foster cooperation." Recalling his unsuccessful efforts at uniting the European computer industry, he suggests that that industry might have been far more successful had it not clung to its anticollaborative mind-set.

Through the late 1960s and the 1970s CDC was the leading maker in the world of peripherals. But that was to change in the early 1980s. Its computer memory device business, fully 35 percent of its computer-related sales, began to sour. The problem started in 1982, when IBM came out with a powerful disk drive. CDC's share of the sale of disk drives to computer makers went down from over 50 percent in 1980 to below 25 percent in 1984. The situation with respect to computers was similarly deteriorating. The firm's share of mainframe computer sales was only 1.5 percent in 1984. The company's sales of supercomputers, one of CDC's first products in the 1950s, were low enough to make it a distant second to Cray Research. By the end of 1984 Cray had installed eighty-six supercomputers to only thirty-one for CDC. During 1985 CDC lost $567.5 million on sales of $3.7 billion.

It was only natural that criticism should focus on founder and chairman Norris. Critics pointed to PLATO, Norris's pet project, which had soaked up hundreds of millions of dollars and had only begun to turn a modest profit in recent years. He was described as too headstrong, as having stayed around too long at the helm. He was called authoritarian and overly idealistic. Someone more pragmatic was needed, the critics said. Norris did step down as chairman and chief executive officer on January 10, 1986. Robert Price, whom he had groomed as his successor, took over the reins.

Within a year CDC had made an impressive recovery due to an overhaul that included getting rid of unprofitable sidelines, placing its focus on computer technology, and reducing its payroll from 54,000 at the end of 1984 to 34,000 in 1986. While CDC showed a loss of $264.5 million in 1986, it was expected to have a profit perhaps as high as $80 million in 1987.

Throughout his career Norris has had a sympathetic press— though he has a reputation for not granting many interviews. Most articles have stressed his unconventional nature, his ability to do the right thing when everyone else was opposed—he likes to say that when he sees someone going south, he generally goes north. While some within the computer industry have been bemused at Norris's fondness for social projects, regarding him as out to save the world or simply crazy, he has received considerable public approbation on this point. He has been called crusty, mean, and gruff, but he prefers the word iconoclastic.

H. Ross Perot

Computerizing the World

12

Ross Perot is not enamored of computers. He appreciates what they can do, but that's as far as it goes. Yet few people have done more to put computers to work. In Electronic Data Systems—EDS—which he founded in the early 1960s, this fabulously wealthy Texan has created the largest computer service firm in the world, providing data services to business and the American government. Apart from being one of America's most successful businessmen, Perot is a much-publicized superpatriot whose adventures have taken him from Laos to Iran. For Ross Perot, making a contribution to the country is what counts. That is why he campaigned to improve the lot of American prisoners of war in North Vietnam, why he personally conducted a rescue mission to save two EDS executives imprisoned in Iran, and why he purchased, for $1.5 million, a rare early copy of the Magna Carta as a gift to the nation. Nor will he cease pursuing new goals. According to his son, Ross, Jr., "A lot of guys would have climbed one mountain and quit. If my father doesn't have a challenge, he starts getting restless."

Ross Perot was born on June 27, 1930, in Texarkana, Texas, where he spent his childhood during the Depression. He has fond memories of his parents, and both amusing and solemn memories of his struggles to earn money. His first job, at age six, was in the employ of his father—breaking horses at a dollar a horse. "The smaller you were, the sooner you could get on that horse." Then, at seven, he sold garden seeds and Christmas cards door-to-door. Here he learned a business lesson he would never forget: the disadvantages of a seasonal enterprise. In the early 1980s someone tried to sell Perot a premier ski resort, but he refused because he did not want to be in a business that could not be operated the year round.

His father was his best friend. He would pick the youngster up from school and they would ride horses together. From September to November the elder Perot was a cotton broker; sitting in the office and watching, his son learned to treat customers fairly. Years later, after General Motors bought Ross Perot's company, he attempted to instill in GM an increased sensitivity to the customer.

At twelve Perot took a paper route. The job involved not merely delivering the newspapers but acquiring and renewing weekly subscriptions; and the neighborhood in which there was an opening was one of poor and often illiterate black laborers. Perot somehow had to convince a sawmill hand to spend 25¢ out of his precious $9-a-week salary for a week's worth of newspapers. The newspaper was so pessimistic about his finding clients that it offered him 17.5¢ instead of the usual 7.5¢ for every newspaper sold.

How did he get sales? He went to the door and asked politely if the person would like to buy a newspaper. He rose even in rain and snow at 3:30 a.m., and placed the newspapers carefully on front porches. Perot's customers would use the newspapers in wall cracks or underneath mattresses as cheap insulation after reading them. Riding a horse to get around, he covered twenty miles a day.

He turned the route into a huge success. The newspaper reacted by trying to change the deal. Because Perot was making too much money, $30 a week, he was informed he would have to take the standard 7.5¢ per newspaper. Fortunately for Perot, he had been on the premises one day when the publisher, C. E. Palmer, had accidentally locked himself in his office. The boy had unlocked the door for his embarrassed employer. Palmer owed Perot a favor. Perot took the rate problem directly to him. "I made a contract with your company, and you folks are trying to change it," he said. Palmer laughed and directed the circulation manager to honor the agreement.

Perot was getting a business education—better, he would say, than going to the Harvard Business School. He was learning how to deal directly with clients. Treat them right, and they would never forget you. When he was fourteen his father needed a kidney operation. Perot was unable to find a substitute delivery boy for the week he would be in Shreveport, where his father was to have the surgery. Explaining his predicament to clients, he could only urge them to subscribe again upon his return. To his surprise they asked him to keep the newspapers and deliver them all at once after he was back. He later referred to this as one of the most touching memories of his life. Perot's customers wanted to help. They understood what it meant not to be paid.

He was a youngster with fierce determination. Once, when an eleventh-grade teacher, a Mrs. Duck, mentioned to him that it was too bad he was not as intelligent as his friends, Perot insisted that he was. Why, then, the teacher asked, did they do better at school? They were simply more interested, he replied. And to prove his intelligence, he informed her, he would get all A's for the next six weeks. In fact, he received A's for the rest of his high-school career.

After graduating in 1947 from Texarkana High School, Perot attended Texarkana Junior College for two years, studying, among other subjects, mathematics and science. He had been trying for three years to win an appointment to the Naval Academy. When no one else came forward in 1949, U.S. Senator W. Lee O'Daniel chose "the boy from Texarkana." Perot "had never been in anything like a military environment, so there was every reason to think that I would have been a square peg in a round hole there." He found that he was not. Studying engineering, he received a solid education in management and leadership as well. He was elected president of his class of 1951–52 and 1952–53, chairman of the Honor Committee, and a battalion commander.

It was at the Naval Academy that he became self-confident and aware that he had leadership potential. Once his peers and senior officers had evaluated him favorably, he felt he had really passed the test: "I had all these different looks in the mirror, three times a year for four years. I knew that I got along with people all right." Of the 925 graduates, he led his class eleven out of the twelve times he was evaluated. "I used to think of leaders as these giants I had read about in history books, and here I was just a Texas boy breaking horses, delivering newspapers, collecting classified ads, and staying busy." He graduated from the Naval Academy with a bachelor of science degree in 1953 and was commissioned an ensign. He served four years at sea aboard a destroyer and an aircraft carrier.

The break that would thrust him into the business world came in 1957 on, of all places, the aircraft carrier *Leyte,* sailing off the east coast of the United States. Perot's job, as assistant navigator, was to remain with the captain at all times. A guest came aboard, an IBM executive, who upon seeing Perot perform his duties was impressed enough to ask if he wanted a job interview. Perot had certainly heard of the company; there were IBM typewriters aboard. What mattered most to him was that somebody had sought him out. Ever since he was six years old he had had to look for every job he held. The IBM man was the first person to offer him a job. He was interested.

Though he had no idea that IBM sold computers when he went for his interview, Perot was hired at $500 a month as a computer salesman, headquartered in Dallas. Piling everything he and his wife Margot owned in their second-hand car, he headed for Dallas. He took the IBM sales training course, finishing first. After all, he had been selling from an early age. And he was a success at selling computers. Oddly, IBM was not pleased that he was making a great deal of money. Perot agreed with management that he was making more then he was worth; perhaps, he suggested as a bluff, they could pay him a smaller commission than the other salesmen? To his surprise IBM took up the offer, paying him twenty percent of what a typical IBM salesman received. This only encouraged Perot to do the job more quickly. As a result he had the largest quota in the western region of the United States; in January 1962 he reached his quota in the first nineteen days of the month. "I had organized that territory. It was like an apple orchard. I just grew apples and picked them every year." IBM was concerned that he was making so much money it would be difficult to promote him. Bothered that he would have to explain why Perot was doing so well, Perot's local manager gave his star salesman nothing to do from January to June. During that time he formulated the idea for EDS—providing computer time to companies in need of it. He tried to sell the idea to IBM but was turned down. And so in June Perot left to start EDS.

He began his company with $1,000 that his wife had saved from her teaching salary. The check, dated August 23, 1962, made out to cash, has been framed and appears on a windowsill in Perot's office in Dallas. He had some of his own money in the bank too; that gave them a cushion for several months. His idea was to purchase unused time on an IBM 7070 and sell it to users who were out of time. Some 110 of these computers had been installed around the country. Such computer time retailed at $150 an hour, but Perot managed to purchase it at a wholesale rate of $60–$70 an hour. The risk in beginning EDS was cushioned by one fallback he thought he could always exploit: the navy repeatedly asked him to become an officer again. One month after he founded EDS, the letters from the navy stopped. Out of curiosity Perot asked why. He was told that at thirty-two he was too old. The escape hatch had closed.

At first he ran into stiff resistance in pushing the EDS idea. With limited funds for travel expenses, he confined himself to the east and west coasts, where these large computers were concentrated. The first seventy-seven potential customers he approached flatly refused. During October of 1962, branching out, he stopped in Cedar Rapids, Iowa, where he discovered a firm called Collins Radio that had just started a large project. It was his seventy-eighth call. "They were out of computer time, and for two months they flew planeloads of tapes and people to Dallas and ran their work on this computer. That was the turning point. When I finished with them I paid my bills." With $100,000 in the bank, Perot began hiring systems engineers. How does he account for that early luck? "Some people are willing to run the risk, others not. I think that's the difference. It has nothing to do with anything except persistence—continuing to make sales calls. . . . The difference between success and failure in most cases is refusing to quit when you get discouraged." Of course, EDS was a sound idea at the right time. EDS made its mark in pioneering the computer services concept of facilities management, through which Perot's firm would become the data-processing department for a large insurance firm, bank, or government agency.

In the beginning, when EDS was small, IBM appeared to be organizing to put Perot out of business, a move he found unpleasant but at the same time flattering. Prospective customers concluded that EDS must be something special to trigger that kind of reaction. Perot decided early on that he would never bring legal proceedings against IBM. "We were tiny. We weren't even nut-sized. I made it my policy, we'll never take IBM to court, we'll beat them in the marketplace. We had to bootstrap the company . . . to take the idea and turn it into a tiny business, make it make money from the early days."

EDS pioneered a number of the data-processing industry's now accepted basics, among them the long-term fixed-price contract, regional computer centers, distributed processing, and the specialization of systems engineers by industry, such as insurance, banking, or health care. The secret of EDS, from Perot's point of view, was its employee training program. Perot believed that if good people were hired and trained properly, they would prove capable employees.

EDS's rise was swift, the company growing at a hundred percent a year during the 1960s. It soon became the leader in handling data processing for insurance and medical claims. In 1969 Ross Perot's stock market holdings were enough to make him a billionaire. All appeared to be going well until 1973, when EDS stock plunged to a low of $15 a share. Perot's attempts to revitalize Wall Street by computerizing the brokerage community had run onto shoals. Because EDS was dependent on a few firms for large contracts, losing a few of them, as it did at that time, brought losses. But Perot kept on building, learning from the disappointments.

In 1977 EDS opened a Washington office, and Perot began bidding for large federal government jobs. He was riding high by the 1980s. EDS grew from 47 customers in 1974 to 122 in 1980. Perot and his new president, Morton H. Meyerson, appointed in 1979, moved EDS into such fields as financial markets, banking, government, and defense.

EDS landed its first megacontract in 1982, when it won a $656-million ten-year contract to redo the computer systems at 47 army bases in the United States. Project Viable, as it was called, was the largest single contract awarded in the computer industry. Also through this contract, EDS had become the first data services company to be a prime contractor on a major federal computer systems integration. The next big development for EDS came in 1983: it landed a $400-million contract to set up an inventory control system for the U.S. Navy over the next eight years. Yet another big contract came EDS's way in October of that year in the form of a seven-year, $200-million contract to create an air mail sorting system for the U.S. Postal Service. By the 1980s EDS was processing over ten percent of all American Medicaid claims. Just under forty percent of its revenues derived from medical claims processing and insurance. EDS was the biggest processor of credit union accounts as well. The commercial part of EDS provided one-third of all its revenues. In 1982 total corporate revenue was $562.6 million; in 1983, $718.8 million; in 1984, $800.5 million. Net income rose from $53 million in 1982 to $67.4 million in 1983 and $71.2 million in 1984. By early 1985 EDS had become the largest computer services firm in the world. It was spread over fifty states and in nine countries.

In one of those strange ironies, Ross Perot has a healthy contempt for computers. To listen to him rail against the machines is to become incredulous that this man has done perhaps more than anyone to computerize American business. He refuses to learn his Social Security number, because he wants to be an individual not a number. "Computers are not a panacea. They're things. We're running the great risk of confusing data with wisdom in this country." Nonetheless, to Perot the computer industry stands above most others: it can benefit man, it's clean, it doesn't pollute the air or streams.

If Ross Perot were simply a pioneer in the computer services field, his story would stop here. But he is much more. During the Vietnam War, at the request of the U.S. government, Perot organized a group called "United We Stand," whose purpose was to improve the treatment of American prisoners of war. He spent $2 million in a series of much-publicized efforts to embarrass the North Vietnamese into taking steps. In 1970 he flew to Laos, where he presented North Vietnamese diplomats with lists of prisoners held in South Vietnam. The campaign appeared to have some effect: POWs were treated better, and the North Vietnamese released their names.

Perot is the subject of a best-selling piece of nonfiction, *On Wings of Eagles,* which describes his personal rescue of two EDS employees, imprisoned in Iran by revolutionaries in 1979. EDS had been under contract to computerize Iran's social security system. The two executives were part of EDS's team in Iran. One was Bill Gaylord, who had designed the computer system for the administration of Medicare and Medicaid programs used in many American states. The other was Paul Chiapparone, the country manager for EDS Corporation Iran.

Perot has been described in various places as the fastest, richest Texan ever; he has been called the man of the grand statement and the flamboyant gesture. How does he react to such descriptions?

"Well, I don't worry about it. I'm just the same guy I was before all this happened. People get paid to write stuff, and if they don't make it interesting, nobody would read it." As for grand gestures, "I don't know what they're talking about. Say if you buy the Magna Carta and you give it to the National Archives [as he did in 1985], is that a grand gesture?"

Perot insists that making lots of money has never been a goal. "People who make money their god typically make a lot of bad decisions." He prides himself on moving through his daily life as other people do, whether it's riding the elevators with EDS employees or appearing on the street unaccompanied by bodyguards. "I decided that I was always going to go wherever I wanted to go and do whatever I wanted to do." J. Paul Getty once asked Perot how he was able to live a normal life and was advised to adopt Perot's carefree philosophy. Not on your life, was Getty's reply. He feared being kidnapped too much.

If his wealth does not keep him cooped up, it does, however, make Perot ponder how best to spend it. He is firm in wanting to use it for society's benefit—apart from his other causes, Perot has made large donations to various Dallas institutions and has been active in the fields of educational reform and drug-abuse prevention—and in wanting to prevent it from making his children weak. He and his wife have five children, Ross, Jr., Nancy, Suzanne, Carolyn, and Katherine. Perot once said he would measure the worth of his life by the way his children turned out. If they exhibited a strong concern for their fellow man and were hard-working, productive citizens, he would be satisfied.

Perot is also sole owner of the Petrus Oil and Gas Company; its reserves plus Perot's substantial real estate holdings are worth hundreds of millions of dollars. In the summer of 1984 he became even wealthier when he sold EDS to General Motors for $2.5 billion in GM's biggest acquisition to date. General Motors clearly needed EDS, hoping that the purchase would enable Perot's firm to straighten out the haphazard data-processing system within the car company. It marked the first time that EDS would engage in systems integration for a private company. For Perot it was a red-letter day. EDS would continue to operate in more or less the same way it always had, remaining an independent unit with headquarters in

Dallas. Perot, who with his family owned some forty-five percent of EDS stock, stood to receive roughly $1 billion from the transaction. He became a director and GM's largest shareholder, with 11.3 million shares.

Why did GM buy EDS rather than simply enter into a long-term contract with Perot's firm? The answer lies in the fact that such a contract might well have cost $3–$5 billion. With over one hundred IBM mainframes in its facilities, GM was the second largest user of computers after the U.S. government; but it duplicated functions, and some computers could not communicate directly with others. GM had a hundred data communications networks and over a hundred data centers before the acquisition; EDS hoped to cut that down to eighteen data centers and one digital network. In 1984 GM had spent the incredibly large sum of over $2 billion on internal data processing and office automation.

EDS hoped to help reduce the time it took to design a car from five or six years to only three. "It takes five years to develop a car in this country," Perot noted in exasperation in July 1986. "Heck, we won World War II in four years. We are spending billions to develop new cars. This isn't a moon shot, it's just a car." Perot took his work at GM with great seriousness. He would sneak into dealer showrooms in Texas and elsewhere in khaki pants and a sports shirt to see how the company was doing at the client level. He advised GM data processors that if anything didn't make sense, they shouldn't be afraid to change things.

GM was a great windfall for EDS, tripling its business, providing Perot's company with seventy percent of its revenues and sixty percent of its earnings. In 1985 EDS earned $190 million on sales of $3.4 billion. Some 15,000 people had to be hired to handle the extra work, raising EDS employment to 43,000. Perot, however, was becoming a thorn in the side of GM. In December 1985 he was the only GM director to vote against the company's purchase of Hughes Aircraft. And by the summer of 1986 he had taken his criticism of GM public. He asserted that the company had failed to capture the full potential of its people. GM, in his view, was a bloated bureaucracy with too many executive dining rooms and chauffeured cars.

GM chairman Roger Smith, who until then had treated Perot with deference, lashed out at him. He replied to the charge of excessive perquisites by saying that Perot's office at EDS in Dallas made his look like a shantytown. The argument had become public, unceasing, and likely to hurt the larger purposes of GM.

Perot, through his attorneys, raised the idea that GM buy him out. There was surprise that Perot, who had rarely backed away from a fight, would choose to step out of this one. But he explained to friends that there was no purpose in remaining, as the tiff with Smith would just drag on and on.

By the fall GM's directors were so angry with Perot that they considered kicking him off the board without a buyout. They rejected that, however, doubting that such a step would end the battle. Finally, on November 25, after two and a half weeks of negotiations, Perot and GM settled on a price for his shares—$700 million—and worked out the other details of the deal. One of the terms forced Perot not to criticize GM upon penalty of a $7.5 million fine. Either because he doubted that GM could enforce the provision or because he simply couldn't resist criticism, Perot almost immediately assailed GM, describing his $700 million as "hush money." At a news conference he chided GM for buying him out when $700 million would have paid for a new car plant. Perot called the buyout "morally wrong." Shareholders were incensed at the "peace for a price" plan: GM had paid about $60, or twice the market rate, for each of Perot's shares.

Roger Smith emerged from the encounter free from Perot's sniping and from the threat that one day Perot might win enough power to replace him. Perot never let on that he coveted Smith's job. But others thought he did. His departure, Perot said, would not solve GM's problems. All that had happened was that GM had shot the messenger.

The buyout of Perot left the future of EDS in question. Part of the deal with GM called for him to resign as EDS chairman. He was permitted to stay on in the post of "founder," though his duties were undefined. There was talk that GM had been trying to prompt some other major firm to purchase EDS. American Telegraph & Telephone had conducted talks with EDS just before the Perot buyout, without result. GM's executives worried that a host of EDS executives might leave their jobs in the wake of Perot's departure, diminishing the value of GM's purchase of EDS dramatically.

Perot seemed never to be out of the headlines. Within days of his departure from GM, he confirmed a *Washington Post* report that he had made millions of dollars available to the U.S. government over several years at the request of Lieutenant Colonal Oliver North, then a staff member of the White House National Security Council, in unsuccessful efforts to free various Americans held hostage by political groups in the Middle East.

Having built EDS into the major computer service organization in the world, having tried to join forces with General Motors, Ross Perot still has challenges before him. But work is all he has ever known, and he wouldn't have it any other way. "If I take a month off," he explains, "at the end of a week I really miss work. I'm happiest really here. This is my life. I understand that a lot of people's life work may be drudgery. But in my particular case I can just come here to my office and do business all day, and enough interesting things will come in through the door to keep the day exciting." Even though he will be lowering his profile at EDS, Perot will undoubtedly continue to be in the news.

Indeed, within a month after winding down his involvement at General Motors, Perot was again making headlines, as he leaped into the arms of fellow computer entrepreneur Steve Jobs, founder of Apple Computers and a key figure in modern computer history. Perot agreed to invest $20 million in Jobs's new firm, Next, Inc., giving the Texan a 16-percent share and a seat on the board. Jobs, in the winter of 1987, was hoping to build a second fortune (his first had come in founding and building Apple) by turning out specialized personal computers for the higher-education market. For Perot, the match-up with Steve Jobs was ideal in combining his interest in higher education with a desire to involve himself in new high-technology investments. However he fared at Next, it was clear that Ross Perot would remain a high-profile computer entrepreneur for some time to come.

Making the Computer Smaller and More Powerful

William Shockley

Co-Inventor of the Transistor

13

It is a simple device, just a small bit of solid material and three fine strands of wire. It is also considered by many to have been the most important invention of the twentieth century; certainly it was a key advance in the computer revolution. This piece of crystal with intriguing electrical properties made possible the minicomputers of the 1960s and the personal computers of the 1970s and 1980s. The transistor, like the vacuum tube, is an electrical valve that is used to control the flow of electricity, enabling the boosting—or amplifying—of electrical signals. Thanks to the invention of the transistor the computer went from room-size to briefcase-size. No longer a mysterious, costly, error-prone machine, locked up in the isolation of an air-conditioned laboratory, the computer could be cheaper, more reliable, and more widely available. The man who led the effort that culminated in the invention of the transistor was William Shockley, one of the most ingenious and controversial figures in computer history. He headed the Bell Laboratories team that devised the transistor and then personally invented the junction transistor, commonly held to be the key device in launching the solid-state era of electronics. For that effort Shockley was a co-winner of the Nobel Prize for physics in 1956.

His father was a mining engineer, his mother a mineral surveyor. They were living in London at the time of William's birth on February 13, 1910, but returned to the United States to live in Palo

Alto, California, three years later. Considering that they could give their son a better education at home, the Shockleys kept him out of school until age eight. Once in school he did not find it enjoyable.

Shockley's mother taught him mathematics, and both parents encouraged his scientific interests; but an especially important influence was exerted by a neighbor in Palo Alto, Professor Perley A. Ross, a Stanford physicist. Ten-year-old Bill was a constant visitor at Ross's house, playing with the professor's two daughters and becoming a kind of substitute son. Ross liked children and enjoyed holding forth with his young audience. Once they talked about radio. Bill was confused about aerial and ground connections: wave aspects of radio were still beyond his comprehension. He thought of the ground as one wire, the air as another. Ross explained the principle of wave coupling to the inquisitive youngster, and suddenly things became clear.

Shockley spent two years at the Palo Alto Military Academy before enrolling in Hollywood High School in Los Angeles. For a brief time he also attended the Los Angeles Coaching School, studying physics. Shockley found he had a special talent for the subject: he devised ways to solve problems that varied from the traditional solutions of his teachers. He was disappointed at not winning the physics prize on graduation from Hollywood High. Although he had the highest marks, the prize was not given to him because he had taken physics elsewhere.

In the fall of 1927 he entered the University of California at Los Angeles. At one point, he wanted to take a course in spherical trigonometry. He had sprained his ankle and thus had an incomplete in physical education. The university had a rule that a student who had an incomplete on his record could not overload his course work. Hence, the registrar turned down his request to take the trig course. Shockley learned a lesson from this experience: "I allowed myself to be stopped in the registration office. I had not realized that one cuts the red tape and goes to the top."

After a year at UCLA he entered the California Institute of Technology, in Pasadena. There he had a number of outstanding teachers and advisers, including William Vermillion Houston, who taught the introductory theoretical physics course, Richard C. Tolman, and Linus Pauling. Shockley earned his bachelor of science degree in physics in 1932. He then went to MIT on a teaching fellowship. His doctoral dissertation was entitled "Calculations of Wave Functions for Electrons in Sodium Chloride Crystals"; this research into one aspect of solid-state physics prepared him for his later pioneering work. Shockley's heroes were the major figures of science, Newton and Einstein. He also admired John von Neumann, for his "elegance and simplicity of writing on abstract subjects."

After obtaining his doctorate from MIT in 1936, Shockley had offers to work at General Electric and Yale University but chose a job at Bell Telephone Laboratories in Murray Hill, New Jersey, because that would allow him to work with C. J. Davisson, whose work in electron diffraction later earned him a Nobel Prize. At the outset Shockley was farmed out to different departments to acquire some general technological knowledge; he then joined the vacuum tube department, headed by Davisson. Shockley remembers a conversation he had with Mervin J. Kelly, formerly head of the vacuum tube department and at that time research director of Bell Laboratories (he would later become president): "He said he was looking forward to the day when they would get all the relays out of the telephone switching equipment and do it somehow electronically. Kelly planted this idea: Can you do something electronically?" Kelly understood that the telephone system would of necessity grow more complex as it came under increasing demands. New technology was required. Kelly was thinking of vacuum tubes, but the conversation nevertheless had an impact on Shockley's later work on transistors.

During World War II Shockley was not at all involved with physics. He took a leave from Bell to serve as director of research for the navy's Anti-Submarine Warfare Operations Research Group between 1942 and 1944 and as an expert consultant for the Office of the Secretary of War in 1944 and 1945. At the Bell field station in Whippany, New Jersey, he did electronic design for radar equipment. Shockley was awarded the highest civilian decoration at that time, the Medal of Merit. Most of his contibutions had to do with using radar in B-29 bomber aircraft.

Shockley returned to Bell laboratories after World War II to resume work in solid-state physics in the hope of finding an alternative to vacuum tubes. Large, costly, fragile, and consumers of lots of power, these devices also gave off great amounts of heat when crowded together in a computer or telephone switching center. The phone company, which used millions of tubes and mechanical relays, grew increasingly frustrated at their unreliability: the tubes would burn out and the relays would malfunction. The hope was to find a way around this by using solid-state components. Now that advances in quantum theory had brought an improved understanding of the atomic and electronic structure, and hence the properties, of solids, Bell was encouraged to press its research on semiconductors.

In July 1945 Shockley became codirector of the solid state physics research program. He became convinced that the solid-state approach might produce a new means of amplification: "The aim was a general one. But we didn't have any doubts of the major potential if it came in."

In the early 1940s Bell staff member Russell S. Ohl had shown that semiconductors had some interesting properties. Specifically, he had demonstrated that a block of silicon could convert light into electric power—an effect now used in the solar cells that power satellites. Ohl was studying the use of silicon crystals as rectifiers to detect radar signals. He found that the block of silicon had two regions. When a beam of light fell on the boundary line that separated them, a difference of half a volt developed between the two regions. Related research provided the theory for this effect: neither region was pure silicon. One contained chemical impurities such as phosphorus and arsenic, which released excess electrons that could move as negative charges under the influence of an electric field. This made the silicon a semiconductor—not as insulating as pure silicon would be but much less conducting than a metal. In the other region, impurities such as boron and aluminum supplied deficits in the electronic structure called holes, which could also move like positive particles. The excess-electron type of silicon with negative-current carriers was called N-type, and that with positive holes was called P-type. And the dividing line between the regions was called a P-N junction. These concepts, developed during World War II, were basic to the program that created the transistor.

After the war the focus once again was on these semiconductors, as part of the quest for a solid-state amplifier. Shockley remembered some of the things he had been exploring before World War II, including attempts to come up with a semiconductor amplifier. He and his team now focused on the two simplest semiconductors, silicon and germanium, at that time the best-understood semiconductor crystals.

One of Shockley's prewar experiments had been his attempt in 1939, along with Walter Brattain, a veteran Bell Laboratories researcher, to produce a semiconductor amplifier by using copper oxide. A tiny controlling grid was inserted into the oxide layer on copper in the hope that it would control the current passing through the semiconductor. This device was called the field-effect transistor. All attempts failed: it was simply impossible to make a solid-state amplifier in this material. This work later led, however, to the now useful Schottky-barrier field-effect transistor.

After the war Shockley came up with a new version of the field-effect transistor based upon semiconductor technology during the war. The results were again failures, but creative failures that helped direct the research toward surface phenomena and surface states. Physicist John Bardeen suggested that Shockley's field-effect transistor had failed because electrons were being trapped at the surface of the semiconductor, thus preventing an electrical field from altering the number of free-charge carries within the semiconductor. More research was needed into surface states, and so for the moment the team shelved the attempt to make an amplifying device. It was at that stage that Bardeen and Brattain realized that a small positive charge on one electrode would inject holes into the semiconductor surface, greatly enhancing its capacity to carry current. Bardeen figured therefore that an amplifier could be made by closely spacing two wire electrodes on a germanium crystal. After Bardeen's experiments, Shockley's team attached two small wires, 1/2000 of an inch apart, to one side of a piece of germanium. When an electrical signal was introduced to the germanium via the wires, the signal was amplified.

The date of birth for the point-contact transistor has been recorded as December 23, 1947, for it was on that day that this technique was demonstrated for the first time by amplifying a human voice. It was John R. Pierce, a Bell electrical engineer, who named the new invention. "Amplister" and "transistor" were both candidates, but Pierce selected the latter because the device operated by transferring current from a low-resistance input to a high-resistance output and thus had the important property of *trans*fer re*sist*ance.

In 1948 Bardeen and Brattain obtained a patent for the invention of the point-contact transistor. Shockley's contributions were underscored by the fact that all photographs of the transistor's inventors included him. Of the ten people associated with the transistor program, Shockley has come to be regarded as the most important. His personality was the most forceful on the team, and he was an undoubted inspiration to the others.

There was hope that the transistor would quickly replace the vacuum tube. But trouble arose immediately. No two transistors seemed to work the same. It was not clear that they could be put to commercial use. Shockley thought a better transistor could be made than the point-contact one, and he came up with the conception of the junction transistor, which in effect replaced the metal-semiconductor contacts by rectifying junctions between P- and N-type regions within one crystal. In Shockley's N-P-N (negative-positive-negative) transistor a thin P-region is sandwiched between two N-areas. A metallic contact is made to each of the three areas; one N-region serves as the emitter, the other is the collector, and the P-region is the base. This was an amplifier that lent itself to mass production. A patent was taken out in 1948, and it bore William Shockley's name. In 1950 Shockley wrote a book that included his junction transistor theory. He led the team that built the first reliable junction transistor in 1951. The inventions in the Bell transistor program attest to Shockley's genius as a research director. He knew how to break a problem down to its basics. In his terse style, whether in writing or in speech, he would shift an experiment into a new, usually correct, direction.

So now the world had the transistor. By its amplifying principles, it could perform fast on-off switching and thus send signals along controlled paths in semiconductor circuits that were essential for computer operations. The transistor had great potential: unlike the vacuum tube, it required no warm-up time, produced no heat, and would not burn out. It would not leak or break. It needed much less power, only one-millionth of a watt compared to a full watt for the vacuum tube. The transistor was faster and smaller than the vacuum tube, paving the way for smaller computers. In the early 1960s Shockley noted: "The things you can do functionally with transistors are almost the things you could do with vacuum tubes. But you can't do it in the same space, with the same power, and probably now you can't do it with equal reliability—although it has taken a long time for the transistors to get to this state of reliability."

Bell Laboratories agreed to license the rights to the transistor to any firm in exchange for a royalty payment. Only hearing-aid manufacturers did not have to pay royalties—a gesture in memory of Alexander Graham Bell, much of whose work had been directed toward helping the deaf. Transistors were used by the public for the first time in 1953, in the form of amplifiers in hearing aids. In 1954 the transistor radio was developed. In February 1956 MIT's Digital Computer Laboratory, in conjunction with IBM, began to build a transistorized computer that was meant to replace the huge, 55,000–vacuum tube SAGE computer. The Air Force, with millions of dollars already invested in SAGE, did not rush to replace it with the MIT-IBM computer. In 1957 and 1958 UNIVAC and Philco brought out the first transistorized computers for the commercial market.

Shockley was named Director of Transistor Physics Research at Bell in 1954. In that year and in 1955 he was a visiting professor at Cal Tech. He also served as deputy director of the Weapons Systems Evaluation Group for the Department of Defense.

Does Shockley agree that the transistor was the major contribution of science in the twentieth century? Certain discoveries in medicine may have been more important, he suggests. And he adds, "I think there was an inevitability about the transistor. I would estimate if I had not been there, it would have been at least a year later." Transistors have been used in such diverse equipment as radios and tape recorders, fire and burglar alarms, ignition systems, beacons for airplanes, mobile telephone equipment, nationwide direct distance dialing, and, of course, computers. In time large numbers of transistors and their associated circuitry would be built into a small chip cut from a thin silicon wafer. By the mid-1980s nearly a million circuit components could be put on a chip—without the cost changing very much over the years. In 1958 Shockley predicted that the dollar sales volume in the semiconductor industry would reach $300 million by 1960; in fact, it rose to $500 million. Ten years after the invention of the transistor, thirty million of them had been made, and the price had dropped from $20 apiece to $1.50.

Shockley shared the Nobel Prize for physics in 1956 with John Bardeen and Walter Brattain, for the invention of the transistor. Shockley was by then living and working in Palo Alto. A Swedish journalist in New York called him on the morning of November 1, 1956, with the news. But the connection was so poor that Shockley could barely understand what the reporter was saying. The man who had done so much to improve telephone communications thought that some of his East Coast friends might be playing a practical joke on him! Soon thereafter the news was announced on the radio. Shockley drove to his laboratory, collected his co-workers, closed up shop, and took everyone to a restaurant for a champagne breakfast.

On December 19 of that year he traveled to Stockholm to accept the prize. The shadow of the brutally suppressed Hungarian uprising hung over that year's ceremonies. Shockley, who almost never spoke from a written text, did prepare his remarks for this occasion in advance. Among those remarks were the following: "Frequently I have been asked if an experiment I have planned is pure or applied research; to me it is more important to know if the experiment will yield new and probably enduring knowledge about nature. If it is likely to yield such knowledge, it is, in my opinion, good fundamental research; and this is much more important than whether the motivation is purely aesthetic satisfaction on the part of the experimenter."

Though Bell Laboratories scientists seldom leave their posts to enter business, Shockley did so in 1955. The Shockley Semiconductor Laboratory, which he founded in a shed in Mountain View, just south of Palo Alto, began as a research and development enterprise, affiliated with Beckman Laboratories, a well-known manufacturer of scientific instruments. It was the first semiconductor firm in what came to be called Silicon Valley.

Shockley hoped to capitalize on his knowledge of solid-state physics. He had a small staff and 6,500 square feet of work space.

His main product was the transistor—a two-terminal, four-layer, subminiature silicon diode. Its main application was as a very fast solid-state switch, a device that performed a function previously requiring five different components. He chose engineers with doctorates and called them "my Ph.D. production line." Enjoying fame as the co-inventor of the transistor, Shockley managed to attract top people.

There are those who feel that Shockley might have done more inventing had he not been distracted by administrative concerns. He was not a successful manager. He tried to put a halt to company secrets by posting everyone's salary. He expected his employees to rate each other regularly. At one point delays were encountered, and Shockley suspected sabotage. He ordered an employee to take a lie detector test, which the person passed. Perhaps the greatest difficulty in business lay in his focus on the four-layer germanium diode, a device that was viewed as basically unmarketable. His colleagues felt he would have done better commercially by concentrating on silicon transistors. When in 1957 seven engineers—including Robert Noyce—left the Shockley Semiconductor Laboratory, the operation suffered. It was purchased by Clevite Transistor in April 1960, with Shockley remaining as a consultant. He had begun lecturing at Stanford in 1958; in 1963 he was named the first Alexander M. Poniatoff Professor of Engineering and Applied Science.

Shockley saw his work as both business and pleasure. But he did take time out for another enthusiasm, mountain climbing. He scaled some major heights in the Alps, including the Jungfrau and—taking along his daughter Alison in 1953—Mt. Blanc. In later life he took up sailing. A serious automobile accident on July 23, 1961, caused Shockley to give up sport and some other activities. In 1965 he returned to Bell Laboratories as a part-time consultant. He retired from that work in February 1975 and from teaching at Stanford the following September.

Morgan Sparks, who was an intimate acquaintance of Shockley's at Bell Laboratories, believed that Shockley's success in science came from an ability to cut through to the heart of a problem: "A particular talent he has is the ability to recognize and ignore the many aspects of the problem that are not of great imporatnce and to analyze the relevant factors quickly and in the simplest possible way."

Later in his life Shockley became the object of great controversy. He campaigned about the threat of what he called dysgenics—retrogressive evolution caused by the excessive reproduction of the genetically disadvantaged. He took an interest in the subject after reading an article about a delicatessen owner who had been blinded by acid by a teenager with a 70 IQ. The teenager was one of seventeen children born to a mother with an IQ of 55. Shockley proposed that private foundations offer cash to those with hemophilia, epilepsy, and low IQ who would agree to be sterilized. This would help to halt what he called "the brutal elimination mechanism of evolution." Particularly disturbing to Shockley's critics were what they considered the racist implications of his views. The Stanford campus was the scene of numerous anti-Shockley demonstrations in the early 1970s.

In 1980 Shockley brought a $1.25-million libel suit against the *Atlanta Constitution* for an article it had published about his ideas on race and intelligence. He accused the newspaper of "falsely and maliciously" likening his ideas to the Nazis' genetic experiments in World War II. Shockley was awarded a token $1 in damages. In June 1982 he announced plans to enter the Republican primary for the seat of retiring U.S. Senator S. I. Hayakawa. He was a single-issue candidate, warning of the threat of dysgenics. He came in eighth, receiving 8,064 votes. In his later years Shockley was far more eager to talk about his theories on race and intelligence than his work on the transistor.

Awarded over ninety patents for his inventions, Shockley once offered some observations on creativity that help to illuminate his way of doing science. In an address at the University of Colorado in August 1969, he said:

One vital conclusion reached by thinking about thinking is that creativity is associated with failure. The mind that creates a significantly new, orderly relationship of thoughts has usually wandered down seemingly unprofitable bypaths and suffered disappointments. However, the actions taken that lead to these frustrations are essential parts of creativity. Taking such actions allows the competent mind to become aware of the concepts that are key attributes of the chaotic situation being faced. Creative failure methodology utilizes a set of search-thinking tools that, even as his early efforts fail, make the investigator aware of the key attributes of the problem. Thus, thinking about thinking encourages tolerance of one's inevitable human limitations and enables the individual to be more creative by recognizing that his failures are often usable building blocks to gain intellectual power in a new situation.

Shockley knows the utility of failure. This understanding, indeed, appears to be something that is part and parcel of the most inventive minds.

Robert Noyce

The Mayor of Silicon Valley

14

It is properly called an integrated circuit, but the name microchip has taken hold in common parlance. Its invention led to yet another revolutionary advance in the development of computers. It became possible to build machines that were complex, yet miniature.

The inner workings of that room-sized primitive, the ENIAC, could be replaced with something as small as a playing card. Now mankind could go to the moon and planets. Now a whole range of products to make life easier and more pleasant was imaginable. The co-inventor of the integrated circuit is Robert Noyce, a major figure in the semiconductor industry whom some have called the mayor of Silicon Valley.

He was born on December 12, 1927, in Burlington, Iowa, the son of a Congregational minister. As a child he spent lots of time in his basement workshop, figuring out how things worked, conducting experiments, and then showing the results to his parents. He loved working with his hands. Scrounging around in the junkyard, he searched for any object—a wheel, a disabled motor—that might conceivably become part of some new contraption. He took an engine from an old washing machine and put it on his bicycle. Chemistry interested him, and he figured out how to make nitroglycerin. He loved model airplanes. He and a friend built some primitive transceivers and sent messages to each other. He liked to take Model T cars apart as well. Noyce has a theory about why life in the rural Midwest of the Depression encouraged youngsters to become engineers: when something broke, it made no sense to wait for a new part to arrive. It would take too long and might not come at all. The best thing to do was make a new part yourself.

Noyce spent most of his youth in the small college town of Grinnell, Iowa. He had such an obvious flair for mathematics and science that while he was still in high school, Grant Gale, a family friend and head of the physics department at Grinnell College, invited him to take the freshman physics course there. Noyce graduated from high school in the spring of 1945 and that fall enrolled in Grinnell, seeking a physics degree.

Bob Noyce seemed to have a hand in everything at college. He was a star diver on the college swimming team and won the Midwest Conference championship in 1947. He also had a role in a radio soap opera. And he was Grant Gale's prize student. Gale had been friendly with John Bardeen, who in December 1947 helped to invent the transistor; Gale managed to get hold of one of the first transistors to show the class. Of all the students Noyce was the most enthralled. He received the news of the invention of the transistor, he says, as if an atom bomb had hit him. Here was proof that amplification could be achieved through means other than the conventional vacuum tube. He was one of the very first to do experiments with a transistor.

He was developing the work habits of an inventor at college as well. Later Noyce would say that one of the main characteristics of an inventor is laziness, because deep down the inventor really doesn't like to do things the hard way. Noyce would work hard trying to come up with the right answer on a physics exam, only to have it come back with large red marks on it. The professor would explain that he had done the problem the hard way, and would show Noyce in a few sentences a much easier solution. That stuck with him. Always look for the easy way.

If Noyce was interested in the new frontiers of semiconductors, he was also a college student with a natural inclination to have fun. In the spring of 1948 he found himself in big trouble. A group of his friends wanted to hold a Hawaiian luau. Noyce and another fellow were chosen to obtain a pig, which they would then roast. Though animal theft was serious business in Iowa, Noyce stole a pig from a nearby farm one midnight. The morning after the luau, he confessed. His father and Gale intervened to prevent his going to jail, but he did have to leave school for one semester. He spent that time working as an actuary for Equitable Life in New York City.

Noyce worked hard on his return to Grinnell and graduated in the fall of 1949. Next he embarked on a graduate program in physics at MIT, where he was disappointed to find that there were no courses available in transistor technology and few people interested in the new invention. He was forced to make what progress he could on his own. His doctoral dissertation was entitled "Photoelectric Study of Surface States on Insulators"; he was awarded the degree in 1954. There was no question that he wanted to do something practical with his studies rather than engage in pure scientific research.

It was only natural that Noyce should turn to industry at this point. Only in that framework was any solid-state research being undertaken. Electronics firms were actively seeking graduate students in physics, and Noyce had received offers from a number of them, including Bell Laboratories, IBM, RCA, and Philco. He chose Philco, located in Philadelphia, because it had just opened a semiconductor unit; he assumed his prospects were best there. He began working for its transistor division. By the end of three years, however, he had become convinced that Philco had little interest in the kind of research he wanted to do. The turning point came in January 1956, when William Shockley, the co-inventor of the transistor, asked him if he wanted to interview for a job with a new firm Shockley was setting up in California to develop high-performance transistors. Noyce could not believe his luck—a phone call from the dean of the semiconductor industry. Not lacking in self-confidence, he arrived in Palo Alto and bought a house near Shockley's laboratory before showing up for the job interview. As it happened, he got the job.

At first Noyce admired his new boss. He identified with Shockley's approach to science, breaking a problem down to its simplest parts. He appreciated Shockley's gift for making the right assumptions about a problem. However, Shockley was concentrating on four-layer diodes while others—correctly, Noyce felt—were focusing on transistors as the ideal semiconductor device. In the spring of 1957 a group of Shockley's engineers, whom he later called the "traitorous eight," tried to oust Shockley as manager of the firm. In their view, he was not a good administrator; his preoccupation with sniffing out conspiracies within the plant, they believed, was contributing to delays in production. The rebels approached Arnold Beckman, financier of Shockley Laboratories, and asked for a change in management. Beckman was in a difficult situation: Shockley had just won a Nobel Prize. He could not simply let him go. The rebels met over the July 4th weekend and decided to quit. By September they had signed an agreement by which Fairchild Camera and Instrument would finance a new company, Fairchild Semiconductor. The group chose Bob Noyce, then only twenty-nine, as its leader. Noyce has always maintained that he was a somewhat reluctant member of the group. Still he wound up as its chief.

Noyce had never dreamed that he would be able to work on any basis other than drawing a weekly salary. Now here was a chance to be involved in a start-up company and perhaps to earn some big money; he quite liked the idea. The parent company retained the right to buy the new firm for $3 million at any time within the next eight years. Fairchild Semiconductor opened for business in a two-story warehouse building in Mountain View, California (just outside Palo Alto), twelve blocks from Shockley's firm. Joining Noyce were Gordon Moore, Jean Hoerni, and five other Shockley defectors. At that time, Shockley and Fairchild were the only semiconductor enterprises in Silicon Valley.

Shockley's efforts soon thereafter deteriorated, and Noyce and company never looked back. They were spurred by the space race. This was 1957, the year of the Soviet Sputnik triumph. Manufacturers, in their desire for subminiaturization, were turning away from vacuum tubes and eager for transistors. To launch and guide rockets, onboard computers were necessary: while it was possible to send commands to a rocket, a good deal of electronics was required on board to interpret those commands. Like other engineers and scientists, Bob Noyce was trying to overcome the Tyranny of Numbers: the more wiring there was in a circuit, the farther electronic pulses had to go; and because there were not a great many ways to make the pulses travel faster—they were unable to go faster than the speed of light—the best way to build faster computers was to cut down the distance the pulses traveled by making the circuits smaller. Noyce looked around his operation at Fairchild in frustration, knowing that the manufacturing process needed improvement.

Fairchild had already begun manufacturing silicon transistors. Workers would make a number of transistors on a single wafer, then cut the wafer apart into small pieces. These would have to be wired back together again—a wasteful, error-prone process that severely limited the complexity of the circuits that could be built. Unable to solve this problem, Noyce turned to a different one having to do with the contamination of the double-diffusion transistors Fairchild was making. Any kind of contaminant, whether dust, a stray electric charge, or even a small amount of gas, could prevent the transistor from working. In 1958 Jean Hoerni came up with a solution: a layer of silicon oxide would be put on top of the N-P-N chip, clinging to the silicon and protecting it from contaminants. They called it the "planar" process, since a flat plane of oxide remained on top of the silicon. Noyce brought in the attorneys to write a patent application quickly.

One attorney thought the planar process might have other electronic uses as well. He suggested writing the application in as broad a language as possible, and was constantly prodding Noyce to think of more things that could be done with the planar process. During the first few weeks of 1959 Noyce's thinking jelled into what would be called The Monolithic Idea. If one transistor, not requiring any moving parts, could be made by putting a few thin wires on a small piece of doped silicon, then perhaps it would be possible to form an entire electronic subsystem on that same silicon chip—it would include numerous transistors, resistors, and other electronic circuit elements. In this way it would not be necessary to wire arrays of transistors together by hand after they were produced. This would overcome the numbers barrier. Otherwise, it was simply too expensive to make a complex electronic device—a computer, for instance—that required tens of thousands of components and interconnections.

The first integrated circuit had been built by Jack Kilby the previous summer, but it was not marketable: it had not solved all the problems. As Noyce later put it, Kilby's was "really more of a brute-force approach, of taking a piece of semiconductor and shaping it so that there'd be the areas that were resistors and then putting wiring from one area to another, still doing a lot of hand wiring." During 1958 and early 1959, Kilby at Texas Instruments and Noyce at Fairchild Semiconductor, without knowing of each other's efforts, were both working toward putting all the transistors on one piece of silicon without wires. Noyce penned his first notes on the subject on January 23, 1959. "It would be desirable," he wrote in his lab notebook, "to make multiple devices on a single piece of silicon, in order to be able to make interconnections between devices as part of the manufacturing process, and thus reduce size, weight, etc., as well as cost per active element."

There was still the interconnection problem to solve. It had proved quite hard to make exact electrical connections to the regions of the N-P-N transistor. Wires were big and it was difficult to get them to fit into the small regions of the chip. Noyce, exploiting Hoerni's planar process, realized that it would be possible to put the process to work to aid in making precise connections to the separate regions of an N-P-N transistor. By using Hoerni's oxide spread on top of the three-layer silicon, connecting wires could then be pushed down through the oxide to the precise place on the chip; the oxide would keep them tightly in place. That idea led Noyce to yet another one. He now concluded he would not need wires at all. He could take tiny lines of metal and print it on the oxide. All of the interconnections of the transistor could be made in one manufacturing effort. Not only could the separate regions of a transistor be connected with these printed metal lines, but two transistors could be put on one piece of silicon and connected in the same way. And once two transistors could be put on a chip, so could other circuit components. In short, an integrated circuit.

On July 30, 1959, Noyce filed a patent for a semiconductor integrated circuit using the planar process. Two years later he won approval. Business took off at Fairchild, thanks to the new silicon chip, becoming a $150-million-a-year enterprise. The microchip set off a revolution in electronics. The goal of miniaturization was accomplished. More important, the microchip provided simplification and reliability, and that meant that everything became cheaper. When asked, years later, what his thoughts of the future had been at the time of his great creativity, Noyce replied, "We were really working day to day to try to get a competitive edge on competitors, and not really looking out at the next decade, but rather the next year. This enormous reduction in the cost of electronics has been impossible to forecast."

The reduction in cost did not happen overnight, however. The first integrated circuits reached the market in the spring of 1961 and cost $120. Who needed them at that price? In May President John F. Kennedy urged that the United States put a man on the moon by the end of the decade. NASA chose Noyce's invention for the computers on board the spacecraft used in the Gemini astronaut program. That gave a huge boost, and orders poured in.

By the time Neil Armstrong had landed on the moon in July 1969, some one million integrated circuits had been purchased for the Apollo lunar flight program. Apollo was the most significant early use of the chip. In 1962 the designers of the second-generation ICBM, the Minuteman II, decided to switch to the chip. In the following three years $24 million in electronics contracts were signed. Texas Instruments would soon sell 4,000 chips a month to the Minuteman people. In 1963 some half-million chips were sold; sales would increase fourfold in 1964, 1965, and 1966. The first integrated circuit sold commercially was used in a Zenith hearing aid in 1964. Until then the only buyer of chips was the government. Almost inevitably, there was litigation over the patent rights of Kilby and Noyce. Fairchild and Noyce won the case. But anyone who wanted to make integrated circuits had to get licenses from both Fairchild and Texas Instruments. Noyce accepted being known as the co-inventor of the integrated circuit.

Noyce had started out at Fairchild as director of research and development; in 1959 he had become vice-president and general manager. He believed in simplicity and efficiency. There were no luxurious private offices, no drivers, no special parking spaces for executives. Work was streamlined. If someone wanted to make a large purchase, he could do so without having to wait for advance approval.

Noyce created a whole aspect of the electronics industry and watched as the competition became fierce. By 1964, a mere five years after he had invented the microchip, inventors were figuring out how to put ten circuits on the same-sized microchip. By 1969 the challenge was in trying to put 1,000 circuits on a chip; in 1975 the figure had jumped to 32,000. People now speak of doubling that figure. Realizing the prospects in the electronics business, Fairchild exercised its option in 1959, purchasing Fairchild Semiconductor for $3 million. Bob Noyce and the other former employees of William Shockley each received $250,000 in Fairchild stock. Spin-offs occurred with growing rapidity in Silicon Valley, and Noyce decided in June 1968 to resign from Fairchild and begin his own firm. Fairchild, in Noyce's view, had been diverting too much of its attention to start-ups that had nothing to do with the semiconductor field. There was a certain amount of surprise when Noyce announced his departure, so identified had he become with Fairchild. By this time he had some twelve integrated circuit and transistor patents to his name.

Noyce and another of the "Shockley eight" group, Gordon Moore, formed a company by investing $250,000 from their own money and $300,000 from the well-known venture capitalist Arthur Rock. Here was an opportunity to take on a new challenge, to start over again. "It was a fertile field out in front of me, which wasn't being addressed in a very aggressive manner by Fairchild or anybody else," recalls Noyce. They wanted to call the company Integrated Electronics, or Intel for short. Someone else was using the name Integrated Electronics, so Noyce decided to stick with the shorter version as the official title. Intel began in a concrete building in Santa Clara, California, where a pear orchard had stood. Rather than compete with Fairchild by making semiconductors, Noyce decided to plunge into one part of the computer industry that had hardly been developed—data storage, or memory. The first major component Intel manufactured was the 1103 memory chip, made of silicon and polysilicon. Thanks to the 1103, Intel was able to make a huge impression on the semiconductor market in the early 1970s. Sales reached $23.4 million in 1972. After Intel's Ted Hoff invented the microprocessor, the company's stock tripled in value between 1971 and 1973. By this time Robert Noyce was worth $18.5 million. Sales had reached $66 million by 1978. In a 1982 advertisement Intel claimed that it had pioneered sixteen of the twenty-two major breakthroughs in microelectronic technology in the previous decade.

In time Noyce would preside over what came to be called the Intel culture, a healthy strain of egalitarianism that was a departure from the hierarchical nature of big business. Executives were given small, unpretentious cubbyholes as offices, employees were encouraged to seek out senior executives directly with all sorts of problems. "It bothers you initially a little," Noyce admits, "the noise around, the clacking typewriters. But it's an emphasis on the pride of accomplishment rather than the accoutrements of power." Like other employees, Noyce wears his name tag on his belt. He puts visitors at ease immediately, with his deep voice, gregarious spirit, and ready smile. He is slender, wiry, square-jawed, with curly hair that has turned gray. He has become the spokesman of the semiconductor industry and is good at it.

Noyce gave up the day-to-day running of Intel in 1974, turning it over to Gordon Moore and Andrew Grove. He became chairman of the board and at the same time took on wider responsibilities as an unofficial spokesman for Silicon Valley. He was chairman of the Semiconductor Industry Association in the late 1970s. He became vice-chairman of Intel in 1979. In 1980 Noyce was awarded the National Medal of Science. Three years later he was inducted into the National Inventors Hall of Fame. By 1983 Intel had sales of over $1 billion for the first time. The figure grew to $1.3 billion in 1985. No one could estimate the size of Bob Noyce's personal fortune. By the mid-1980s he was involved in many activities outside the semiconductor industry, among them serving as a regent of the University of California and as a member of the Presidential Commission on Industrial Competitiveness (the Young Commission). "My time is fractionated, which makes it difficult. Unfortunately that means that you don't do things as thoroughly as you should. But at the same time I find these issues fascinating enough that I want to be involved in all of them." Noyce has four children from his first marriage, to Elizabeth Bottomley, which ended in divorce in 1974 after twenty-one years. He acknowledged once that his work had contributed to his divorce. In 1975 he married Ann Bowers, Intel's personnel director, who would later work five years for Apple Computer.

As for the future, Noyce sees a world in which computers take on an increasing number of jobs that people don't want to do. "We don't put coal on the fire any more, to turn up the heat. Someone else does that for us. More and more I don't remember telephone numbers. I push a button and there's a code to look up that number and dial the person I want to talk to. So I think that getting away from the routine things that could be assigned to some other intelligence would free us to do things that human beings can do that computers can't do."

Jack Kilby

Co-Inventor of the Integrated Circuit

15

The Problem, as they called it, still loomed large. Solve it and the sky was the limit. If computers were to work faster, somebody would have to figure out how to cut down the distance the electronic pulses traveled—in short, how to make the circuits smaller. A large, profitable market awaited the first to find the answer. Jack Kilby had all the time in the world that summer of 1958 to work on the Problem. All the others at Texas Instruments had gone off on vacation. Kilby was free to think, and he had reason to think hard.

Everyone, it seemed, was hungry for more progress now that the transistor had arrived. After the Sputnik launch in 1957, there was a lot of talk of playing catch-up with the Russians, of getting into space. But first, the computer had to be made small enough to fit into the nose cone of a missile, and reliable enough to be sent on a trip to the moon or the planets. The issues of size and reliability of components had to be considered along with that of speed.

Kilby could feel the breath of other would-be inventors down his neck. Once he had arrived at step one of his solution, it seemed more important to get it down on paper and be the first than to work out steps two and three. Later he would have time to be thorough.

And so he recorded his idea carefully in his laboratory notebook, the handwritten remarks, the sketches of circuits. When his boss, the well-known silicon researcher Willis Adcock, returned from vacation, Kilby approached him. Would he go for the idea? It would take a certain amount of courage and money. Adcock would have to justify to the others his allowing Kilby to be diverted from other tasks. Adcock was a little skeptical, but he said all right, give it a try. Now Kilby had the chance to make a prototype. It would be one of the oldest—and most famous—prototypes in the history of computers and science.

Jack Kilby talks slowly, quietly. He is large—six feet, six inches—his hands are large, and so are his shoulders. He seems to stoop a little. He appears to be someone who has never lost his temper. He has a round, rough-drawn face, with gray hair popping up from the sides of his balding head. The sentences come snail-like, there are long pauses before a thought emerges. He seems to have all the time in the world. He is someone who has spent a lot of time alone, a lot of time thinking out problems by himself. So it is appropriate that he seems in no great rush to do things, to talk, to end a conversation. But he's interested in people, and glad to talk about himself and his inventions.

Kilby makes an interesting distinction between engineers and scientists. Most inventors, he says, would rather be known as scientists than as engineers. Scientists think great thoughts, engineers put things together and are hungrier for tangible results—including money. Kilby considers himself an engineer, and has no qualms about it. He counts himself among those practical-minded people who want to make things work better, cheaper, and more easily, and who want to sell their improvements to the public. Of course, inventing something new is not easy. There's no school that teaches courses in invention, there's only hard work. Jack Kilby's tried and proven method is not at all complicated: the trick in solving a problem, he explains, is to get to the core as quickly as possible, and make sure that what you identify as the core of the problem really is that. A poorly defined problem inevitably leads to failure, to trying to solve the wrong problem. Another pitfall to be avoided is that of coming up with the obvious solutions, the ones others have thought of before. Kilby has tried to eschew solutions that appeared self-evident, looking instead for the unexpected ones, even though they may violate scientific conventions. But solving the problem isn't enough; it must also be done with an eye for cost. Creating a new product that no one can afford to buy, even if the product performs miracles, is of no use whatsoever. The public has to be able to afford your new invention.

In thinking about developing an integrated circuit, Kilby was motivated primarily by the idea that it would have a dramatic impact on the way electronic equipment was built. He was thinking like an engineer, not a scientist. If he could see his product in the marketplace making a difference in the short run, he would be a happy man. In fact, one of the first things he did, once the integrated circuit idea had taken shape in his mind, was to skim through the records of patents issued in Washington over the past few years, just to make sure no one else had come up with the same thing.

Kilby has said that he could never have invented anything if he had had first to consider its cosmic implications. An important corollary is his pronouncement that a successful inventor must have the ability to pick his targets. Spreading oneself too thin can be very dangerous to an inventor. Vowing to live with total creativity would drive the best person nuts by noon. "If you want to be totally creative, you've got to decide on a radically different way of getting out of your bed every morning, a radically different way to comb your hair and brush your teeth."

Ironically, Kilby doesn't seem receptive to the high-tech world he has helped to create. He shuns computers; he still keeps his slide rule (though his invention of the hand-held calculator made it obsolete). He dislikes wearing a digital watch. He has used the same Hasselblad camera for twenty years. Jack Kilby was born on November 8, 1923, in Jefferson City, Missouri, and lived there until the age of four, when he and his family moved to Salina, Kansas. At that time his father, an electrical engineer, became president of the Kansas Power Company. In 1935, when the company's offices moved to Great Bend, the Kilby family moved as well. During the summers Jack tagged along on his father's visits to the power company's facilities throughout the western part of Kansas. Crawling with his father through generation stations, searching for faulty equipment, he was introduced to the wonders of electricity.

In 1937 Kansas was hit by a major blizzard, and Jack's father used a ham radio to stay in touch with distant power stations. Jack put on the earphones and took an immediate liking to the radio. He studied hard and soon became a fully licensed ham radio operator, with call letters W9GTY. Scavenging for parts, he built his own radio. Even during high school he knew that he wanted to study electrical engineering. Then in June 1941 he took the MIT entrance exam. The passing grade was 500, and Kilby received a 497. This missing out by just three points was something he would never get over. He had not applied elsewhere, so he had to push to get into the University of Illinois, his parents' alma mater. Four months after he entered the school, the Japanese attacked Pearl Harbor; Kilby became a corporal, assigned to work in a radio repair shop on an army base in northeastern India. He put his knowledge to work, setting up and maintaining the transmitters used to contact agents in the field.

After the war he returned to the University of Illinois, hoping to learn about the progress that had been made in electronics during the war. The university did not offer courses in solid-state physics, so he took those electronics courses that were available. He graduated in 1947 with grades that were good, but not excellent. There were some jobs open in electronics in the utilities, but none appealed to Kilby. When Centralab in Milwaukee, a producer of electric parts for television, hearing aids, and radio circuits, offered him a job, he took it. He began working on silk-screening techniques for printing a substrate onto which germanium transistors could be soldered. It was only a partial solution, inasmuch as the transistors were made separately and then had to be soldered into place. From this Kilby became aware that integration of a circuit was worth pursuing. He stored the idea in his head for possible future use.

In the early 1950s the transistor was the coming thing. Jack Kilby read all he could about it. He took graduate courses, and he listened to John Bardeen, the Nobel Prize–winning physicist who had co-invented the transistor (along with William Shockley and Walter Brattain), give a lecture at Marquette University. Then in 1952 he was sent by Centralab to take Bell Laboratories' first ten-day seminar in transistors. Centralab had paid the $25,000 license fee and thus would become one of the first firms to produce transistors. After Kilby returned, Centralab organized a small, not highly profitable transistor manufacturing operation, selling components to hearing-aid manufacturers. As excited as he was by the transistor's prospects, Kilby quickly realized its limitations. He would design something—a hearing aid, a radio amplifier—but then the factory workers would have trouble building the circuits: there were too many parts and interconnections, they were too close together, the human hand just wasn't capable of handling the work, the numbers were too large—it was the Tyranny of Numbers. Transistors could do wonders, but somehow The Problem had first to be solved. Kilby wanted to try.

As for computers, they were fated not to get much faster as long as The Problem was unsolved. The more wiring there was in a circuit, the farther the electronic pulses had to go. There weren't too many ways to make those pulses travel faster: they could only go as fast as the speed of light. Putting in more transistors enabled the computer to do more, but it cut down speed. The distance the pulses traveled had to be reduced—the circuits had to be made smaller. Early electronic equipment had had few components, so it was not a problem to hand-solder them together; costs were kept reasonable, and the equipment worked adequately. But as electronic equipment became more complex, it became expensive to manufacture, and unreliable as well. A B-29 aircraft needed almost a thousand vacuum tubes and tens of thousands of passive devices. It had become clear by the close of World War II that the future of electronics was limited unless the problems of cost, size, and speed, and reliability could be overcome.

Kilby's career in Milwaukee had been satisfactory. He had twelve patents to his name, including the steatite-packaged transistor and the reduced-titanate capacitor. But perhaps, he thought, he could aim higher in the world of electronics. For that he needed to be part of a firm that was totally dedicated to electronics—not just marginally, as Centralab was. At age thirty-four he looked around for a candidate and was soon offered work at Texas Instruments in Dallas.

The company Jack Kilby joined in the spring of 1958 had played an important role in the transistor field. It had produced the first transistor radio in 1954. In that year too it had produced the first silicon transistors, selling them for $2.50 each, a sixth of the cost of germanium transistors. By May 1958 Texas Instruments was earnestly experimenting with an idea called the Micro-Module in order to overcome the Tyranny of Numbers. The goal of the project was to interconnect miniaturized components—complete electronic circuits—by standardizing their size and shape and stacking them vertically, with wires running through the stack. A prototype had been successfully developed. Kilby had been hired with the general understanding that he would work on miniaturization. He had no enthusiasm for the Micro-Module project, however, feeling that it would be far more efficient to use a horizontal layout, and more cost effective to dispense with germanium and use only silicon. Instead of joining the project, therefore, he began experimenting with an intermediate-frequency amplifier called an IF strip, a device that was used commonly in radios. He wanted to make components in a tubular form rather than the flat wafers that were part and parcel of the Micro-Module plan. He spent a few months on this, making some models, but concluded that the device would require too much hand assembling.

It was then—in the first few weeks of July—that almost everyone at Texas Instruments took off for vacation under the company's mass vacation policy. Because he was too new to have earned any time off, Kilby was left alone in the semiconductor lab. He feared that he would have to begin working on the Micro-Module once vacation was over—unless in the meantime he could come up with a better idea. The IF-strip approach had not proved fruitful, so he looked around for alternatives.

If all the parts of a circuit—the resistors, the capacitors, and the transistors—could be made of the same material, Kilby reasoned, they could be manufactured in a single, monolithic block; then there would be no need to wire anything together. The connections could go inside the chip. By avoiding the wiring and the connections, one could put a great many components on the chip. The best material for the purpose, Kilby felt, was silicon: by 1958 it had become clear that its properties made it more useful as a semiconductor than germanium. The latter was easy to work with but unsatisfactory for many applications inasmuch as it could not function at high temperatures; silicon, on the other hand, though thought to be too brittle and too hard to purify for transistors, at least could withstand high temperatures. Knowing of the military's strong interest in miniaturization in electronics, Kilby was confident that the first circuits would be sold to the armed forces. Given silicon's higher temperature capability, it had already become the military's preferred choice. Beyond that, Texas Instruments had invested millions of dollars in equipment and techniques to purify silicon as well as to build silicon transistors. Whatever Kilby would invent, it would be most practical for him to use silicon as a building block.

Exactly what could he do with silicon? At the time no one would have thought of making components out of a semiconductor material. Nonetheless, Kilby though the idea exciting. He knew that it had been possible to make diodes and transistors out of silicon if properly doped with the right impurities to conduct electric charges. Were the silicon to have no impurities, its electrons would be bound in place and no charges would flow through it; indeed, it would block current in the same way that a standard resistor would. Kilby thought of building a silicon resistor, realizing that a strip of undoped silicon could in fact act as a resistor. He sensed that it would not be as good as a standard carbon resistor—but it would work. And, for that matter, capacitors could be made out of silicon as well. They wouldn't work as well as the standard metal-and-porcelain ones—but again, they would work. However, even with all the elements formed within a silicon chip, interconnections would be required. Some of these could be internal, but others would have to be on the surface.

Kilby felt confident enough to write in his lab notebook on July 24, 1958, that "the following circuit elements could be made on a single slice: resistors, capacitor, distributed capacitor, transistor." He made some sketches showing how the components could be arranged out of N-type and P-type semiconductor material. Although he believed it would work, he could not be sure. He needed to build a model. Approaching his boss, Willis Adcock, right after the vacation period, Kilby found him only mildly interested in the idea: Adcock was knee-deep in Micro-Modules and not eager to divert people to the Kilby scheme. But, sensing that his new employee might well be on to something big, Adcock worked out a deal with him. If Kilby could make a working resistor and a working capacitor from separate pieces of silicon, Adcock would go along: he would authorize the building of an integrated circuit on a chip, a far more expensive proposition.

By creating a circuit called a phase-shift oscillator—a device that oscillates signals at a given rate—Kilby did his part, and so

Adcock lived up to his end of the deal. Texas Instruments gave Kilby some money to build a prototype. The Kilby test device, actually an oscillator on a chip, was ready on September 12, 1958. A half-inch long, it consisted of two circuits built in one piece of germanium. (Kilby had used germanium rather than silicon because at the time it was better understood.) Texas Instruments executives came in to see the show. A nervous Jack Kilby hooked up the wires from the battery to the circuit, then from the circuit to the oscilloscope. He played with the dials on the oscilloscope, made a last-minute check of the connections, breathed deeply, and pushed the switch. A bright green light undulated across the screen—a perfect sine wave. The experiment was a success. The microchip was born.

A market for the new device seemed waiting—the digital one. Because digital circuits have the great advantage of being very repetitive, it was possible to build even the most complex computer from a single building-block element. Turning the invention into a product, however, proved a long and frustrating task. Building those first circuits in the late summer and fall of 1958, Kilby had been so intent on integrating all the components into one chip that he had not addressed the question of interconnections. He had connected the components on the chip by hand with small gold wires. To be able to market the integrated circuit, someone would have to solve the interconnection problem. Aware that he needed to indicate that his new circuit would not require wiring by hand, Kilby added a paragraph in his patent application: "Instead of using the gold wires in making electrical connections, connections may be provided in other ways. For example . . . silicon oxide may be evaporated onto the semiconductor circuit wafer. . . . Material such as gold may then be laid down on the [oxide] to make the necessary electrical connections." The five-page application, together with four pages of pictures, was turned over to the U.S. Patent Office on February 6, 1959. At an industry convention in New York City in March 1959 Texas Instruments announced "the development of a semiconductor solid circuit no larger than a match head." More than two years later, on April 26, 1961, Kilby learned that the patent had been granted—not to him, but to Robert Noyce.

Kilby had outlined a process for providing interconnections on the surface of a chip. But the Court of Patent Appeals had ruled that his description was not adequate, and that Robert Noyce's was. Although Kilby had been the first to come up with the idea of integration, it has been Noyce who, in the early months of 1959, had first solved the problem of interconnections. Kilby and Noyce engaged in a ten-year struggle over patent rights, which Noyce ultimately won. By the time the verdict was in, however, both Texas Instruments and Fairchild Semiconductor (Noyce's employer at the time of the invention) had decided it was better to make a deal so that both would be assured a part of the integrated circuit market. Kilby and Noyce would be called the co-inventors of the integrated circuit.

Does Kilby accept the term co-inventor? "Not readily, I think that's really Dr. Noyce's term. I don't think anyone questions that I was the first to design what are now called monolithic circuits and to build some. And I think I would say that Dr. Noyce was the first to do something which I had intended to do but was not done at the time the patent application was filed—which was to provide interconnections between some of the components with evaporated metal leads on the surface of the chip. Dr. Noyce feels this was such a radical departure that it really constituted starting the process over again. I suspect that he feels a little charitable in including me as a co-inventor if he really did start it. I don't share that feeling."

Part of the cool reception accorded to the integrated circuit when it was first shown off on March 24, 1959, had to do with the difficulty people had in believing that resistors and capacitors could be made out of silicon. Nichrome was supposed to be the best material for making resistors, and Mylar the best for capacitors. Further, it was feared that integrated circuits would be hard to make. Another concern was that circuit designers at computer firms would become unemployed once Texas Instruments and Fairchild began to sell integrated circuits. In time the annual sales of integrated circuits exceeded $25 billion, and a good part of the $100-billion electronics industry would rest on the wondrous chip.

The new chip cracked the military market first. The Minuteman missile program had been using transistors, and these had developed a reputation for reliability. When the integrated circuit replaced the transistor in the Minuteman project—each missile required 2,500 integrated circuits for guidance control—people began to take the device seriously. There was a growing desire on the part of its manufacturers to penetrate the consumer market as well.

Thus it was that in the mid-1960s Texas Instruments turned to Jack Kilby to invent something that would be good for the consumer, a miniature calculator that could fit in one's hand. Kilby had been promoted a number of times and was now deputy director of the Semiconductor Research and Development Laboratory. The company had in mind something that would cost under $100 and would fit in a coat pocket; calculators at the time were the size of office typewriters and cost $1,200. The machine should add, subtract, divide, multiply, perhaps do square roots—and be battery operated. The project was treated with great secrecy.

Kilby and his team had to start from scratch. Existing calculators were irrelevant as models. Kilby was involved in most of the design decisions other than the logic design. The major problem was to design a set of components—logic, keyboard, output, and power supply—that were electrically compatible and sufficiently small for the purpose. The most difficult aspect was the output, and to solve this Kilby invented a thermal printing system. A low-power printing head "burned" images into heat-sensitive paper.

Late in 1966 the prototype worked for the first time. But it would take until April 14, 1971, for the first pocket calculator, the Pocketronic, to be put on the market. It weighed 2.5 pounds, could add, subtract, multiply, and divide, and was priced at $250. It was a huge success. In 1972, five million pocket calculators were bought in the United States. The price dropped to below $100 by the end of 1972, to $25 in 1976, and to $10 in 1980. Sales doubled each year. A standard model became available for $6.95 in the mid-1980s; worldwide, 100 million calculators are bought annually in what has become a billion-dollar business. The second most popular application of the integrated circuit was the digital watch, introduced in the fall of 1971. Millions would be bought in the next decade.

Kilby worked at Texas Instruments from 1958 to 1970. Until 1968 he was in charge of integrated circuit development work. He notes that he had a long string of titles, but the content didn't change very much; his title as of 1968 was Assistant Vice-President and Director of Engineering. Since 1970, when he took a leave of absence, he has worked as both an independent inventor and a consultant. He has done some advising to faculty and graduate students at Texas A&M as well. From 1975 until 1984 he worked largely on a solar energy project which was novel in that the means for collection and storage of energy were combined. Texas Instruments acquired the rights to the idea, and the U.S. Department of Energy funded it for four years, during which time several large systems were produced, demonstrating its feasibility. It was never produced commercially because of the drop in oil prices and a slackening of interest in solar projects.

Marcian E. (Ted) Hoff

Inventor of the "Computer on a Chip"

16

"Announcing a new era of integrated electronics . . . a micropro-grammable computer on a chip." That was Intel's advertisement in the November 15, 1971, issue of *Electronic News,* introducing the 4004 microprocessor. It was ingenious, it was revolutionary, but at first no one knew quite what to do with it. In just a couple of years, however, it would become clear that the change Ted Hoff had wrought in inventing the microprocessor would turn the computer industry on end. Charles Babbage's mighty mill had appeared in microcosm.

A large part of the mystery of computers would now evaporate. They could be made small and versatile, and they could be standardized. The arrival of the microprocessor made people recognize, in Hoff's words, "that the computer, a little chunk of intelligence, was a very marketable building block." Indeed, Hoff has always felt that the invention of the microprocessor was not nearly as significant as the perception that a market existed for it.

Prior to the microprocessor a different integrated–circuit chip was required for every application; a cheap and compact central control system didn't exist. Now, however, there could be one standardized design for numerous applications—no longer did chips have to be custom-designed. The beauty of the microprocessor lay in the fact that its program could be put on a separate memory chip. Simply by replacing a small program chip with new instructions, one could command the microprocessor to do a variety of tasks. So crucial was his invention that Hoff has been called one of the greatest scientists of the twentieth century.

The chip was small enough and cheap enough to fit into almost any "thinking" device. Elevator controls, cameras, calculators, vending machines, and electric typewriters with memory could use it; it could run a watch or steer a spacecraft. Hoff was amused to learn what people were doing with microprocessors at first: one of the earliest applications was in monitoring the amount of water cows were drinking in farm experiments. A major asset of Hoff's microprocessor was its versatility: one firm, Pro-Log Corporation, of Monterey, California, designed a demonstration device that started out as a digital clock and then, when the program chip that ran the clock was taken out and another put in its place, played a tune. Most important to our story, the microprocessor paved the way for the personal computer.

Ted Hoff was born in Rochester, New York, on October 28, 1937. He grew up outside of Rochester near the village of North Chili and went to Churchville-Chili Central High School. His education began in a one-room schoolhouse; one teacher taught seven grades, thirteen students in all. From his father, who worked for the General Railway Signal Company, Ted acquired an interest in electricity. From his uncle came an enthusiasm for chemistry. Hoff remembers being about five years old and watching his uncle pour two colorless liquids together, making them turn bright red. Enchanted by this phenomenon, he took up the study of chemistry on his own. He took the New York State chemistry examinations without having taken a high school chemistry course, and achieved a score of ninety-five. His uncle gave him some advice, however: Jobs in chemistry were limited. He was better off studying chemical engineering. Hoff recoiled at the idea, thinking there was too much "plumbing and standard design" in that subject. His uncle did him another favor that proved more rewarding: he gave him a subscription to *Popular Science*. Hoff sent away for an Allied Radio catalogue, and that got him started in electronics, a subject he found thoroughly engaging during high school.

Hoff entered Rensselaer Polytechnic Institute, in Troy, New York, in 1954. Through his father he was employed every summer during college as a technician in the electronics lab at the General Railway Signal Company in Rochester. There he worked on an electronic track circuit, making some suggestions for part of the design that were eventually used—and so his name appeared on the patent application. Another project involved lightning protection schemes for the track circuit, for which Hoff also received credit in the patent application. The actual granting of the two patents came in 1959, a year after he graduated from college.

In 1958 Hoff received a bachelor's degree in electrical engineering from Rensselaer. His undergraduate thesis was on transistors. Moving on to Stanford University, he received his master's and doctoral degrees in electrical engineering while acquiring two more patents.

Hoff's classmates at Rensselaer remember him as brilliant but modest. "He had the uncanny ability to work out complicated electrical engineering problems in a fraction of the time it took the rest of us," recalled his friend Harold Hoyt in a recent alumni bulletin. On one occasion Hoyt spent an entire weekend working on a very tough engineering problem that was due at a 1 p.m. Monday class. "I ran into Ted at about 11 and asked if he had done it. 'No,' was his answer, 'not yet.' But in class, less than two hours later, he had finished it. . . . He had this natural ability, an inquisitive nature, a creative approach to solving problems. Yet he was not overbearing."

Hoff had some minor contact with computers as an undergraduate; he took a computer course and was aware that Rensselaer possessed an IBM 650 that was largely off limits. But his interest in computers intensified at Stanford. He was intrigued by the problem of pattern recognition and image processing. To do his thesis he worked on an IBM 1620, newly acquired by Stanford. That gave him his first opportunity to program. He obtained his master's degree in 1959 and his doctorate in 1962. His doctoral thesis was entitled "Learning Phenomena in Networks of Adaptive Neurons."

Hoff spent another six years at Stanford as a research associate. Among other pursuits, he worked with his thesis adviser, Bernard Widrow, on an electrochemical memory element that led to some patents. He began working at Intel, a brand-new semiconductor firm, on September 1, 1968, as manager of applications research. He was the company's twelfth employee. He had been hired by Robert Noyce to come up with commercial applications for the semiconductor memory chips that Intel was manufacturing.

The story of Ted Hoff's microprocessor really begins back in the late 1950s, when two computer experts, Jack Kilby of Texas Instruments and Robert Noyce, then of Fairchild Semiconductor, working apart from one another, figured out that large numbers of transistors and their connections could be etched on a piece of silicon. This integrated circuit contained an entire section of a computer—a logic circuit or a memory register, for example. More and more transistors were crammed in by designers, so that eventually a tiny silicon chip would have hundreds of thousands of transistors etched on it. This was known as large-scale integration, or LSI. LSI had one flaw: circuits were rigidly fixed in the silicon, so the chips could perform only the jobs for which they were designed—they were, in engineering terms, "hardwired."

No guiding light ordered a major research effort designed to lead to the microprocessor. No one decided that it ought to be invented. Rather, the microprocessor came about indirectly. Early in 1969 Ted Hoff was given the job of helping a group of Japanese engineers produce a set of miniature components for programmable desktop calculators: a Japanese firm, ETI, planned to market the final product. While others were routinely making devices that contained 500 to 1,000 transistors, the ETI engineers wanted to put 3,000 on some of their chips of random logic. ETI spoke of putting all the required circuitry on just twelve silicon chips.

It appeared to Hoff that coming up with that kind of calculator, with its complicated design, would tax all of his and his colleagues' design capabilities. Hoff knew it was possible to store in a memory chip a program that would run a tiny computing circuit. Though ETI had no desire to build a minicomputer, Hoff still felt that it was preferable to build a general-purpose computer that would be programmed by the read-only memory to perform the specific function of a calculator. The user of the calculator need not know that there was a general-purpose computer inside the equipment. Hoff therefore suggested that the ETI engineers employ the read-only memory to implement subroutines, thus enabling them to reduce the amount of logic. The general response was, "Go away, don't bother us. We know what we're doing. If we need your help, we'll ask for it." Intel's Noyce advised Hoff that if he thought he had an idea, he should pursue it as a kind of back-up to what the Japanese were doing. Then came the breakthrough.

Hoff put the entire central processing unit—the CPU—of a simple computer on one chip. He attached two memory chips, one a read-only memory and the other a read-write memory. Another chip was added later, primarily an input-output chip. The microprocessor—actually a highly complicated printed electric circuit—became known as the "computer on a chip" because it had put all the logic functions and arithmetic of a computer on a chip the size of the head of a tack. Reducing the number of parts wasn't important, design was. Says Hoff, "The real key was not necessarily the number of components or the number of features, but the organization, the architectural concept in which you take a general-purpose computer and build it into a system."

Hoff's breakthrough was designing the architecture of the chip set (not the chips themselves, which were designed by Federico Faggin, another Intel engineer). The architecture included the arrangements of registers, the instruction set, and the interconnections between the chips. The crucial chip would have most of the calculator's arithmetic and logic circuitry on it. Only the input-output and programming units would go on separate chips. Instead of having individual chips for keyboard control, display control, printer control, arithmetic, registers, and so on, Hoff suggested the design of a single-chip CPU that would be able to run conventional computer programs. Hoff's CPU measured just 1/8 inch by 1/6 inch and contained 2,300 transistors. Its power was the equal of ENIAC's. It performed as well as those $300,000 IBM machines of the early 1960s—each of which needed a central processing unit the size of a large desk.

Although the ETI engineers recognized the problems with their chips, they were still not interested in Hoff's new approach. Matters came to a head in October 1969. The senior management of ETI visited Intel, and the Japanese engineers made their presentation. Then Hoff made one of his own, noting that his device had the advantage of performing many other functions besides that of a calculator. He argued that the calculator chips were so specific in the way they did arithmetic that they really weren't useful for much else, whereas his chips were highly versatile. The ETI managers were convinced; Hoff was given the go-ahead to produce his computer on a chip.

Hoff's architecture was realized in silicon by Federico Faggin.

The chips themselves—the actual placement of the various transistors in the chip layout—were Faggin's work; he developed the specifics of the chip size and transistor count, in the spring of 1970. The microprocessor was ready in early 1971. The ETI calculator, containing Intel's first microprocessor, was produced under the name Busicon. ETI had financial troubles, however, ending in bankruptcy—a setback that had the effect of pushing Intel to look for other applications for the microprocessor.

One other Intel invention accelerated the development of Hoff's chip and enhanced its marketability. This was the EPROM—Erasable Programmable Read-Only Memory—invented by Dov Frohman, an Intel researcher. Heretofore, computer memories had been virtually permanent; they could be altered only with difficulty. Now, thanks to the EPROM, it was possible to erase the memory of one function and have it reprogrammed. Until the EPROM was invented, the only types of memory were the volatile read-write memory, the read-only memory ordered from the factory, and a one-time-only programmable read-only memory. Now one could reprogram memories with the EPROM and not have to discard misprogrammed parts.

Hoff and other Intel engineers hoped that the microprocessor could become an Intel proprietary chip—in other words, that they could sell it to other customers besides ETI. After all, the design being implemented was Intel's and not ETI's. But the marketing people preferred to avoid the difficulties associated with selling computers. They explained to Hoff that he was a latecomer to the computer business, that only 20,000 minicomputers were sold a year, and that Intel, if it sold his chip, might get perhaps ten percent of that market. For 2,000 shipments a year it was not worth the headaches of providing support for such computers. Another question was how computers sold with this new chip costing only $50 to $100 could cover the software cost. At this stage small computers were not popular at all, so the public's appetite for the microprocessor was nonexistent. The concept of the microprocessor was so new that no one—not even Hoff and his colleagues—could foresee that it would revolutionize the computer and electronics industry. People were used to thinking of computers as million-dollar items, requiring experts to run and repair. The idea that one simply replaced a defective chip with a new one at no more cost than that of a fluorescent lightbulb (by the end of the 1970s the microprocessor was selling for less than $5) was too alien for many to grasp.

By 1974, however, Intel had become aware that there was an almost limitless number of applications for Ted Hoff's microprocessor. The Intel 8080 chip, the first true general-purpose microprocessor, was a major advance. A far more highly integrated chip than its predecessors, it was capable of executing about 290,000 operations a second. The 8080 became an industry standard, and Intel quickly took over the 8-bit market.

In 1974 Hoff became active in Intel's telecommunications products. He helped design the architecture of an "analog" microprocessor—an EPROM digital signal processor with analog input and output interfaces. In 1978 he was promoted to Intel Fellow. Late in 1982 Hoff surprised the electronics industry by announcing that, after fourteen years, he planned to leave Intel. He felt he needed a change. He became vice-president in charge of corporate research and development at Atari in Sunnyvale, California, with a mandate to investigate new products. Hoff was attracted to Atari because it was putting computers in the home, something that interested him very much. But eighteen months later, in July 1984, the company was sold and Hoff left to do some independent consulting and research. He works in his garage-turned-lab at home in Sunnyvale, where he says he can build almost anything he wants. On being asked recently what kind of research he was pursuing, he remained vague except to say, "I've been looking at several aspects of interface and ways of bringing the computer into greater use." Hoff envisions a time when computers will handle a significant portion of the drudgeries of everyday life.

In 1983 Ted Hoff became the third recipient of Rensselaer Polytechnic Institute's Davies Medal for Outstanding Engineering Accomplishment, in recognition of his invention of the microprocessor.

The Hardware Designers

Gene Amdahl

Mainframe Designer Par Excellence

17

He is considered one of the greatest computer designers of all time. He was a major reason for IBM's dominance of the mainframe computer industry in the 1950s and 1960s. When he could not get IBM to follow his wishes, Gene Amdahl challenged the computer giant, and did well. His company, Amdahl Corporation, was the first to create alternative mainframes compatible with IBM equipment.

The similarities between Gene Amdahl and supercomputer builder Seymour Cray are considerable: both have sought to change the way large computers are built, both have distinct, individual visions of how computers should be made, and both have made huge impressions on the industry. But whereas Cray—a man whom Amdahl admires but has never met—has concentrated on specialized computers with a small market, Amdahl has produced general-purpose data-processing machines intended for a large segment of the marketplace.

Amdahl was born on November 16, 1922, in Flandreau, South Dakota. He entered South Dakota State College (later South Dakota University) in the fall of 1941, remaining there until the spring of 1943. He then taught physics in the U.S. Army's advanced specialized training program before serving in the Navy from mid-1944 to mid-1946; in the Navy he taught electronics. He returned to South Dakota State College in the fall of 1946 and two years later received his bachelor of science degree in engineering physics.

Amdahl did his graduate work, in theoretical physics, at the University of Wisconsin. In 1950 he was asked by a professor to work with two other graduate students to determine whether a proposed intranuclear particle force could describe the bound state of the simplest three-body nucleus. For thirty days Amdahl and his two colleagues employed a desk calculator and a slide rule to provide two more significant digits in order to calculate the lowest energy level for any value of the parameters. They became frustrated, discovering there was an almost-bound state but not quite a bound state. In short, the proposed intranuclear force could not possibly describe the nucleus adequately. "So," recalls Amdahl, "I decided there was a terrible bind, that we needed better tools."

He decided to build a computer. The one he put together was known as WISC—the Wisconsin Integrally Synchronized Computer. It contained both a floating point and a partially parallel instruction execution facility. There were four instructions being executed at the same time. Amdahl remembers it as "really quite an interesting computer." His doctoral dissertation was an account of its design and construction. The building of the machine became a training tool for electrical engineers at the university; Amdahl did not see the fully finished product until 1978.

He received a doctorate in theoretical physics from the University of Wisconsin in February 1952. It was in June of that year that he joined IBM, working at first on simulation studies and machine design for character recognition. He went to IBM's plant in Poughkeepsie, New York, where the finishing touches were being put on the 701, the Defense Calculator. IBM had sold nineteen of these machines, and although they were advanced, the company wanted something more powerful. Amdahl worked on the design of the IBM 704, introducing indexing and floating-point—features that had been explored in earlier computers but never included in machines sold commercially. In November 1953 Amdahl was made chief planner and project engineer for the 704 development program. Among its other features, the 704 was the first computer with a programming language.

Amdahl was the first planner of the IBM 709, the successor to the 704. When, in December 1955, he was denied a leading role in the STRETCH (the IBM 7030) project, he left IBM. For nine months he worked for a start-up called Ramo-Woolridge in Los Angeles, preparing several military and internal proposals in the data-processing field. He also did the system planning for what became the RW440 process-control computer, a minicomputer offered by Ramo-Woolridge in the late 1950s. It was his first taste of working for a new venture; he remained there only briefly, leaving in August 1956.

Amdahl next went to work for Aeronautics, a Ford Motor Company subsidiary in Newport Beach, California. There he ran the commercial data-processing department. Rejoining IBM in September 1960, he went first to Yorktown as director of experimental machines, then to Poughkeepsie to direct the preliminary engineering and software aspects of the System/360, one of the most successful mainframe computer product families. He had planned to stay east for only six months, but it stretched to four years. That was a difficult time, as he had to work on several computers at once. Amdahl was in charge of defining data flows, achieving performance and cost objectives, and, most important, defining the systems' architecture.

Amdahl wanted to return to the West Coast, and IBM agreed to transfer him there. In February 1965 he was made an IBM Fellow: he was permitted to spend the next five years on whatever projects he wished. He served as director of the new institution he helped to found, IBM's Advanced Computing Systems Laboratory in Menlo Park, California. In 1969 Amdahl and IBM had a falling out over Big Blue's computer-building strategy. IBM had all along based the prices of its machines on their computing power, not on their production costs. That led the company to reject any proposal to build a bigger computer, as the high price it would have to bear would diminish the market and not make the effort worthwhile. Amdahl had been working on a larger machine in the hope that he could convince IBM to veer from its strategy. In the summer of 1969 he asked for a meeting with IBM's three top executives, T. Vincent Learson, Frank Carey, and John Opel. "They graphed on the board why IBM was right, that it would be more costly to them to go with the computer I wanted to build." There was little Amdahl could do. He spent the next year thinking about the pricing difficulties of IBM's high-end products, and concluded that IBM would always try to compromise the high-end offering to improve its general financial picture. The System/360s that Amdahl had designed were doing well in sales, and IBM saw no reason to cut into those sales. "Basically, I left IBM that second time because I wanted to work in large computers. . . . I'd have had to change my career if I stayed at IBM—for I wanted personal satisfaction."

An incident in the summer of 1970 helped Amdahl make up his mind to quit. For the previous five years he had been a director of a consulting firm called Compata, founded by his brother. Until that summer IBM had not objected. But then it learned that a company named Compata had developed a minicomputer, appearing to put Amdahl in violation of IBM's conflict-of-interest rule. When IBM realized that the firm in question was a different one from Amdahl's, it apologized to him, but urged him to quit the Compata board anyway. Compata being at the time in financial trouble, Amdahl felt he should stay on. He decided to quit IBM and found his own firm, Amdahl Corporation. On turning in his letter of resignation, he had yet another inconclusive meeting with the IBM brass. One vice-president hurried after him in the hall as the meeting broke up to advise him not to go into the large computer systems business. There was no money to be made in it. Nevertheless, Amdahl started the new firm that fall.

Ideas come to the silver-haired computer designer at all hours of the day or night. "Sometimes I wake up in the middle of the night and I'll be going sixty miles an hour on the way to a solution. I see a mental picture of what is going on in the machine and I dynamically operate that in my mind. Sometimes I am in the middle of a conversation that triggers a bright idea, and for a while there I completely forget about the conversation. When I finally realize what has happened, I might make some comment to make the person think I've been following things, even though I had missed a bit of it." How does he explain his success? "What's always mystified me is that there are many people who have very good ideas on computers and somehow or other I always managed to be the one who got the chance to work on the better program." Gene Amdahl is the holder or coholder of numerous patents on such developments as an analog-to-digital conversion device, a message display and transmission system, a stored-logic computer, a large-scale shifter, a memory protection system, and the IBM System/360.

In founding Amdahl Corporation in October 1970, Gene Amdahl set out to create IBM plug-compatible mainframes—computers designed so that they could operate with equipment and systems designed by other manufacturers. If these new mainframes were truly going to be an answer to Big Blue, as Amdahl hoped, why not describe his own firm as Big Red? So there was Amdahl red on his machines and on the office phones, and there was no doubt what he was saying by doing this. For fifteen years computer products had been made that were plug-compatible with IBM computers. Now Amdahl would make mainframes that would be plug-compatible with IBM machines. Rather than try to build a distinct computer, he planned to be the first to actually copy the IBM computer's operations. As a result he was able to deprive IBM of a good portion of the market. Amdahl was a bit miffed when he was accused of taking an entire technical team from IBM with him: in fact he took only a young financial man and two secretaries.

The building of Amdahl Corporation was Gene Amdahl's proudest achievement. He greatly enjoyed "getting those first computers built and really making a difference, seeing it completely shattering the control of the market that IBM had, causing pricing to come back to realistic levels. I really felt that was the contribution to make. We had the world's first large-scale integrated circuits in early 1971. The problem was how do you get a lot of circuits on a chip and have it producible." IBM had been working on medium-scale integration, trying to get 25 to 30 circuits on a chip, but not 100. It had been able to make the sophisticated chips, but it could not bring the design time to an acceptable minimum. The work could only be done by hand, so it all depended on finding someone who knew how to route the interconnections on the chip. Amdahl eventually realized how to solve the problem: As the semiconductor industry made devices finer, smaller, and with finer resolution, it kept reducing everything, so the space between the transistors was getting smaller as the transistors became smaller. There simply wasn't room to route. "You tried to put more transistors in this area and the number of wires increased relative to the number of transistors so it became too crowded." There was a constant desire to make chips as small as possible. Amdahl sensed that this was the wrong approach; instead, "what you really have to do is put these transistors on and leave enough space."

Did Gene Amdahl walk away with IBM secrets? Some thought he had. But he defends himself vigorously. IBM, in his view, had simply not solved the high-performance problem, and he had. He was proposing large-scale integration for the new computer he wanted to build, and IBM had not even been successful in medium-scale integration. In any event, IBM never accused him of taking its secrets.

Amdahl Corporation spent over $40 million before shipping its first system. A lot of effort went into developing a memory system, but production on that was suspended and replaced by the virtual memory model. A one-megabyte system with sixteen channels was priced at $3.65 million. In the first full year Amdahl had sales of $96 million, in its second year $190 million, and in its third year $320 million. Gene Amdahl's first computers, the Amdahl 470 family, were generally thought of as the highest-capacity general-purpose business computers yet made. IBM's System/360 had seen the technology outrace it. No longer were the 360's integrated circuits, hybrids that they were, the latest thing; Gene Amdahl was now using large-scale integration, and so his new computers were faster, smaller, more powerful than the 360s or the new 370s—and cheaper.

In October 1971 Amdahl was able to announce the first high-performance large-scale-integration chip, which was the key to his most significant early computer, the 470 V/6. The computer cost $40 million to develop. Gene Amdahl had done it, he had used large-scale integration—LSI—to cut down the computer's size so that it was a quarter as big as existing computers. For the first time LSI logic had become cost-effective: the computer was three times more powerful than IBM's 360/165 but was priced the same, at $3.5 million. When it appeared in the mid-1970s, it was indeed the answer to the IBM 360/168. The blue-chip enterprises, including AT&T, General Motors, and NASA, lined up to purchase the 470 V/6; by the spring of 1977 Amdahl Corporation had installed some fifty of them. In March of that year IBM announced its 3033 processor, which was twice as fast as its predecessor the 360/168 but cost two-thirds as much. In response Amdahl reduced the price of his V/6 and came out with two new machines: the 470 V/5, which was plug-compatible with the 370/168, and the 470 V/7, plug-compatible with the 3033 and one-third faster than the IBM machine, while costing only three percent more.

Gene Amdahl's connection with the venture bearing his name lasted until September 1979, when he became Amdahl's chairman emeritus and a consultant to the firm. Amdahl Corporation had become the most successful plug-compatible mainframe firm in the computer industry but then had suffered, as did other plug-compatible firms, when IBM convinced buyers that its new mainframes would be cheaper than those of its competitors. Selling a good deal of his stock to Japan's Fujitsu to raise cash, Gene Amdahl lost control of Amdahl Corporation in the process.

In August 1980 Amdahl cut his remaining ties with Amdahl Corporation and began a new venture aimed at challenging IBM's virtual monopoly at the top end of mainframe computers. This put him into competition with Amdahl Corporation, competition over a small market: since 1978 the total plug-compatible mainframe market has been at $600 million, only twenty percent of the plug-compatible peripherals market. With his marvelous reputation, Amdahl was able to raise $85 million in about a year; investors put up over $200 million in the first four years, making this Silicon Valley's largest start-up. The new firm was named Trilogy; its three founders were Gene Amdahl, his son Carlton (a former chief designer for Magnuson Computer), and former Amdahl chief financial officer Clifford Madden. Trilogy would design, manufacture, and market large-scale, high-performance computer systems. Gene Amdahl wanted to create a new standard—of price and performance—for the industry, and he was so confident that he would succeed that he boasted he would have sales of $1 billion within two years after the product came out—less than half the time it took Apple Computer.

IBM and Texas Instruments had not succeeded in similar efforts before him, but Amdahl thought he could. He would build a computer that was more powerful and far less expensive—$4 million—than the biggest mainframes produced by IBM and Amdahl Corporation. Gene Amdahl thought of the pivot of this system—the silicon superchip—when lying in a sickbed recuperating from back problems in 1980. He planned to rely on a unique semiconductor technology called "wafer-scale integration": rather than wire together thumbnail-size silicon chips, he would etch the circuitry onto silicon wafers 2.5 inches square. Only twenty wafers would be necessary, rather than 1,000 to 2,000 separate chips. The key premise in wafer-scale integration was that it was inefficient to cut apart chips and then solder them together again on a printed circuit board. Moreover, each time information was taken from a chip and sent through the circuit board to another, a major time loss resulted.

Finally, moving the information around on the wafer itself, as opposed to moving it among many chips, took a fraction of the power.

Trilogy ran into problems. It went ahead with the computer design in the winter of 1983–84 without a full appreciation of the characteristics of the twenty wafers that would comprise the central processing unit. In the event, some of the essential circuitry—especially those sections dealing with arithmetical calculations—was split between two wafers. As a result much speed and power was lost.

Then in the winter of 1984–85 in putting together the extra-thin aluminum that would connect all the integrated circuits together on the wafer, Trilogy made a bad alloy choice, and so short circuits occurred. Constrained by time and money, Amdahl was forced to announce by spring 1985 that the date for marketing the new computer would now be 1987, three years later than first hoped. He was, he said, saddened and disappointed: he truly believed that the American computer industry needed an alternative to IBM. That summer he was forced to give up plans to make mainframes. He still planned to develop a high-speed wafer-scale chip that would be a hundred times more powerful than a standard chip.

In the spring of 1985 Trilogy decided to merge with Elxsi, a private Silicon Valley firm that had spent five years and $30 million trying to develop a super minicomputer but had lost $7 million on sales of $18.5 million. The merger was valued at up to $60 million. It means that Elxsi's backers could own nearly half of the new firm. Through the purchase of Elxsi, Amdahl hoped to offer a computer that would fill the gap between minicomputers and supercomputers. Trilogy also made a deal in April 1985 with Ross Perot's EDS—now a unit of General Motors—to have EDS manage Trilogy's computer-aided-design facility.

During the winter of 1986 Amdahl began to see some light, thanks to a technical breakthrough that linked the power of the new Elxsi mini-supercomputer with the DEC VAX minicomputer. Heretofore, users of the VAXes had an undesirable choice once they reached the limits of the VAX's computing power: they could either connect to a second VAX or purchase a more powerful machine from DEC rivals. Hooking up to a second VAX did not mean getting twice the computer power, even though the financial investment doubled. And turning to a rival's computer meant not being able to run the software bought or developed for the VAX. Out of such frustration was born Gene Amdahl's new computer, the new Elxsi, which was more powerful than the VAX but not more expensive—and it accepted most VAX software.

Through the new Elxsi computer, Gene Amdahl hopes to salvage what he can for Trilogy shareholders. While he has talked about retirement in recent months, there is so far no sign that he is about to take such a step—at least until he is satisfied that he has put Elxsi on the right path.

Seymour Cray

The Hermit of Chippewa Falls and His "Simple, Dumb Things"

18

His name has long been associated with the awe-inspiring world of supercomputers. The world in which man precisely foretells the weather and simulates nuclear explosions. It's a world that Seymour Cray, recluse, builder of the speediest computers around, has molded largely on his own.

Cray's single purpose has been to build the fastest computers available, enabling others to simulate physical phenomena via differential equations. The growth of the supercomputer industry has been due in large measure to this man of mystery: of the 130 supercomputers in use in the world by January 1986, some 90 had been made by Cray's publicly held company, Cray Research. That firm has its headquarters in Minneapolis, while manufacturing is done in Chippewa Falls, Wisconsin. The number of supercomputers is startlingly high considering that only eighty potential buyers were once thought to exist.

What is a supercomputer? Well, a computer that can perform over 20 megaflops—20 million floating-point operations per second—is one. The CRAY-1, Seymour Cray's pioneering supercomputer of the mid-1970s, had a peak processing speed of some 100 megaflops. In comparison, the IBM Personal Computer, which came out in August 1981, is in the 0.0005-megaflop range. The biggest IBM mainframe does 3 or 4 megaflops. Supercomputers tend to be expensive. Each one costs between $4.5 and $13 million.

Thanks to the supercomputer, scientists and engineers can undertake the mathematical modeling of dynamic events occurring in the real world—the way air moves over an airplane's wing, for example, or the flowing of water through an oil reservoir. The air flow around supersonic aircraft can be simulated, saving time and money in testing. Nuclear weapons can be refined—without having to test them. Or, in a more peaceful realm the effects of changing the money supply on the federal deficit can be explored. The path of a weather system, even one as complicated as a hurricane, can be predicted accurately.

Seymour Cray always knew that the larger and faster super-computers were made, the fewer the clients. Still, there would be clients. The issue was whether the costs of a machine could be recovered. But no matter what the problems were, cost, clients, whatever, Cray liked the technical challenge, and so he built the machines. In the 1950s he was imagining a computer that could perform 150 to 200 million calculations per second. That would represent 20 to 100 times the capacity of general-purpose computers of the 1970s.

Cray was born in Chippewa Falls, Wisconsin, on September 28, 1925. His father was a city engineer in Chippewa Falls. After a few years as an electrician in the army, Seymour began his college education at the University of Wisconsin in Madison; he soon transferred to the University of Minnesota. He found electrical engineering generally primitive. Certain parts of the curriculum, such as the study of electric motors, did not interest him at all, and there was little mathematics. After receiving a bachelor's degree in electrical engineering in 1950, Cray took another year in applied mathematics, winning a master's degree in 1951.

From 1950 to 1957 he worked for Engineering Research Associates (ERA) in St. Paul and for its successors, Remington Rand and Sperry Rand. ERA was a pioneering computer firm started in 1946 by a small group that included William Norris. Cray involved himself in circuit, logic, and software design—a collection of subjects that few could do all at once—and designed his first computer, the ERA 1101, one of the first scientific machines. He was also largely responsible for the design of the UNIVAC 1103. But Sperry's UNIVAC division was more interested in increasing computer sales than in improving computing power. It was time for Cray to move on.

In 1957 Cray and eight others, among them Bill Norris, Frank

Mullaney, and Bob Kisch, left Sperry Rand to start a new company, Control Data Corporation (CDC). Cray was given free rein to build supercomputers, having persuaded Norris that a relatively cheap, powerful solid-state computer built from printed circuit modules would make the new firm money. The computer could be sold at the Department of Defense, aircraft firms, universities. Such clients didn't need heavy investment in support or marketing; they would want quality and would prefer to do their own programming. Cray presided over the building of the CDC 1604, which was among the first commercial computers to use transistors instead of vacuum tubes. Developing the 1604 was a distinct gamble, since CDC was still in its infancy. Faced with serious cash shortages at CDC, Cray went to an old electronics distributor in Minneapolis and bought the cheapest parts he could obtain to build the computer. The 1604, announced in 1958, could do high-speed, extremely accurate arithmetic, and it had the advantage of costing less than other computers with similar capabilities. The 1604 had succeeded, so had Cray, and so had CDC. Indeed, few mainframe firms could boast, as CDC did, that in less than two years it was showing a profit.

Seymour Cray's reputation soared. Eventually, however, he tired of too many administrative, too many ceremonial chores. He wanted only to build the fastest computers in the world, and for that he needed peace and quiet. He announced to CDC chairman Norris that he planned to go home to Wisconsin and start his own firm. A few weeks later Norris persuaded Cray to stay with CDC and agreed that CDC would take its 6600 computer development program to Chippewa Falls.

Norris built Cray a laboratory in 1962 on a forty-acre piece of rural land Cray owned near his home town. The lab was within walking distance of Cray's house. Cray became a recluse, reportedly allowing Norris to visit him only twice a year—by appointment only. Cray would visit CDC's headquarters in Minneapolis every few months. At times, VIPs would come to Chippewa Falls to hear Cray lecture. They would gather at a local diner, where Cray would quickly eat a hot dog and then beg off so that he could get back to work. It was said that he put together his computers on a card table on the porch of his cottage on Lake Wissota. Grabbing a basket of computer chips, a pair of tweezers, and a soldering gun, he would assemble the parts. The truth is that Cray builds computers by using only a pencil and paper. Each day he goes through a pad of 8½-by-11-inch paper. He takes his calculations to thirty people who form his development team, and the work is then translated into a computer module of microcircuit chips.

By August 22, 1963, the hermit of Chippewa Falls had proved that his isolation was worth it. That was the day Control Data announced the CDC 6600, the most powerful computer of its time; when this made CDC the industry leader, IBM was livid. The new computer was three times as powerful as STRETCH, a supercomputer IBM had given up on a few years earlier, and far cheaper and smaller—but was priced at only $7.5 million. The Atomic Energy commission and the U.S. Weather Bureau, both eager for as much computer power as possible, were considered the most likely customers. The 6600 was to be delivered to the AEC's Livermore Laboratory in February 1964. But with problems of debugging (the 6600 had 350,000 transistors) it was six months late. The 6600 was the first computer to employ a freon cooling system, to prevent the densely packed components from overheating.

In 1967 sixty-three 6600s—the bugs worked out of them—were in the hands of elite customers. These computers became pivots of scientific research in their time. Seymour Cray had gone ahead with plans to build the 7600 (price: $7.5 million), which when it came out in 1969 was considered by many the first supercomputer. Later, Cray designed the 8600, but CDC chose not to market it. Meanwhile, CDC was diversifying into commercial applications, relegating the scientific computers or supercomputers to a lowered status. Cray felt the constraint of working for a firm that was not devoted exclusively to supercomputers. So he decided it was time to go out on his own. Taking Frank Mullaney and some other CDC employees with him, he founded Cray Research in 1972, insisting that the firm build only supercomputers and that it build them one at a time. Each new design would be a compatible add-on as well. CDC generously contributed $500,000 as start-up money to Cray Research. In 1973, when he left CDC, Cray received a compliment of sorts: CDC abandoned building supercomputers for the next few years (though it eventually tried to catch up). Cray Research had become the dominant force in supercomputers by the late 1970s.

The move to go public in early 1976 may well have saved the company. Some believed at the time that Cray Research—a company without a product—had only forty-five days to raise capital before it would have to close down. An overture to Wall Street produced surprisingly good results from investors who had missed out on previous high-tech opportunities and who had trusted Seymour Cray from his CDC days. On St. Patrick's Day 1976 Cray Research went public, a bold step for a firm that had not yet completed its first unit—a unit that would cost $8.8 million and for which there seemed to be only eighty potential customers. At that point Cray Research had no sales, no earnings, and a $2.4-million deficit. But when the firm offered 600,000 shares of common stock on the over-the-counter securities market, it generated $10 million almost immediately. Thus Seymour Cray could complete his first computer for his own firm.

The first CRAY–1 was shipped to the Los Alamos National Laboratory in March 1976. The supercomputer was indeed unique: it was the first practical and effective example of vector processing, in which the computer works on many different parts of the problem at once. This high-speed parallel processing is meant to increase processing rates. The CRAY–1 was also the world's fastest scalar processor (in scalar processing, each computation is performed discretely, in contrast with vector processing). It has a capacity of one million 64–bit words and a clock period of 12.5 nanoseconds. The CRAY–1 used only three types of integrated circuits, and its creator had managed to cut the maximum wire length to 4 feet and the cycle time to 12.5 nanoseconds, via a remarkable packaging design. It was 6 feet high and 8 feet in diameter. Some 60 miles of wiring, more than 200,000 semiconductor chips, and 3,400 integrated circuit boards went into its interior. Its cylindrical design, a Seymour Cray conception to cut down the length of internal wiring, was unprecedented. Some called it "the world's most expensive loveseat." During the building of the CRAY–1, Cray would work with his associates at the plant for a few hours in the middle of each day, go home at 4 p.m., and return at night to work alone into the early morning hours. He has only one rule when beginning a new project, and that is to start all over, to avoid repeating what he did the last time. He instinctively knows it won't work a second time, having exhausted all the possibilities of the old design.

Cray did not believe the CRAY–1 was a revolutionary machine; he had not been trying to accomplish everything when he designed it. In 1979, having sold a total of six CRAY–1's (including one in 1978 to Cray Research's first commercial customer, United Computing Systems of Kansas City), Cray Research announced the decision to build the CRAY–2, which was to have four to six times as much power as the CRAY–1. The first production model of the $17.6-million machine went through its paces in the spring of 1985 at the Lawrence Livermore National Laboratory in Livermore, California. It had the largest internal memory capacity of any computer—2 billion bytes—and a speed of 1.2 billion floating-point operations per second, made possible by its four processors, which run together. This made it 6 to 12 times as fast as the CRAY–1 and 40,000 to 50,000 times as fast as a personal computer. What scientists and engineers were spending a year to do in 1952 could now be done in a second.

The CRAY–2 is to be used for such work as the study of the intense magnetic fields required for fusion reactors and the design of heat shields for future space trips. It has 256 million words of central memory, compared to a maximum of 1 million in the CRAY–1. The CRAY–2 occupies less area than its predecessor because of 3-D chip modules that allow for shorter interconnections than on the traditional boards; Cray managed to pack 240,000 computer chips into a C-shaped cabinet that is 53 inches across and 45 inches high. This reduced the critical factor in supercomputers, the amount of time required for electric current to travel from one section of the computer to the other. But in doing that Seymour Cray created another problem: the heat generated by those electrons flowing through the densely packed circuit boards could quickly melt the computer. So he flooded the circuits with Fluorinert, a liquid coolant. Someone has called the CRAY–2 a computer in an aquarium.

A maximum wire length of 16 inches cut cycle time to 4 nanoseconds. Thus, the CRAY–2 can execute scalar operations roughly 6 times more quickly than the CRAY–1, and vector operations about 12 times faster. In the midst of designing the machine, Cray decided that metal-oxide-semiconductor (MOS) technology—which permits much greater computer memory—would be worth including in his new computer, and so he made the change to MOS.

The company had become profitable by 1977. In 1980 it sold nine supercomputers, thirteen in 1981, and fifteen in 1982. In that

The CRAY-2

year Cray Research had earnings of $19 million on revenues of $141 million. In 1983, fifteen CRAYs were sold; twenty-three were sold in 1984. Roughly half of these computer systems went to government research organizations and half to commercial customers. By October of 1984 Cray Research claimed it had seventy percent of the supercomputer market. Cray was selling more supercomputers because technological advances had made it possible to cut prices as much as $5–$10 million.

Concerned over the diminishing amount of time he was able to devote to building supercomputers, Seymour Cray decided to turn over the management of the firm to others. In November 1981 he relinquished the chairmanship of the board of Cray Research to the president, John Rollwagen, remaining a member of the board of directors and becoming the company's sole research-and-development contractor. Once again he could concentrate on, as he put it, the "thing" part of computers, rather than the "people" part. He worked out an agreement with Cray Research that allowed him to pursue any idea that interested him, even if the company was not interested in it. By the spring of 1985 he owned 1.6 percent of Cray Research stock, worth at that time $17 million.

Cray's particular talent is that he is not a particularist—whereas most inventors in the computer business specialize. Dealing with all the parts of the computer requires tremendous patience, and Cray has demonstrated that patience. He thinks of the design of super-computers as an art: being logical doesn't seem to work. There is an inexplicable thought process in which he will mull over all of his ideas and, as he describes it, try to hear what is going on inside. If it sounds good, he proceeds. Generalist though he is, Cray's forte has been innovative packaging, the way the components are put into the computer. He says that his goal is to build the machine as compactly as possible—and for good reason. To be fast, a computer has to be small. Every inch is important.

Cray's method of building computers is to keep the number of people involved as small as possible. The more people involved, the smaller the chances of success for the project. In his view the ideal number is one; but that is unrealistic, so the maximum should be twelve. Cray's computers are designed very simply—conceptually they are even simpler than microcomputers and minicomputers with their elaborate hardware sequences. Cray proudly notes that his computers do no more than add, subtract, multiply, and divide.

He is appalled at the notion of a national effort in computer research. To Cray the ideal situation is many independent people doing their own thinking, experimenting on their own. Competition within the same firm is healthy, he notes. Though he is certainly an individualist, Cray does not consider himself a pioneer. Indeed, he says, he wouldn't want to be one: pioneers make mistakes, and he would rather follow in their wake so as to benefit from those mistakes. Oddly enough, Cray doesn't like to call his super-computers machines. He describes them as "simple, dumb things."

In April 1982 Cray Research announced the CRAY X-MP series of computer systems, the first CRAY computers not totally designed by Seymour Cray. The X-MP series, designed by Steve Chen, in effect enhanced the original CRAY−1 supercomputer. The top price was $20 million. By the spring of 1985 some fifty had been sold. The CRAY X-MP was unique in having more than one central processing unit. Its clock cycle time was 9.5 nanoseconds. An even faster version, introduced in 1984, had ten times the speed of the CRAY–1 and could perform one billion calculations a second, more than double the most advanced Japanese models. An Apple IIe, in contrast, can perform 500,000 operations a second.

By early 1985 Cray was working on a follow-up to the CRAY–2, to be known as the CRAY–3. The new computer is to be five to ten times faster than the CRAY–2. It is due in 1988, and Cray hopes it will have an 8-billion-byte memory. Plans call for the CRAY–3 to be based on gallium arsenide technology—marking the first time that Cray, ever the one for simplicity and tried-and-true components, has gambled on a relatively new technology. Because gallium arsenide is so brittle, it is harder to make into chips than silicon; but its speed makes the effort worthwhile. Gallium arsenide has an electron mobility four to five times that of silicon, permitting faster switching speeds and lower power consumption. Components can thus be stacked more densely than with silicon, reducing the distance the electrons must travel. The longest wire connection in the CRAY–3 will probably be only 3 inches. The CRAY–3 will be small—one-fifth the size of the CRAY–2—and has already been dubbed "the breadbox computer." Its CPU will take up only 16 square feet of floor space. Aircraft manufacturers hope to use it to simulate an entire airplane in flight; even with state-of-the-art supercomputers, they must still piece together separate simulations—of the wings, the fuselage, and the tail.

In a rare public appearance in the spring of 1985, Cray pointed out that whereas in the past he had been proud to make factor-of-four improvements from one generation of machines to another, now progress was by factors of ten. The CRAY–1 had one processor, the CRAY–2 had four, and the CRAY–3 may have sixteen working at the same time. There's even a name for these new multiprocessor computers: ultracomputers.

Cray regularly turns down invitations to speak to scientific or business groups. From 1976 until 1981 he did not meet with a single journalist. In 1981 he relented, because he was concerned lest his resignation from the chairmanship of Cray Research be construed as a sign of a rift between him and the management of the firm. Cray rarely lets the staff at Cray Research know when he is going to drop in on them. He disconnects his phone every afternoon. Company officials say his uncommunicativeness reflects not so much a preference for solitude as a need to shut out distractions from his work.

Though he has little time for noncomputer pursuits, Cray has in recent years devoted some of that leisure time to sports; windsurfing is a favorite. Three times a year he makes a trip to the tropics. He refuses to waste his attention on trivialities: when he needs to buy a new car, he picks the first car to the right of the showroom door.

Cray Research earned $229 million in sales in 1984, having sold twenty-three supercomputers. Its profits were $45 million—more than twice the 1982 figure. Profits climbed to $75.6 million in 1985, out of $380.2 million in revenues. The company's work force had grown to almost 3,000, and its market value was up to $1.5 billion.

Ironically, Cray Research was not selling a Seymour Cray supercomputer in the mid-1980s. As for Cray himself, he was little heard from in 1986 and early 1987, laboring to build his next supercomputer, the CRAY–3. The silence is characteristic of this quiet, reclusive inventor. When he has something to say, he will say it. When he has a computer to show the world, he will show it. The world will just have to wait.

Gordon Bell

Launching the Age of the Minicomputer

19

Computers in the mid-1950s were huge, intimidating, and remote, kept in sterile, air-conditioned rooms out of the reach of ordinary man. They were immovable, unfriendly, and cost at least a million dollars each. A firm that purchased one of these giant-sized electronic brains thought the occasion so historic that it sent out press releases. In 1957 a new company came along called Digital Equipment Corporation, and it aimed at selling smaller, cheaper computers. Within a few years the founders had signed on a young engineer whose talents for computer design would have a major impact on the industry. On the strength of the computers he would build for DEC, Gordon Bell would launch his own kind of revolution, the age of the minicomputer.

The computers Bell conceptualized, designed, and sponsored—the PDP-4, PDP-5, PDP-6, PDP-8, PDP-10, and PDP-11—turned the industry upside down. They gave performance and power, but they cost tens or hundreds of thousands of dollars, not millions. He obtained miniaturization not through the large-scale integration of components—that development came after his pioneering efforts—but through his engineering skills.

When Ken Olsen, founder of DEC, began his assault on the mainframes in 1957, he was not surprised to encounter plenty of resistance—from those who thought computers wouldn't sell, big or small, and from those who thought nothing would dent IBM's dominance of the industry. Olsen was proved right, however. Clients responded favorably to machines that sold for under $1 million and that interacted with the user via a video or keyboard terminal. Bell was DEC's second computer engineer, joining in 1960. The very first DEC computer, shipped in November of that year, was the PDP-1, whose design and software library Bell helped finish. In 1963 he was appointed manager of computer design.

Gordon Bell was born on August 19, 1934, in Kirksville, Missouri. Starting at age six, he worked in his father's appliance and electrical contracting business. At that age he installed a plug on a wire. Within a few years he was wiring houses, fixing motors and appliances. Bell attended MIT as an undergraduate, studying electrical engineering. There were then two courses available on digital systems; he took them both. As a participant in the five-year co-op plan, he worked during four terms and three summers for various power companies and manufacturers, including General Electric. In his spare time he built an audio amplifier.

On graduating in 1957, with both a bachelor's and a master's degree in electrical engineering, Bell went off to study in Australia on a Fulbright scholarship. This represented a welcome postponement of what he called "the going to work problem." Large companies like General Electric seemed too sterile, too bureaucratic. He would feel lost among all those engineers. He needed a way to express himself as an individual, and he knew deep down that he wanted to be an inventor.

While at the University of New South Wales Bell wrote software and, with a fellow Fulbright scholar, gave the school's first graduate course on computer design. There he met his future wife, Gwen, another Fulbright scholar. They were married on their return to the United States in 1959. Gwen Bell was later to become director of the Boston Computer Museum.

Bell now confronted a choice between going to work for Philco in computer design and returning to MIT to complete his doctorate. He decided against Philco, because he doubted that he would be able either to work independently there or to learn a great deal from Philco personnel. He chose to try to learn something at MIT. For his thesis for a second master's degree, Bell built a statistical sound survey meter to deal with acoustical control and noise reduction. His thesis adviser, Kenneth Stevens, suggested that it might be interesting for him to work on the TX-0, a new MIT computer, later commercialized as DEC's first minicomputer. Bell interfaced speech input equipment to the TX-0 and wrote speech analysis and recognition programs. One, Analysis by Synthesis, is still in use. The Analysis by Synthesis technique, however, was but one small part of what is needed in speech recognition. Bell realized after a year of trying to write the speech recognition program that this would take him twenty years, far too long a time for him, as he was less interested in research than in engineering.

During this period he learned of Digital Equipment Corporation, a new firm started by MIT graduate Kenneth Olsen that sold system modules compatible with the TX-0. Bell had been using DEC's modules to build a tape controller for the TX-0 to give it secondary memory for the speech laboratory and other labs. In 1960 he was hired by DEC, to do programming, architecture, and logic design. The DEC people had become convinced that most computer users did not need the computing power of a mainframe, that most jobs could be handled with smaller machines. Not only that. Most computer users would be delighted to have access to a computer that performed chores in real time.

DEC called its first machine the PDP-1. PDP stood for Program Data Processor: DEC was reluctant to use the word *computer* because it might scare off customers. The PDP-1 was packaged in four 6-foot cabinets. It weighed 250 pounds, one-quarter the weight of other computers. With its reduced size and price ($120,000), the PDP-1 was useful for a wide range of tasks, including manufacturing control, electrocardiogram analysis, oceanographic research, and signal processing; it could serve as a small multiple-user system.

People could now stop worrying about the high cost of computer time. These new, smaller computers would not be used for great number-crunching jobs—only the mainframes could do those—but for mathematical formulations, for scientific inquiry, for the broader purpose of just getting to know what a computer could do. DEC had got its start just as the computer industry was switching from vacuum-tube technology to transistor-based technology. Although the transistor had been around for over a decade and was already being used in radios, the PDP-1, when introduced in 1960, was one of the first computers to be designed with transistor technology.

Sales of the PDP-1 were slow at first—in part because it was, as Gordon Bell acknowledges, an unorthodox machine, with its high speed, short word length, and lack of the built-in floating-point arithmetic that characterized scientific computation. DEC's unproven track record worried some would-be buyers as well. But between 1965 and 1980 more than 50,000 computers were bought implementing the PDP-1 design. The choice DEC had offered was between buying a PDP-1 for $120,000 and renting a medium-sized computer from IBM. Half of the fifty PDP-1's built between 1960 and 1965 were sold to ITT, as the ADX 7300, for message switching. The PDP-1 handled as many as 256 telegraph lines, switching them to other telegraph lines. Getting the ITT order was a great stroke of luck for DEC, as it had the effect of making the PDP-1 a standard product. While working on that project, Gordon Bell developed the UART—Universal Asynchronous Receiver Transmitter. The receiver portion sampled an incoming, serial teletype line and converted it to a parallel code, while the transmitter portion did the reverse.

Bell was the architect of the PDP-4, which was shipped in 1962. He felt that this machine should be 12-bit, but at the last minute the design was switched to 18 bits, as in the PDP-1. The PDP-4 was much simpler than the PDP-1; simple machines with few instructions perform almost as well, Bell believed, as machines with more instructions. He was proved correct. The PDP-4 took less than half the space of the PDP-1 and offered 5/8 the performance for half the price.

The PDP-4, like the PDP-1, was to be used largely for process control, for pulse height analysis in labs, and for data gathering. Though priced at only $65,000, it did not sell as well as had been hoped: it lacked software and a hardware option base, as was true of so many other first machines of a series, and that dissuaded some buyers.

In 1963 Bell was instrumental in developing the PDP-5, designed in response to the Atomic Energy Commission's need for nuclear reactor data gathering. It was used in conjunction with a PDP-4 as the main control computer. Bell decided that in this machine DEC would build the world's smallest computer. Its price was small, too—$27,000. Ed DeCastro, who later founded Data General, was the project engineer. The beauty of the PDP series lay in its convenience to users, who could upgrade the machines as their problems became more difficult to solve; other key characteristics were its generality and modularity.

The PDP-6, appearing in late 1964, was DEC's first stab at the large multiprocessor computer and was built for time sharing. Bell was the architect of the hardware and software, the principal logic designer, and the head of the project. The PDP-6 created a new market for technical users; later it was used for conventional data processing. The machine was hard to build, and only twenty were produced.

The main thrust of the company was established when DEC in April 1965 introduced the PDP-8, the first successful mass-produced minicomputer. DEC could charge only $18,000, half the cost of the nearest competitive machines, because of the arrival of integrated circuits. New core memory technology permitted the memory cycle time to drop from 6 microseconds in the PDP-5 to only 1.6 microseconds in the PDP-8. The cost of logic had dropped sufficiently to permit the program counter to be moved from the memory to a separate register, with the result that instruction execution times were greatly reduced. The computer was the size of a very small, eight-cubic-foot refrigerator. For the first time a computer could be put on top of a lab bench or built into equipment. In time DEC would come out with a scaled-down version of the PDP-8, selling for under $10,000. Over 100,000 PDP-8's and successor models were built, and an 8-on-a-chip was still embedded in word processors twenty years later.

The PDP-8 was much easier to interface, much faster, and much smaller than the PDP-5. It sold so well because it had one of the highest levels of performance relative to price then available. Of course, the PDP-8 was quite limited in comparison with mainframes. It could run only a single program at a time; it handled data in 12-bit words in contrast with the 32-bit words of the more powerful mainframes; it contained a mere 4K of memory. But the price gave the PDP-8 its special appeal. No longer did anyone have as the only option an expensive, largely inaccessible mainframe. The PDP-8 was everywhere, in laboratories, in offices, even on submarines, keeping watch over bank accounts, controlling the flow of chemicals or the operations of machine tools in factories, keeping track of inventory, and, of course, running programs in computer centers. Now it was possible to have bank branches process daily transactions and at the end of the day send their records to the bank's central computer at headquarters. A term was coined for this activity: it was called distributed processing.

After the PDP-8 hit the market, DEC's fortunes soared. In 1966, the year after that first minicomputer was shipped, DEC sales were $25 million. The success of the minicomputer spurred other firms to get into the business, and by 1971 there were some seventy-five companies making the minis. By 1977 DEC sales would reach $1 billion. The PDP-8 had been Gordon Bell's baby, and he was proud of it, proud to have built one of the best computers around. He insists, however, that computers are not particularly complex devices. "All that happens is that you have basically a mechanism in the machine that picks up instructions, looks at them, and then does them. That's all that computers are about. All computing is a set of those layers."

By 1966 Bell was tired of building computers. He took a job as an associate professor of computer science at Carnegie-Mellon University in Pittsburgh, though continuing to consult for DEC. In fact, he was involved in computer design at Carnegie-Mellon, too: he was one of the principal architects of C.mmp, a multiprocessor of sixteen processors sharing a common memory and based on the PDP-11, and Cm*, a hierarchical multiprocessor of fifty processors that could be expanded up to a hundred processors. Both were used for research in parallel and distributed processing. In 1971 Bell wrote a book called *Computer Structures* with Allen Newell. It became a standard textbook for graduate students in the field.

While Bell was away, DEC was going forward with more computers. The PDP-10, based on the PDP-6 and costing between $300,000 and $400,000, appeared in 1970. It was designed for time-sharing systems. Bell was the main architect of the PDP-11, which also reached the market in 1970. This was the first minicomputer to support modern programming constructs, through its general registers and last-in–first-out information retrieval architecture. The PDP-11 allowed DEC to regain the minicomputer market. This permitted the flexible design of memories and peripherals, and the easy configuring of a range of systems. The PDP-11's unibus was the forerunner of all modern mini- and microbus designs, including the Intel multibus, VME, and all of DEC's buses. The Chicago

Police Department, which in the mid-1970s was monitoring more than 4.5 million per calls per year, used the PDP-11 to find the address and phone number from which each call on the 911 emergency telephone line was made, enabling an operator to dispatch assistance quickly. The PDP-11 was a great favorite in laboratories, largely for its ease in handling.

The year 1972 was supposed to provide the time for Gordon Bell to take a sabbatical and write another book—this would be the "ultimate" one on designing digital computers—but DEC's president, Ken Olsen, asked him to return and become vice-president in charge of engineering. Bell had been thinking a lot at Carnegie-Mellon about the new technologies—large-scale integrated circuits—and knew that they would make possible even more powerful computers at an even lower cost. He had never really abandoned computer design, and he was ready to go full-time again. Exciting things were about to happen at DEC because of large-scale integration, and Bell wanted to be involved.

By April 1, 1975, Bell and his engineering team had defined and designed the next computer, the VAX-11. VAX stood for "virtual address extension," and "11" was a reminder to everyone (especially the engineers) that DEC was extending the PDP-11, not just starting from scratch. With virtual memory, the hallmark of the VAX system, much more working memory was available, enabling the writing of larger programs. Bill Strecker, Bell's doctoral student at Carnegie, was responsible for the VAX architecture. VAX would develop into one of DEC's major trademarks. The computer industry having already built a number of 32-bit superminicomputers in the 1970s, DEC was at a disadvantage in not producing its own until 1978; when VAX appeared that year, however, it soon captured forty percent of the market.

In 1978 Bell thought about forming a company that would produce personal computers. He never managed to implement the idea, because he was too busy working on the VAX project—something he felt in retrospect to have been far more important than starting a home-computer firm. Bell designed what was called the VAX strategy, which called for the use of VAX throughout a firm as the dominant style of computing—a homogeneous network. VAX would become the industry standard, dominating the scientific and engineering communities. The VAX strategy, which was completed in 1985, called for personal workstations (the MicroVax II), traditional minis for departmental computers, and large, tightly coupled computers (called VAX clusters) that formed a single system—all interconnected via Ethernet, DEC's primary local-area network. Digital's sales went from $1 billion in 1977 to $4 billion in 1983 on the basis of its sales of VAX. Thousands of VAXs were sold; the VAX-11/780 became one of the most popular super-minicomputers. By 1985 VAX accounted for nearly all of DEC's revenues. The VAX line illustrates DEC's general approach, which has been not to produce the fastest equipment but to concentrate on satisfying the client and offering low cost with high performance.

In 1982 Bell grew worried over the threat posed by the Japanese in the computer field. Unless there were a proper American response, he believed, America's computer industry might not even exist in ten years. Of course, it was difficult to get a consensus on what that response should be; but some suggested a joint venture among several of the big American computer firms. The semiconductor industry had such a venture under way—the Semiconductor Research Cooperative. Bell was delighted to take part in a second group, the Microelectronics and Computer Technology Corporation, spurred by Control Data Corporation's William Norris. He attended the founding meeting in Orlando, Florida, in the spring of 1982. It will take some time to evaluate its degree of success; there have been promising developments.

By the early 1980s Bell had become tired of working for such a large organization. He felt there wasn't much more that he could do at DEC because of the solid VAX strategy. Owing in large measure to the computers he had helped build, DEC had become the world leader in the minicomputer field. Bell had had six thousand people working for him. He had achieved a lot and fulfilled the basic contract he had made in 1972: to build a first-rate semiconductor group and VAX. The bonus was a VAX architecture that was more pervasive than even IBM's 360/370 series. In February 1983 Bell had a heart attack. Once he had recovered, getting away from DEC and from computer design seemed indicated. So he went to Stanford in the spring and spent a month there. He thought of returning to an academic environment. Ed Feigenbaum, head of Stanford's Heuristic Programming Project, suggested that he and Bell write a proposal to DARPA—the Defense Advanced Research Project

Agency—to build an artificial intelligence machine based on parallel processing. But Bell didn't really want to go through the process of writing proposals. He had enough of that at Carnegie. Teaching would have been fine, but not proposal writing.

Bell left DEC in July 1983. At the time he was head of all engineering. He began a new company, Encore Computer, with two others, Kenneth Fisher, who had been president of Prime Computer from 1975 to 1981, and Henry Burkhardt, whom he had hired at DEC and who was a founder of Data General. Encore, it was hoped, would come out with a computer that would in effect create a new machine class: called Multimax, it would use a multiprocessor design and permit the handling of a number of different programs at once. It was to have a base cost of $112,000 to $340,000, depending on the number of processors. Bell predicted that by 1990 all computers in the price range of $20,000 to $2 million would employ the Multimax basic structure. At the outset he was vice-chairman of the board and chief technical officer, responsible for overall product strategy. In January 1986, feeling that his part of the start-up—the design of the computer—was completed, Bell decided to leave Encore. He became involved in another company, this one called the Dana Group, in Sunnyvale, California, helping this start-up firm to make a personal supercomputer—Bell called it a "very high-performance vector machine"—in the $50,000 range.

In June 1986 Bell moved to Washington, D.C., to become the assistant director of the National Science Foundation for computer and information science and engineering. He directs the NSF's funding of American computer science.

The Software Specialists

Grace Murray Hopper

Bugs, Compilers, and COBOL

20

Grace Hopper was there at the beginning, programming the Harvard Mark I, literally taking the bugs out of Howard Aiken's computing engine. She came to computers late in life—in her forties. Programming was her specialty. Indeed, she was among the first to figure out how to put a program together. In effect, she created the field of high-level programming languages. She also played a major role in the building of the most popular business language, COBOL. This was the language that made computers accessible to nonmathematicians. But beyond that she has been one of the most engaging and colorful personalities of computer history, a spokesperson, an educator, a strong-willed dynamo who has loved two things above all else, computers and the U.S. Navy. Her subordinates affectionately call her Amazing Grace.

Grace Brewster Murray was born on December 9, 1906, in New York City. Her father's father was a rear admiral in the U.S. Navy, her mother's father the senior civil engineer of the city of New York. Hopper says it was her maternal grandfather who got her interested in geometry and mathematics. He took her with him on the job, permitting her to hold the red and white surveying pole. If Grace had thoughts of becoming an engineer, she quickly cast them aside, realizing the profession had no place for a woman. From early childhood she had a curiosity about gadgets. In the Murray family's summer home in Wolfeboro, New Hampshire, were seven alarm clocks; to find out how they worked, Grace, age seven, dismantled a clock one evening. But to see how to put that one back together, she found she had to dismantle a second; reassembling the second required taking apart a third, and so on. Her parents let her off unpunished, approving of her youthful curiosity.

All three Murray children, Grace, the eldest, her sister, and her brother, showed talent in mathematics. Grace in particular shone. Her father developed hardening of the arteries, and both legs had to be amputated. His illness and long hospitalizations spurred his oldest child to do well in school. Mathematics was her favorite, and especially geometry: "When I did geometry problems, I could use all the colored pencils."

She attended a series of private schools for young ladies, and in 1924 entered Vassar College in Poughkeepsie, New York. Her main interests there were mathematics, physics, and engineering. After graduating in 1928 she went to Yale, where she received a master's degree in 1930 and a doctorate in 1934, in mathematics and mathematical physics. Her doctoral thesis was entitled "A New Criterion for Reduceability of Algebraic Equations." ("I proved it geometrically, which upset everybody, but I always liked geometry better.")

Getting a doctorate in mathematics was a major accomplishment—only 1,279 were awarded in the United States between 1862 and 1934. Nonetheless, a female mathematician could not expect to find teaching work above the high-school level. Yet Grace Hopper managed. Beginning in 1931 she taught at Vassar, first as an assistant in mathematics, then as an instructor, then as an assistant professor, and finally as an associate professor, remaining there until World War II. She had married Vincent Foster Hopper—whom she had met at Wolfeboro, where his family spent the summers—on June 15, 1930; they were divorced in 1945.

In 1941 Hopper was awarded a Vassar Faculty Fellowship to study for a year at the Courant Institute of New York University. In 1943 she taught at Barnard College. Then, like thousands of other American women, she decided to join the armed forces. She was sworn into the U.S. Naval Reserve in December 1943 and, after thirty days' training as an apprentice seaman, attended the USNR Midshipman's School at Northampton, Massachusetts. On graduation in June 1944 she was commissioned with the rank of lieutenant, junior grade.

On the same day that she was commissioned, Hopper was assigned to the Bureau of Ships Computation Project at Harvard

University. She had never thought of going into work on computers—not surprising, as there were hardly any around at the time. She spent the weekend after she was commissioned with her family. She took a large sheaf of flowers and visited the grave of her grandfather, the rear admiral. It was all right for a woman to be a naval officer, she explained to him. She thought that if she hadn't offered the explanation, he would have rolled over in his grave. Arriving on Monday in the basement of the Cruft Laboratory, Hopper was met by a somewhat piqued Howard Aiken, director of the Computation Project. Aiken asked her where she had been. She thought he was talking about her lost weekend. But he was referring to the previous two months. When Hopper explained that she had been at midshipman's school, Aiken growled, "I told them you didn't need that. We've got to get to work."

Aiken set her to her tasks immediately. "When I walked in to the Mark I installation, wonderful Commander Aiken waved a hand at the fifty-one feet of Mark I and said, 'That's a computing engine.' " All Lieutenant Hopper could say was, "Yes, sir." But she thought to herself that it was the prettiest gadget she had ever seen. She kept quiet, sensing that Aiken would not appreciate the remark. She had no idea what she was looking at—it was in fact the first programmable digital computer made in America. Next thing she knew, she was handed a code book and Aiken was asking to have the coefficients for the interpolation of the arc tangent by the following Thursday. It was a sudden entry into the word of computers.

She was to work with a pair of ensigns, Robert V. D. Campbell and Richard Bloch, neither of whom seemed very happy at her arrival. They had apparently been told that the white-haired old schoolteacher would be joining them. They bribed each other to keep from having to sit next to her. But when it came time to help her with her first computation, they did so. She was almost immediately introduced to the work of Charles Babbage. Aiken, an expert on Babbage, would assign Hopper and the others to read appropriate sections of the nineteenth-century computer pioneer's writings.

The Mark I was in its time a marvel. It could do three additions every second, super-fast for the 1940s. And just such speed was needed, because of new dependence in American weapons systems on rapid computation. For example, Hopper explains, "Before

World War II, you had a mine, and it had horns on it, and the ship had to hit the horns before it went off''; with the development of acoustic and magnetic mines, however, it was possible to detonate a mine when a ship was nearby. With a computation of exactly how large an area each mine influenced, a mine field could be laid so that all approaching ships would be destroyed.

One of Hopper's most difficult experiences on Mark I was writing the manual for the computer. Aiken came up behind her one day and announced that she was going to write a book. Startled, she replied that she could not. "You're in the navy now," was his terse reply. And so she set about producing *The Manual of Operation for the Automatic Sequence Controlled Calculator*. Recalls Hopper, "Every day I would have to read him ten pages aloud."

The first work in programming was done without much rhyme or reason, and Grace Hopper was there from the very start. The Mark I was the first computer to be sequentially programmed, giving it great significance. But that meant that errors could be easily made. In writing programs, a Δ could be mistaken for a 4, a B for a 13. At times, people simply wrote the wrong thing. To get around this, Hopper and her colleagues at Harvard would collect programs known to be correct and write them in a notebook; this gave them a library of subroutines—one did the sine, one the cosine, one the arc tangent. "We had notebooks, and we had a piece of code that we had already checked out. We would rewrite it starting from zero. We would borrow each other's code that was already written. I might want a cosine to nine digits and would yell 'Dick.' And if I wanted a cosine to six digits, well, probably Bob had that. And we would copy them in the new programs."

The work on the Mark was uplifting but demanding. Grace Hopper found Howard Aiken a tough taskmaster: "If the work wasn't done, and it was dinner time, you stayed there. I slept nights on a desk to see if my program was going to get running." One morning after Hopper had spent the entire night with Mark I and Mark II, Aiken asked her what she had been doing there all that time. "Chaperoning these two damned computers," she snapped.

Most WAVES returned to civilian life after the war—to marriage and child raising. Grace Hopper was divorced and had no children. She wanted to remain in the navy and continue her work. She asked to be transferred from the reserves to the regular navy, but because she had turned forty in 1946 and the age limit was thirty-eight, she was refused. She had an invitation from Vassar to return as a full professor, but instead she remained at the Harvard Computation Lab with the title of Research Fellow in Engineering Sciences and Applied Physics. This was the time when the Mark II and Mark III computers were being built for the navy. It was in 1946 that Hopper was given the Naval Ordnance Development Award.

Grace Hopper will go down in computing history as the lady who coined the term "bug." She contends that she doesn't deserve this honor, but rather dutifully accepts it. It came about in the following way. During the summer of 1947 the Mark II computer, successor to the Mark I, was acting up, giving some erroneous information. The faulty relay was located, and there, inside it, was discovered the cause of the malfunction: a moth, beaten to death by the relay. The moth was taken out of the relay with a pair of tweezers and scotch-taped onto a page of the logbook. An operator wrote in the logbook, "First actual bug found." Aiken liked to come into the laboratory and ask, "Are you making any numbers?" When little work was being accomplished, Hopper and the others would say they were "debugging" the machine—a handy excuse. Thus the term stuck.

Aiken had encouraged the Prudential Insurance Company shortly after World War II to use the Mark I in actuarial work. Hopper helped to write a program for Prudential, and this got her interested in the business side of computers. Using computers for business purposes was very new. "I realized," remembers Hopper, "that it was going to be far more complicated to use computers in business applications than in mathematical, science, and engineering applications, because there were no formulas. Because every time you got up to something it would spread in five different directions."

Hopper had taught mathematics at Harvard as a fellow for three years but was not permitted to stay longer, so in 1949 she sought a new job. Weighing several offers, she went with the Eckert-Mauchly Corporation, the Philadelphia firm run by John Mauchly and J. Presper Eckert, the co-inventors of ENIAC. This was a company about to have a working computer, the UNIVAC I, and that appealed to her. She joined the firm as a senior mathematician.

At the time she joined the firm, Mauchly and Eckert were nearing completion of the BINAC, to be used for the then-classified Snark Missile project. In mid-1949 Hopper was part of a small team from Eckert-Mauchly that traveled to Hawthorne, California, to instruct Northrup Aircraft personnel how to use the computer. Because BINAC was programmed in octal—base-8 arithmetic— Hopper taught herself to add, subtract, multiply, and divide in this code. She became proficient in it. For three consecutive months during this period, however, she had problems balancing her checkbook. She consulted her brother, a banker, who, after several evenings of labor, told her that occasionally she had been subtracting in octal!

Hopper stayed on with Eckert-Mauchly as a senior programmer even after it was purchased by Remington Rand and later merged into the Sperry Corporation. In 1952 she was appointed Systems Engineer and Director of Automatic Programming for the UNIVAC Division of Sperry. She held that post until 1964.

Hopper was troubled by the inherently mistake-filled nature of code writing, and she decided to do something about it. What she developed was a new kind of program called a compiler—a piece of software that would translate an entire set of programmer's instructions, written in a higher-level symbolic language, into an organized program in the machine's binary language, and would then carry out that program. The first compiler was called A-0 and was developed by Grace Hopper and her staff at Remington in 1952.

She solved one problem in the writing of computer languages—how to jump forward to a segment in a program that hadn't been written yet—by alluding to her days as college basketball player. Under women's basketball rules, dribbling was permitted only once, so it was necessary to employ the forward pass— one would throw the ball to a teammate and then run down court to receive it again. Hopper used this routine as a model for solving the problem of forward jumps. She tucked a small section called the "neutral corner" down at the end of the memory, and when she wanted to jump forward from the routine she was working on, she jumped to a spot in that neutral corner.

She ran into cynics who argued that her compiler would not work, that computers could do arithmetic but not programming. This gave her the chance to prove not only that compilers were valuable but also that women were as capable as men of doing this kind of work. (For her part, Hopper believed that women made better programmers than men: men tended to rush off to a new problem before completing the solution of the first.) She decided to show that she could make a computer do anything she could define. By 1954 she had developed the first operational analytical differentiator. Hopper invited people to bring functions for the program to differentiate. One man arrived with a particularly complicated function, on which he had worked six months, obtaining the first fifteen derivatives. She gave them to him in eighteen minutes. The man then insisted that she had someone behind the computer feeding the answers in! Hopper had shown that the computer was not merely an arithmetical gadget, but much more. The computer, as she puts it, is "basically a symbolic manipulator. When it's doing numerical mathematics it is manipulating arithmetic symbols, and when it's doing data processing it's manipulating data processing symbols."

As another demonstration of the value of compilers, Hopper wrote a small inventory/price program that could be translated into machine code and then wrote a routine that could translate the same program written in French or German into machine code. Management refused to believe it: "It was absolutely obvious that a computer made in Philadelphia, Pennsylvania, could not understand French or German." She finally won out, and Flow-matic was put together by Hopper and her staff at UNIVAC in 1957. At first known as B-0, it was the first English-language data-processing compiler—the first computer language employing words. In 1958 the manual for running Flow-matic was ready. It had the first complete set of commands, including "add," "execute," and "stop." Flow-matic was later incorporated into COBOL, the most widely used business computer language, another Hopper contribution.

By 1957 leading figures in the computer world were disturbed that, while the scientific community had been given the computer language FORTRAN, nothing of the kind existed for business. Furthermore, there was a need for standardization. Once Flow-matic had come out, IBM announced Commercial Translator, Honeywell announced Fact. The prospect of having more than one standard business language was appalling to Hopper and to others in the industry. But standardization could be viewed as a breach of the antitrust laws. It was for that reason that the meeting that launched COBOL—Common Business-Oriented Language— was held at a university, a neutral site.

Six people, Grace Hopper among them, convened on April 8, 1959, in the office of Professor Saul Gorn at the University of Pennsylvania's Computer Center. Academics, computer users, and computer manufacturers were represented. They talked of developing the specifications for a common business language for automatic digital computers. The next and crucial meeting was held on May 28 at the Department of Defense, chosen partly because the Defense Department was a major user of business applications for its computers and partly because it was another neutral (i.e., nonbusiness) site. From that two-day meeting emerged marching orders and the organization that would eventually develop COBOL. Hopper had been referred to as the "mother of COBOL." Although the language in its final form came out of a committee of which she was not a working member, the committee members acknowledged that her Flow-matic language greatly influenced their thinking.

COBOL was designed to make programs easy to read; it was also supposed to be independent of whatever computer it happened to be running on. In contrast with FORTRAN, which uses a briefer and more mathematical approach, COBOL uses syntax and terms that come close to natural English. Some find it wordy. COBOL, as distinct from previous languages, is very clear in separating processing from the data parts; thus, if a programmer decides to change the program, he need only alter part of the previously written code, not all of it. The language has received high marks for its file-handling capability: it supports sequential and direct-access files and is particularly suited to managing large amounts of data stored on tape or disk.

One of COBOL's big advantages was that it was not identified with any specific manufacturers: thus, both government and private industry were more inclined to use it. Still, it got off to a shaky start. Within the first year a rumor spread that it was dead. Howard Bromberg of RCA, a member of the program language committee, was so angry that he shipped a tombstone with the word COBOL on it to the Pentagon. But COBOL caught on, and Grace Hopper would declare in the 1980s that "it's going to keep on for a long time for the basic data processing and file processing. For people who want access to the data, it will do the grind work. There is nothing else to replace it so far."

In 1964 Hopper assumed the title Staff Scientist, Systems Programming, in the UNIVAC Division of Sperry Corporation. She remained active in the Naval Reserve until 1966, when with great sadness she retired, with the rank of commander. But the navy soon found it couldn't get along without her: its payroll program had been rewritten 823 times—and enough was enough. So, seven months after her retirement, Norman J. Ream, then a special assistant to the secretary of the navy, called her to say she was needed to standardize the high-level languages and get the entire navy to use them. "Mr. Ream," replied Commander Hopper, "the first job is finite, the second job is infinite. But I will be glad to try."

Thus, at the age of sixty, Grace Hopper returned to active duty in the navy on August 1, 1967. The normal retirement age for a military officer is sixty-two, but Hopper remained on active duty for nineteen more years, under the procedure approved by Congress that permits annual extensions. She liked to boast that she was on the longest temporary duty in navy history. In 1969 the Data Processing Management Association selected her as its first computer sciences "Man of the Year." She retired from Sperry in December 1971, at which time the UNIVAC Division initiated the Grace Murray Hopper Award for young computer personnel, to be given annually by the Association for Computing Machinery. In 1973 she was promoted to captain on the retired list of the Naval Reserve, and on December 15, 1983, in a White House ceremony, she was promoted to the rank of commodore. In March 1984 she became a special adviser to the chief of the Naval Data Automation Command.

Grace Hopper had become one of the U.S. Navy's greatest public-relations assets. She traveled widely, speaking about computers on the navy's behalf, exhibiting an honest pride in the navy and her country, and talking vividly and forthrightly about the work she loved. She enjoyed chiding her computer colleagues for playing it safe. The most dangerous phrase employed by computer people, Hopper would say, was "But we've always done it that way." To stress that, she kept a clock in her office that operated in counterclockwise fashion. After a while people realized they could learn to tell time that way, and there was no reason why clocks had to run clockwise. She encouraged people to be innovative. One of her favorite pieces of advice was, It is easier to apologize than to get permission.

She was apt to be the butt of some of her best jokes. She liked to tell audiences about the time she was moving through a baggage checkpoint at an airport and the security guard asked if she was in the navy. She said yes. The man stared at her for a long time, a tiny puppet of a lady, incongruous in her military attire. "You must be the oldest one they've got," he finally blurted out. And so she was. When Admiral Hyman Rickover retired from active duty in January 1982 at age eighty-two, Grace Hopper became the oldest naval person. She gave as many as two hundred lectures a year, preferring young audiences. She believes her greatest contribution has been in training young people.

In her lectures Hopper lashed out at the computer industry on several counts. Its lack of standards—for programming languages, computer architecture, data structure, and networks—was costing the government hundreds of millions of dollars a year in hardware and software that had to be thrown out because of incompatibility. Either a consortium of vendors or the government should come up with one standard—but certainly not, she said, a dominant firm. She also condemned the notion that larger computers were automatically superior. As an analogy, she pointed out that when a farmer had to move a big, heavy boulder, and one of his oxen alone wasn't strong enough to do the job, he didn't try to grow a bigger ox. He added another ox. Likewise, large volumes of data were better handled by multiple users than by a bigger machine. Hopper was concerned too about the fact that with so much information being processed, people were growing less critical of the quality of that information. Finally, she was angry at the computer industry for making computers binary rather than alpha decimal. Binary was better for numerical computations, being faster—but not, in her opinion, for data processing. One disadvantage of making the early computers binary was the effect on the public. "When computers were thoroughly binary, we told everybody, 'Oh no, you can't understand that; you don't know binary.' We pushed people away. We wouldn't explain, we created a barrier. Now we're trying to break that down again."

In November 1985 Hopper was promoted to rear admiral. Then on August 14, 1986, she retired from the navy at the age of seventy-nine. At her retirement ceremony in Boston, aboard the U.S.S. *Constitution*, she asked the young white-uniformed sailors in attendance, "Do you realize I'm the last of the World War II WAVES to leave active duty?" She reminded them of how she had been told at forty that she was too old to join the regular navy, but had remained in uniform for nearly another four decades. "It's just as well to be told you're too old at forty," she chirped. "Then you're out of it." But Grace Hopper would never be out of it. On September 1, 1986, she began working for Digital Equipment Corporation in public relations.

John Backus

The Man Who Invented FORTRAN

21

To use a computer in the early 1950s, one had to possess a great deal of expertise, ingenuity, and patience. All sorts of tricks had to be employed to make a program run quickly enough to justify the cost of running the computer—or even to make a program run at all. John Backus knew there must be a better way. In 1953 he set out to create the first practical high-level programming language, with the aim of making computers easier to use and more widely accessible. Backus thinks his personal motivation was that he was lazy. He didn't like the drudgery of programming. So he designed FORTRAN.

To appreciate the genius of John Backus, one must imagine the computer world in its dinosaur age, the 1940s. The first generation of computers—ENIAC, the IAS machine, the Mark I at Manchester University, IBM's 701, and Whirlwind—were programmed either in machine code (consisting of binary numbers) or in assembly language (letters, numbers, symbols, and short words). Programs written in one of the assembly languages would be fed into the computer and translated automatically into machine code. An operator then had to reenter the resulting machine code, which had been punched on tape or cards, into the computer. As one example of the complexity of early programming, a wiring diagram served as the program for the ENIAC, requiring two to three days to set up. A programmer in those days had to know the interior of the machine in order to function. Stored-program computers, replacing ENIAC in the late 1940s, did away with the need to play with the computer's wiring. It became possible to use punched-card readers or magnetic-tape decks to put instructions directly into the computer. With the advent of elementary operating systems, programs became automatic in the sense that it was no longer necessary to reenter the assembled machine code via cards or tape.

Still, programmers labored hard, using up valuable time writing subroutines—segments of programs—that indicated to the computer how to perform floating-point operations and how to compute memory addresses (the latter operation being known as indexing). The programmers of the day were eager to automate the drudgery of indexing, floating-point, and input/output operations, so that they could turn to more creative tasks. But automation alone was not enough. The new automatic programs would have to perform faster than programmers using the old method of writing and debugging subroutines by hand.

One early attempt was Grace Hopper's A-0, written in 1952; it automatically performed floating-point operations and other tasks. It could also understand words, phrases, and mathematical expressions. But automatic programming, though it helped sell some computers, was still quite inefficient, producing programs that ran very slowly—and in those days machine time was scarce and expensive. Automatic programming systems were not considered to be cost-effective, inasmuch as they slowed down the computer by a factor of five or ten. The main reason for the slowdown: these programs spent most of their time in floating-point subroutines.

Then IBM's 704 appeared in May 1954, helping to simplify programming. With its built-in floating-point and indexing, the 704 cut operating time dramatically. But there remained other inefficient aspects to programming. If someone could write a compiler that would translate simple high-level instructions into machine code—and do it as well and as efficiently as the hand code of a programmer—that would be a real breakthrough.

Enter John Backus. Born in Philadelphia on December 3, 1924, he grew up in Wilmington, Delaware, and entered the University of Virginia in the fall of 1942, planning to major in chemical engineering. He was thrown out of the school in the first semester, for cutting classes, and in early 1943 was drafted into the army. He first served in an antiaircraft program in Georgia and then, as part of the army's specialized training, studied engineering at the University of

Pittsburgh from September 1943 to March 1944. At that time he and twenty others were sent to a hospital in Atlantic City for six months of premedical training. While at the hospital Backus was operated on to remove a bone tumor. In March 1945 he entered Flower and Fifth Avenue Medical School in New York City, but after six months he realized medicine was not for him. He spent from December 1945 until May 1946 in Halloran Hospital on Staten Island, where a new plate was inserted into his head to replace the defective one that had been put in at the time of the first operation.

After leaving the U.S. Army in May 1946, Backus lived in an $18-a-month apartment in New York. He was interested in building a hi-fi set, so he enrolled at the Radio Television Institute in New York, a training school for radio and television repairmen. While there he met an instructor who stimulated in him an interest in mathematics. Backus began taking courses in math at Columbia University. He received his bachelor of arts degree from that university in 1949. A master's degree in math followed in 1950. A teaching job seemed the likely next step, but he had no desire to teach. He had heard about IBM, which had offices in New York City, and he applied for a job there. Rex Seeber, a co-inventor of the Selective Sequence Electronic Calculator—the SSEC—hired him as a programmer.

Backus knew next to nothing about computers when he started at IBM in 1950. He worked on the SSEC for a year and then led a small programming team that developed an assembly language for the 701, introduced in 1952. Called Speedcoding, this language made the 701 look to the user like a floating-point machine with index registers. He also helped to design the IBM 704 and to build floating-point and indexing hardware into it.

John Backus at this point asked, "Can a machine translate a sufficiently rich mathematical language into a sufficiently economical program at a sufficiently low cost to make the whole affair feasible?" Translating a scientific source program into an object program that ran only half as fast as its hand-code counterpart would be inadequate. So the design of the translator was in Backus's view the major challenge—not the design of the language.

Backus had been disheartened by the whole programming game. He was stymied by the technical dilemmas. But he also sensed that programmers had themselves kept the art from advancing—and from spreading into the wider public realm. "Today," he wrote in 1980,

a programmer is often under great pressure from superiors who know just how and how long he should take to write a program. His work is no longer regarded as a mysterious art, and much of his productive capacity depends on his ability to find out what he needs in a 6-inch-thick manual of some baroque programming or operating system. In contrast, programming in the early 1950s was a black art, a private arcane matter involving only a programmer, a problem, a computer, and perhaps a small library of subroutines, and a primitive assembly program. Existing programs for similar problems were unreadable and hence could not be adapted to new uses. General programming principles were largely nonexistent. Thus each problem required a unique beginning at square one, and the success of a program depended primarily on the programmer's private techniques and invention.

Furthermore, programmers of the early 1950s were too impatient to hold onto an idea until it could be fully developed or a paper written. "They wanted to convince others," Backus continued. "Action, progress, and outdoing one's rivals were more important than mere authorship of a paper. Recognition in the small programming fraternity was more likely to be accorded for a colorful personality, an extraordinary feat of coding, or the ability to hold a lot of liquor well, than it was for an intellectual insight."

If there was one preeminent reason for the creation of FORTRAN, it was the economics of programming. Programming and debugging accounted for up to three-quarters of the cost of running a computer, a ratio that would increase as computers became cheaper. So when John Backus wrote a letter to his boss, Cuthbert Hurd, in December 1953, proposing to develop a practical high-level programming language, the response was enthusiastic indeed. Backus and his team were to work unhindered by demands that they project or justify costs.

Backus set up shop in a small office in the Jay Thorpe Building on Fifth Avenue, near IBM headquarters at 590 Madison Avenue. A few months later, in May 1954, the FORTRAN project moved to a room on the nineteenth floor of the 590 Madison Avenue annex—next to the elevator machinery. At first Backus had only one colleague, Irving Ziller. Then came Harlan Herrick, followed by another half-dozen people, including mathematicians and a technical typist named Robert A. Nelson, who would become an important contributor. One team member, Lois Haibt, had just graduated as a mathematics major from college, and the only thing she knew about computers was that they existed. There was an atmosphere of excitement surrounding the project: even though they little thought that their programming language would ever be used on machines other than the IBM 704, the participants knew that, if they should succeed, their work would have an enormous impact on the computer scene. Just coming up with a faster, cheaper, and more reliable way of programming the 704 would be enough to jolt the industry. Backus didn't anticipate that people would make compilers for other machines that would accept the FORTRAN language; later, he realized it was inevitable.

They were inventing as they went along with no tested principles to fall back on. When someone asked them how long it would take to finish, they would always give the same reply, six months, come back in six months. They honestly believed the project would end then. But in fact it took three years. They worked under crowded conditions, desks crammed together in one room—no partitions, no peace and quiet, one small family.

They knew they would have to give the language a name and found inventing names a pleasant diversion on slow days. Backus thought of some pretty trite ones, only to be knocked down each time by a colleague. But one day he offered Formula Translation—FORTRAN. The reaction was decidedly cool, but it was accepted in the absence of anything better.

Why did Backus and his team succeed? Hurd pointed to Backus's ability to think (as Hurd put it) tops-down and bottoms-up; Ziller pointed to an ability they all seemed to have to associate freely, to interrelate things; Herrick noted a lack of inhibition in the group, linked to a willingness to discard the frustrating notion that something can't be done; Backus suggested they were all willing to ask new questions, to examine an aspect of a problem that had gone unnoticed. But above all, in Backus's view, there was the willingness to fail, the willingness to keep generating ideas even when one knows that failure is the likely result.

The critical problem for Backus and his team was not the design of the language but rather the design of the compiler that would produce efficient programs. They would make up the language as they went along, hoping to produce one with which scientists and engineers could feel comfortable in writing programs for the 704. With the fall of 1954, Backus had become manager of the Programming Research Group, as his FORTRAN team was called. On November 10 they published their first paper, "Preliminary Report, Specifications for the IBM Mathematical FORmula TRANslating System, FORTRAN."

Backus and his team exuded a great air of optimism in that first report. Whereas up to that time "systems which have sought to reduce the job of coding and debugging problems have offered the choice of easy coding and slow execution or laborious coding and fast execution," the programs produced by the compiler they were laboring to write "will be executed in about the same time that would be required had the problem been laboriously hand-coded. . . . FORTRAN may apply complex lengthy techniques in coding a problem which the human coder would have neither the time nor inclination to derive or apply."

In late 1954 Backus, Herrick, and Ziller gave a half-dozen talks about their plans for FORTRAN to groups of IBM customers who had put in orders for the 704. The FORTRAN agents traveled to Washington, Albuquerque, Pittsburgh, Los Angeles, and a few other cities. The "Preliminary Report" had been published, but the compiler was not expected to be completed for another six months. (In fact, it would take another two years, until April 1957.) The purpose of the sessions was to hear from the customers what some of their needs and complaints were—those that might have a bearing on FORTRAN. The customers said little; no one was willing to believe that Backus and his group would really come up with a compiler that produced efficient object programs. There were no suggestions, no feedback, no criticism. Show me, don't talk about it, was the attitude of the listeners.

In the summer of 1956 they got most of the system functioning. This was a difficult period for the team members. They would sleep in rented rooms in the Langdon Hotel on 56th Street during the day so as to run programs on the computer during the night when it was free. The compiler, when it began to work, produced some unanticipated good results, but it also had some bugs that didn't seem to want to go away. As the team approached the end, the frustration level grew. Word got around the industry that John

Backus and his team were on a merry-go-round and didn't know how to get off; the project was a year late. Those in the know understood that a year's delay in a program was not a fiasco, but quite reasonable.

The compiler was finished in April 1957. It consisted of 25,000 lines of machine code and was stored on magnetic tape. Every IBM 704 installation got a copy, complete with a smart-looking 51-page manual. The originally distributed program contained many bugs, but in time there was success.

When FORTRAN was ready, Backus's team sensed they had a language that was easy to learn. The notation was specifically written for mathematicians and scientists, and as time would show, it would remain a good big language for scientific programs for a long time. No one would fault FORTRAN for having no application outside of the scientific, mathematical, and engineering realm. Soon there would be other languages (among them, COBOL and BASIC) for other applications.

With FORTRAN a language and its compiler existed that allowed people to deal with a computer without knowing the internal workings of the machine and without knowing its assembly language. IBM had scored a major coup that would help enormously in selling its computers. Backus is modest about his own role in the FORTRAN project, noting that others wrote the major sections of the compiler. It was their invention of numerous techniques—which they incorporated in the compiler—that enabled the compiler to produce efficient object programs. Even in the mid-1980s John Backus still derived joy from FORTRAN's longevity: FORTRAN has lasted for thirty years. What computer has survived for more than five years? What program has been the best of its kind for more than two or three years? And yet, the original FORTRAN compiler produced the most optimized program of all the compilers written over the next two decades.

Backus counted among the successes of his first ten years of research—1950 to 1960—two major ones, the development of FORTRAN and (in 1959) the notation for describing ALGOL, called Backus-Naur Form. The latter, a recursive description of how to assign a set of strings to variables, has subsequently been adapted for quite a number of other languages. He counted among his failures an earlier programming language for the 701. In his second decade of research, beginning in 1960, Backus attempted to come up with a mathematical concept of the "structure" of a family of sets that would be useful for solving a variety of problems. "I worked very hard during those ten years," he recalled in a lecture given in 1983, "and kept proving enough theorems to keep me thinking I was making progress. But in the end, I had to face the fact that I wasn't going to get the results I had hoped for, that I just had to quit." Since 1960 he had been at the IBM Research Division, which supported him throughout that decade with "a bit of understandable reluctance." The failure of this project was painful. "I had enjoyed the work very much, but it is hard to describe the feeling of discouragement, even despair, that I felt as I filed away those notebooks for the last time."

In 1970 he began the third and most recent phase of his research career. He began to work on finding a better way to program, coming up with what he calls function-level languages. His goal is to make it easier for computer users to tell computers what they want them to do. Backus considers programming in the 1980s still too slow and expensive. Moreover, the fact that it is difficult keeps the average user from controlling the computer. Little has changed in programming since the 1950s. Indeed, computers are becoming less accessible to the non-expert, he insists, as programming languages get more complex. The real problem originates in the way computers are organized.

Computers have been designed to operate only on individual words; complex operating systems are needed. If serial computers are difficult to program, parallel computers are even more perplexing. But the largest problem is that computers do not make good use of the capabilities of Very Large Scale Integration (VLSI) circuits. Backus notes that millions of people will want to use the increasingly cheap computers, but if they are to do so effectively they must be able to write programs themselves.

It is one's concept of what a program is, says Backus, that determines how one programs and how one designs machines. According to the prevailing concept, a program is basically a mapping of one "store" onto another. It is a transformation of a set of named cells into another set, with some cells having new contents. The key thing wrong with this concept, in Backus's view, is that programs then depend on storage plans. It is not enough to know the action or purpose of a program to use it; one must also know its storage plan. One must know the names of all its inputs and its outputs. This means that independently written programs cannot be put together to build new ones—not, that is, unless they have a common storage plan or unless one alters their storage plans to conform with each other. Adds Backus in a recent article,

The functional approach rejects the model of computing conceived by the mathematician John von Neumann and others. The von Neumann model is based on a computer consisting of a central processing unit (CPU), a store or memory, and a connection between them that transmits a single unit of data, or "word," between the CPU and the store. Because today's programming languages are modeled on such computers, programs are complex, concerned with the smallest data entities, and seldom reusable in building new programs.

Backus points out that while computing power increases and hardware costs decrease every year, the writing of software becomes more expensive. Those costs and the needed expertise to write programs discourage countless numbers from touching a computer.

Of the new function-level language, Backus wrote in a 1978 article,

An alternative functional style of programming is founded on the use of combining forms for creating programs. Functional programs deal with structured data, are often nonrepetitive and nonrecursive, are hierarchically constructed, do not name their arguments, and do not require the complex machinery of procedure declarations to become generally applicable. Combining forms can use high-level programs to build still higher level ones in a style not possible in conventional languages.

The life of a researcher can be frustrating and lonely, the benefits difficult to see. "I'm in the business of failing," says Backus. "You work on something and it fails and you try again. It's very painful and so you constantly search for distractions." Still, he does not sound as if he wants to trade his career for anyone else's. His failures have been easier to take after his great breakthrough with FORTRAN. The recognition he received for pioneering that language was a tonic that had a lasting effect. Then too there is the simple fact that he loves research.

John Kemeny   Thomas Kurtz

John Kemeny and Thomas Kurtz

Handling the Computer—BASICally

22

In the beginning all a computer was expected to do was—compute. If it took less time over an operation than a human being took, it had performed a miracle. But as the hardware began to reach down to larger audiences in the 1960s, as computers became less expensive, less remote, expectations changed. Users had to be able to converse with their computers, or else why buy the arcane objects? Assembly languages were difficult to learn: any idea, however simple, required complex instructions. Merely to print a number, a whole series of codes had to be typed. And yet the only high-level languages around—languages employing simple English words rather than codes—were for very specific purposes. There was FORTRAN for the scientific community, COBOL for the business world. Both of these intimidated most amateur computer users.

It was this fertile territory that John Kemeny and Thomas Kurtz began to plow. These two Dartmouth professors of mathematics knew what computers could do, but they chafed at the way computer centers effectively kept people from getting to computers. What a wonderful research environment the computers could provide—but first they must be accessible. And so Kemeny and Kurtz set in motion the then revolutionary concept of making computers as freely available to college students as library books were. John McCarthy, who had been developing the concept of time sharing at MIT during the early 1960s, urged Kurtz to get involved in the same thing at Dartmouth. In contrast with the old system of batch processing, which allowed only technicians to get near a computer, time sharing permitted students to have direct access to the machine. For the Dartmouth community time sharing would be a life saver. To work with computers, one had to punch programs on cards and carry them to the nearest computer center, which in this case was a 135-mile train ride away. Then one had to wait hours or even days for the results. Kurtz passed McCarthy's advice on to John Kemeny. "Let's do it," was the immediate reply.

Because of the time-sharing system, Dartmouth students, though largely nontechnical, had far more experience in the 1960s with computers than students elsewhere. Kemeny and Kurtz did not want to train computer scientists; their idea was rather to put the computer at the disposal of large numbers of generalists. A few Dartmouth academics attacked the introduction of the "machine age" soon after the computer system was installed, but resistance among faculty members was short-lived.

There was a direct connection between the Dartmouth time-sharing project and the development of BASIC—Beginner's All-Purpose Symbolic Instruction Code. It became clear to Kemeny and Kurtz that a high-level language would be needed for the non-expert users of the system. Nothing like that existed. Kemeny was the one who suggested to Kurtz, while they were implementing time sharing, that they ought to come up with a more user-friendly language. While certain that they could invent such a language, Kurtz was concerned lest Dartmouth students get stuck with a language they couldn't use outside the school. After all, IBM's FORTRAN dominated the scene in those days. "I occasionally kid Tom about that worry," notes Kemeny, "because, as you know, that's not quite what happened."

The road to BASIC was a long one. Kemeny and Kurtz had come up with DARSIMCO—DARtmouth SIMplified COde—Dartmouth's first real attempt at a computer language, in 1956. Because FORTRAN appeared soon thereafter, however, it fell into quick disuse. In 1962, Kemeny, assisted by Dartmouth student Sidney Marshall, wrote a language called DOPE—Dartmouth Oversimplified Programming Experiment—which was a precursor to BASIC. It was not a success. At one point Kurtz preferred trying to modify ALGOL and FORTRAN. But he quickly concluded that it was not possible to construct subsets of these languages that would be easier to use. So he eventually adopted Kemeny's attitude, which was to create a whole new language.

In 1963 Kemeny designed an introductory computer course but soon realized that batch-processing systems were not adequate for the course assignments. He started to work on a compiler for a draft version of BASIC in September of that year, even before the Dartmouth time-sharing system was put together. Working at the General Electric offices in Lynn, Massachusetts, he was permitted to take over a computer similar to the one Dartmouth had ordered for an hour every once in a while, a rare event in those days of batch processing. It took Kemeny until the following spring to write BASIC.

Dartmouth students were the first to use the language. If they had trouble with a command, they could tell one of the authors about it and almost at once a correction would be made. The first program in BASIC was a compiler, whereas all subsequent versions were interpreters. Kemeny and Kurtz chose a compiler for the following reason: Although most compilers were notoriously slow in 1963, they knew that fast "load and go" compilers could be written. They had in fact written several themselves. Although an interpreter gave quicker initial response, on any moderately long-running program the compiled version did much better (even counting the compile time). They knew that after a brief learning phase their students would be writing substantial programs. Finally, their two-processor time-sharing hardware configuration did not lend itself to efficient program editing using an interpreter.

The first BASIC program ran on May 1, 1964, at 4 a.m. on the time-sharing system, implemented on the GE 225 computer. The name for the language was derived from Kemeny's and Kurtz's wish to have a simple acronym that meant something as well. Says Kurtz, "We wanted a word that was simple but not simple-minded, and BASIC was the one."

Neither Kemeny nor Kurtz thought in grand terms then. They only hoped that BASIC would help students work with, and learn something about, computers. The two men put their invention in the public domain right away, and so they made no real money from it. Dartmouth copyrighted BASIC but made it available free to anyone who wanted to use it. Its great advantage was that it was easy to learn. One didn't need a background in programming or mathematics, as did someone who wanted to use an assembly language. Any computer user could benefit from it, not just scientists or businessmen. John Kemeny even envisioned below-average students learning it easily.

It was ideally suited to become, as it did, the most popular computer language. BASIC became the key factor in persuading educators that computers could help students in their education. Some ten to twelve million schoolchildren have learned it. Professional programmers have exploited it to make millions of dollars in applications. More people have learned BASIC than Norwegian, Danish, and Swedish combined. By enabling the average person to use a computer in the 1960s, BASIC helped bring on the personal computer revolution of a decade later. And indeed, BASIC soared in popularity in 1975 after a pair of youngsters in a Harvard dormitory, Bill Gates and Paul Allen, managed to get it working on one of the earliest personal computers. Gates and Allen's version became the most widely used BASIC. Oddly enough, Kemeny and Kurtz were not aware of this project until much later; during the mid-1970s the two Dartmouth inventors were in fact unaware that personal computers were even being developed. With their free time-sharing system at the college they had no need for personal computers.

Following the Gates-Allen success BASIC spread to the Commodore, Apple, TRS-80, Atari, IBM PC, and even the Sinclair. Eventually it would run on nearly every microcomputer and serve as the basis for thousands of applications. Nowadays it is often embedded in a machine's memory, and comes free with many computers. Rather than typing those complicated assembly-language codes to print numbers, in BASIC one simply typed PRINT followed by the number, and the computer went to work. If a command contained INT, for another example, the computer understood that it had to consider only the integer part of arguments. In BASIC the rules link abstract algebraic expressions with English words like LET, GO TO, FOR/NEXT, INPUT, PRINT, and END. BASIC, using 200 words, was translated inside the computer into instructions that the computer could understand. Once the computer recognized a one-word instruction, it performed a particular operation.

BASIC had a few major differences that made it easier to apply than earlier high-level languages. In the past one had to memorize a complicated vocabulary and syntax, no longer true with BASIC. The number of statements was reduced to just a dozen or so, allowing programmers to write concise, efficient programs. Because BASIC was interactive, it provided new programmers with an instant response to lines typed into the computer, easing the process of debugging and modifying programs. On seeing an error message, one could quickly correct a faulty line. It could solve a small problem with a small solution, something that would take many more programming lines in other languages. In short, it was efficient. Another advantage was its built-in random number generator, which allowed youngsters to write games easily.

The elder of BASIC's two authors, John Kemeny, was born in Budapest on May 31, 1926. Though others thought him unduly alarmed, Kemeny's father believed that Hitler's march into Vienna in early 1938 augured worse things, and so he left on his own for the United States. Eighteen months later, in early 1940, he sent for his wife, daughter, and teen-aged son John. After a Budapest-to-Genoa train ride, the family sailed to America without incident. ("Other than getting seasick," Kemeny recalls, "nothing happened.") The one misadventure of the trip concerned their heavy luggage: it was put on an Italian freighter that never sailed, as Italy was about to go to war. Young Kemeny attended school in New York City. In 1943 he entered Princeton, where he studied mathematics.

During his junior year, turning eighteen, Kemeny was drafted and sent to Los Alamos, where organizers of the Manhattan Project had undertaken a crash program to accelerate development of the atom bomb. Here he was assigned to what was known as the project's computing center; in fact, it used IBM bookkeeping calculators. Kemeny joined others working eight-hour shifts, twenty-four hours a day, six days a week. "It took us about two weeks to get a numerical solution to one partial differential equation. I would estimate that all the work we did—twenty of us in a year—could have been done by a Dartmouth sophomore in one afternoon after we had the time-sharing system in place. And while he was doing that, 250 other people would be using the same computer." Kemeny remained at Los Alamos through 1945 and 1946.

After the war he returned to Princeton to do a doctorate. During 1948 and 1949, while completing his dissertation, Kemeny served as Albert Einstein's research assistant at the Institute for Advanced Study; Einstein always had a mathematician as a research assistant. Kemeny worked three or four days a week with Einstein, who at the time was completing his work on unified field theory, trying to choose which of three possible versions was the best. Kemeny spent a good deal of time checking Einstein's calculations. "If we both got the same answer, the chances were overwhelming that it was right. And in the way the pleasant part of the job was that I was the person with whom Einstein could talk when he wanted to think out loud." One day, coming out of the Institute, Kemeny and Einstein met John von Neumann. "You have made the wrong kind of computer," Einstein told von Neumann. "Why don't you invent a computer that would help me in my work? I don't need a numerical computer." What Einstein required was a symbolic machine— one that could perform symbolic differentiation, among other tasks. In the course of the lengthy discussion that followed, von Neumann predicted that one day computers would do the kind of work Einstein wanted. And he was right, of course.

After Kemeny received his doctorate, he taught mathematics for two years and philosophy for another two years at Princeton. He joined the Dartmouth faculty in 1953 and has been there ever since, teaching mathematics and philosophy, serving as chairman of the mathematics department from 1956 to 1968 and as president of the college from 1970 to 1981. He was a consultant to the Rand Corporation during the 1950s, on computer science and other matters. In 1979 he took time out from his duties at Dartmouth to serve as chairman of the President's Commission on the Accident at Three Mile Island.

Thomas Kurtz was born on February 22, 1928, in Oak Park, Illinois. He graduated in 1950 from Knox College in Galesburg, Illinois, where he majored in mathematics. Like Kemeny, he went to graduate school at Princeton, where he did his doctoral work in statistics, receiving the degree in 1956. His thesis was on a problem of multiple comparisons in mathematical statistics. In 1951 he spent a summer working with computers at UCLA in the Institute for Numerical Analysis, a branch of the National Bureau of Standards.

Kurtz arrived at Dartmouth in 1956 and began teaching mathematics. Almost immediately he became involved with computers.

In his first year he would travel to General Electric in Lynn, Massachusetts, to use its computers. For the next two years he used an IBM 704 at MIT. He was director of the Kiewit Computation Center at Dartmouth from 1966 to 1975. From 1974 through 1984 Kurtz served as chairman of American National Standards Committee X3J2, which aimed at developing a standard for BASIC. He is still at Dartmouth, teaching both mathematics and computer science.

There were several milestones along the way to BASIC's ultimate success. One came in 1965 when General Electric adopted the language for use on its time-sharing system. Another occurred in the late 1960s and early 1970s with the proliferation of small time-sharing systems in education and other fields. BASIC spawned a series of languages that were variants of the original Kemeny-Kurtz effort. With the added capabilities of the new personal computers, BASIC spread from machine to machine, with a host of dialects popping up. There were MITS BASIC, Tiny BASIC, SWTP BASIC, Applesoft BASIC, RM BASIC, BAZIC, BASIC-09, Better BASIC, Professional BASIC, Macintosh BASIC, BASICA (GW-BASIC), and the pathbreaking Microsoft BASIC. Kemeny and Kurtz called these "street BASICs" to express their disdain.

One unhappy result of this variety has been the difficulty of transporting a BASIC program from one machine to another. Some of the dialects, according to Kemeny and Kurtz, should not be considered part of the BASIC family, for they violate one or more of their original criteria. For example, some permit several statements on one line or a single statement continuing over several lines. Kurtz is appalled upon seeing in these variants the lack of structured features, the reliance on line numbers, and the manner in which lines are scanned for key words. Kemeny is horrified that microcomputer BASICs insist on changing one's entire program to capital letters. None of the authors of these programs have asked Kemeny or Kurtz for advice on whether they were violating essential criteria. Instead they have taken ideas from other BASIC variants, and not surprisingly, the core ideas of the Kemeny-Kurtz BASIC have become garbled.

With machines getting smaller, compromises have had to be made to squeeze the language into tighter space, compromises that became a feature of the variants. Kemeny and Kurtz know there was no way they could have controlled the proliferation of these BASICs once the language entered the public domain. Lingering in Kemeny's mind is a sense of regret that the two men permitted this. Yet it never occurred to them in 1964 that BASIC would become as widespread as it did, and that maintaining quality control would become so difficult.

In 1978 the American National Standards Institute (ANSI) published the first standard for BASIC, but it was largely ignored by the computer industry. The BASIC it described was too minimal to be adequate for the expanding capabilities of the new computers. Work on a new standard has begun, with Thomas Kurtz serving as chairman of the technical draft committee.

Kemeny became aware of the problem of proliferating BASICs only after completing his term as president of Dartmouth. It hit home to him when the College Board decided that the language it would use on the advanced college placement exam in computing would be PASCAL. Kemeny was furious and hoped someone would write a version of BASIC that would be considered an improvement over PASCAL. In the summer of 1983 he and Kurtz decided to do the job themselves.

Critics of BASIC have noted that while ideal for short programs, it can lead to confusion if long programs are written; this is especially true when the GO TO command, enabling programmers to instruct a computer to jump from one program section to another, is used. Because it was not written as a structured language, BASIC cannot be broken up into discrete parts, so it is more difficult to read, modify, and debug. (Kemeny and Kurtz have not permitted their students to use GO TO statements for many years.)

With PASCAL gaining increasing acceptance in the high schools because it was structured, and BASIC more and more in disfavor, Kemeny and Kurtz decided during the summer of 1983 to produce a new version of their original language. They would call it True BASIC. What particularly annoyed Kemeny and Kurtz was that although they had personally turned BASIC into a structured language years earlier, the original BASIC and its unwanted children, the variants, encouraged the impression that BASIC was inferior to the new, structured languages. Soon enough they would remedy that.

True BASIC, the new effort of Kemeny and Kurtz, was shipped on March 5, 1985. A more powerful language than BASIC, it incorporates interactive graphics—the original BASIC did not have graphics—a window manager, formatting tools, and a high-level debugger. It has an interface and command structure that is identical regardless of what computer is being used; this was meant to overcome problems that arose with the original BASIC, requiring different versions for different computers. The Kemeny-Kurtz goal, in short, was to eliminate the babble of BASIC. Kemeny and Kurtz were gambling that graphics capabilities would entice current BASIC users to switch to True BASIC, as would the fact that the new program was to conform to the proposed ANSI standards.

Kemeny is chairman and Kurtz vice-chairman of True BASIC, Incorporated, with headquarters in an office on the main street of Hanover, New Hampshire, near the Dartmouth campus. Kemeny and Kurtz hope that True BASIC will replace PASCAL as the major language taught in computer science departments. Kemeny feels that at least it will give them a choice. The two authors will not be as charitable with the new language as they were with BASIC; they have copyrighted True BASIC. Kemeny insists, however, that they are not out to get rich; they want most of all to provide a good version of BASIC for schools and colleges. True BASIC has been published by Addison-Wesley and sold at the outset for $149.90.

In May 1986 True BASIC, Inc., introduced the Kemeny/Kurtz Math Series, a line of high school and college-level software packages for a number of personal computers. Two months later the firm began shipping a new version of True BASIC to support the Commodore Amiga.

In June 1986 Kemeny received some good news. He had been given the Computer Pioneer Award by the Computer Society of the Institute of Electrical and Electronics Engineers, in recognition of his contributions to computer science.

Meanwhile, Tom Kurtz has only one nightmare. It is that the experience with BASIC will be repeated with True BASIC, that someone will write a rotten implementation of the new language. So far, his bad dream has not come true.

Gary Kildall

Making It Easier to Use a Computer— with CP/M

23

In the early 1970s—the infancy of the personal computer age— computer companies were popping up, seemingly ten a day, build- ing microcomputer systems and eager for software for their machines. They had one big problem: their interfaces, controllers, and disk drives were incompatible with existing software. A com- puter manufacturer had no alternative but to have his own propri- etary software designed, for the control and management of the interior of his particular computer. Programs written for one ma- chine could not easily be switched to another; users required retrain- ing to switch from one machine to another. Standardization of computer operating systems had been a dream for a long time. But with the drop in the cost of hardware and the concurrent rise in demand for software, the call for a means of making the equipment converge became clamorous. That was where CP/M came in, Gary Kildall's revolutionary operating system—which was, by his own admission, not the best-designed program.

It was by no means the only operating system around. But it was special. CP/M—Control Program for Microcomputers—was the first disk-based systems software product designed for mi- crocomputers. Until its advent, a personal computer user would have to write a program, or copy another user's, to do the routine things one expects from an operating system. But now, in Gary Kildall's marvelous new program, the personal computer user had at his disposal an operating system that would work on any 8-bit computer, as long as it had 16K of memory and contained an 8080, 8085, or Z80 CPU.

CP/M caught on because it was easy to adapt, because it eliminated the need for manufacturers to design their own individual operating systems, and because it was, at the time of its introduction, the only operating system designed to control floppy-disk drives. In Kildall's words, CP/M "carried the basic building blocks" that enabled the equipment of the whole computer industry to become more uniform. In time some two thousand computer firms would use the program to one extent or another. By 1979 CP/M had become the de facto industry standard for computers based on 8-bit microprocessors.

Gary Kildall is one of the major figures in the computer software field. He has for the past decade been associated with Digital Research of Monterey, California: he founded the firm and is its chairman, president, and chief executive officer. Since 1984, however, he has reduced his role at Digital in order to explore the possibilities in optical-disk publishing, through his new venture, KnowledgeSet Corporation.

Kildall was born on May 19, 1942, in Seattle, Washington, where he lived until he was twenty-seven. No star student in high school, he preferred working on gadgets and cars. He designed and built an automobile burglar alarm, a machine to practice Morse code using a tape recorder, and a flip-flop binary switch; his tinkering with telephones bordered on the obsession that latter-day hackers have found with computers. But it was electronics that interested him the most.

Beginning in 1960, for two years prior to college Kildall taught at his father's navigation school in Seattle. There he acquired a strong interest in mathematics. But navigation was a field rooted in the old technology; college promised a taste of the new. He went to the University of Washington, at first intending to become a high school mathematics teacher. His interest in numerical analysis led him directly to computers. During his junior year he took a couple of courses in computer programming—and that decided him on his future. He had begun his studies in numerical analysis using old-fashioned hand calculators, but by the time he had completed his course work he had dabbled in FORTRAN programming. Bitten by the computer bug, he spent nights working at the university's computer center.

In 1962, Kildall married Dorothy McEwen. After more than twenty years together, the couple separated; they have two children.

With the Vietnam war on, Kildall was liable to be drafted into the army. He joined the naval reserves so that he could continue with his schooling, spending two summers at Newport, Rhode Island, in Officer's Candidate School. In 1967 he received a bachelor's degree in computer science; he stayed on at the University of Washington in the graduate computer science program. At the university's Computer Center Kildall worked evenings on a Burroughs 5500 computer. He learned many interesting concepts from it, including a mass-storage allocation technique. Late at night the machine was virtually his own. He handled the maintenance of the ALGOL compiler for the Burroughs 5500, and this provided him with experience in compiling—the focal point of his graduate studies.

On receiving his master's degree in 1969, Kildall was called into active military service and given the choice of going on a destroyer to Vietnam or teaching computer science at the Naval Postgraduate School in Monterey, California. "It took me a couple of microseconds to make a decision about that." For the next three years, while teaching computer science to naval officers, he pursued his doctorate, completing it in May 1972. His research was on compiler code optimization; his dissertation was entitled "Global Flow Analysis." Flow analysis is used to determine how to make machine code as concise as possible.

After a brief period at the University of Washington he returned to Monterey to continue teaching at the Naval Postgraduate School as a civilian associate professor. There he found the inaccessibility of computers frustrating. One always had to go through time sharing or computer operators who were usually hostile. Kildall turned to Intel's microcomputer systems.

His acquaintance with the Intel's devices came about in the following way. Shortly after receiving his doctorate in 1972, Kildall had come upon a note on a bulletin board at the University of Washington advertising a microcomputer for $25. He purchased it, a 4-bit microprocessor known as the Intel 4004—it was the very first computer on a chip. Until then he had been working with an IBM System/360 mainframe at the naval school that had cost $3 million. Mostly for fun he wrote a simulator and assembler for the 4004 on the System/360 mainframe. Kildall had bought the $25 chip, not because he thought the microprocessor would soon replace the huge mainframes, but rather because this was a new technology that one ought to explore more fully. But how? He asked Intel to send him the 4004 manual.

Kildall planned to use the chip to build a navigation calculator. His father had always wanted a device that could compute navigational triangles. Kildall tried to write some arithmetic subroutines on the 4004 but soon realized that its instruction set was very limiting. He went to Intel to ask if they were interested in the programming he was doing on the 4004. Although navigation applications didn't particularly interest Intel, they found his mathematics programs intriguing.

For the next several years Kildall consulted for Intel part-time, while continuing to teach at the Naval Postgraduate School. First he convinced some Intel people to exchange his 4004 simulator for an early personal computer, the Sim-04 (which had the 4004 chip and other electronic circuitry). Possessing much of what a mainframe had, the Sim-04 contained a central processing unit, memory, and input/output capability. For the input/output it needed a teletypewriter with a paper tape reader/punch. Toward the end of 1973 Kildall developed a simulator for Intel's new 8-bit microprocessor, the 8008. He persuaded the firm that it required a systems implementation language tailored to the 8008. This was what he would call a Programming Language for Microcomputers, or PL/M. When PL/M came out in 1973, it was well received. It was used a good deal for developing systems software such as word processors, editors, and assemblers. Kildall then began working on a variant of PL/M for the 8080 microprocessor—the chip that replaced the 8008 and truly began the microcomputer revolution.

The need for time-sharing systems decreased significantly. Performing calculations or handling data could be done just as well with a microprocessor chip as with a mainframe. Still, using a high-level language like PL/M was expensive. Microprocessor systems did not use magnetic tape as did mainframes. They still used the more unwieldy punched paper tape devices, which made them much slower. A connection to a time-sharing service was required, and that could be costly. During the summer of 1975, for example, while working on a project for Signetics, Kildall paid a time-sharing service a total of $25,000—his fee for the entire project. Kildall's goal was to put the kind of programming language on a microcomputer that would make time sharing unnecessary. A back-up storage device was needed. The major challenge was to put a disk drive on a small computer—thus providing it with relatively fast mass storage, making it unnecessary to turn to the less desirable forms of memory. The dawn of CP/M was about to break.

Disk drives had been used in mainframe computers since 1956; at first they were two feet in diameter. A controller, in fact a circuit board, was the device that linked the disk drive to the computer. Disk drives were superior to magnetic tape: one had to wait for hundreds of yards of tape to pass by a fixed point to get at a particular piece of information on the reel, but one could access any information in a matter of seconds using the disk. A derivative of the disk drive called the floppy disk was invented in 1972. It would become the dominant storage medium for personal computers; but through the early 1970s they used paper tape, running at ten characters per second. Disk-drive performance was equivalent to reading paper tape at the rate of 25,000 characters per second.

When Kildall embarked on his new project in late 1973, cheap floppy disks had just become available. Al Shugart, the founder of Shugart Associates, was a major supplier of floppy-disk drives. Kildall contacted Shugart Associates and told them he wanted to put a disk drive on a small computer system and then use that as a back-up storage device for PL/M development. Sensing that Kildall's idea would be good for Shugart Associates, the company gave him a used $500 drive. He labored hard to get the drive hooked up to a computer, but what was needed was a controller. Kildall spent a month trying to build a controller, with no luck. He then tried to connect his computer to a cassette recorder, but that didn't work either. He noted later that had the cassette recorder worked as a replacement for paper tape, he might not have explored floppy-disk storage—which was to become a major feature of CP/M. Kildall had a controller designed, but it cost $2,000, four times as much as the $500 disk drive. He made some further efforts at building a controller, but without a background in electrical engineering he could not do it.

Kildall was not especially interested in hardware. He preferred working on the operating program that would be required for diskette storage management once a way was found to connect the drive to the microprocessor. So he started to write software in his PL/M language, using a simulation run on a larger computer system. The software provided a high-level access to the diskette and was a compact operating system. Under simulation the operating system worked, but Kildall could not be certain it would work with a floppy disk until he had a controller. In 1974 he enlisted the aid of a friend, John Torode (later president of Digital Micro Systems), who had just obtained his doctorate at the University of Washington. Torode succeeded in getting the drive to work. Kildall went back to Shugart Associates and persuaded them to give them another drive, which he put in a box with the controller and the development system. Once the hardware interface was built, the whole system came together and operated pretty well. This was the first CP/M system. It took Kildall a month or two to write it. One of its great advantages was that it required only 3K.

Kildall knew that having an operating system was not enough for program development: he added extra utilities such as a text editor, a dynamic debugger, and a simple assembler. It was not until 1975 that he had a full set of utilities for CP/M, which included PIP (Peripheral Interchange Program) for copying files. With CP/M it was possible to transfer data from a disk to the microcomputer, print data on a printer, and perform all operations that the microcomputer system was physically capable of handling.

Kildall and Torode sensed that having floppy disks connected to small computers was a fantastic thing. But should they undertake the risks of marketing their system? Where exactly was its market? The first commercial use of CP/M was not terribly successful. Very few recall Gary Kildall's astrology machine. Yet it was that machine that launched the CP/M. In1975 Kildall ran into Ben Cooper, president of Micromation, a San Francisco firm. Cooper wanted to build an astrology machine, and he hired Kildall to handle the mathematics necessary for calculating star positions. Kildall did the assembler, the debugger, and the BASIC interpreter, using his CP/M system. Once at the machine someone could inset a quarter and then turn the dials to his birthday. The machine would print out the right astrology chart. Some machines were placed around San Francisco, but the dials were very complicated and the paper often jammed.

Most of the initial buyers of CP/M were hobbyists. The Homebrew Computer Club, an amateur group that began meeting in March 1975, bought one that year. These were computer buffs who had built their own systems with their own controllers—no two alike. Then in 1976, Jim Warren, editor of the computer hobbyist magazine *Dr. Dobb's Journal,* and the future founder of the West Coast Computer Faire, suggested to Kildall that he sell CP/M through ads in the *Journal.* So he did—and at $75 it caught on quickly.

That same year Kildall gave up his post at the Naval Postgraduate School and, along with his wife, founded Digital Research. (The firm started out under the name Intergalactic Digital Research, but the first word was dropped after a Sausalito firm with the name Digital Research closed.) They began selling CP/M in packages. Sales were slow at first. Some of the early clients landed big bargains. One firm, Gnat Computers, purchased the right to use CP/M as the operating system for any product it developed. Only a year later a CP/M license would cost in the tens of thousands of dollars. By the end of 1976, however, Digital Research was flooded with orders for the product. Within a short time some hundred firms were using CP/M. By the late 1970s over nine hundred firms had become clients. CP/M became the standard for which most application programs were written. This lasted until the early 1980s, when MS-DOS replaced it as the most popular operating system. Thanks to CP/M, Digital Research for a time had a virtual monopoly on the operating software that told 8-bit computers how to store and retrieve data.

Kildall and his wife, Dorothy, had no previsions of great success. Says Dorothy McEwen, "There was never any thought of having a big company. It was just something that happened. It seemed like the right thing to do." She doubted, that first year in 1976, whether the new firm would earn more than $15,000; in fact it earned between $60,000 and $80,000. During the first five to six years the firm doubled its earnings each year. In 1981 sales grew to $5.2 million. Three years later they reached $44.6 million.

No real marketing of CP/M was done. It was, in Dorothy McEwen's words, "kind of like a grass-roots effort," aided by the pleasant fact that competition didn't exist for the first four years. The principal obstacle was getting clients away from the idea that they needed to develop unique operating systems or to develop something in house. Digital Research had to convince potential clients that it was to their advantage to have a generic operating system, as that would ensure that applications would work.

The real breakthrough came in 1977 when a San Leandro, California, firm named IMSAI purchased CP/M for $25,000. At that point Kildall had produced about five versions of CP/M, all customized for different computers with different disk drives. He sat down one afternoon with Glen Ewing, an ex-student of his and now an IMSAI employee, and said, "Look, I'm going to make this one little piece of it [CP/M] called the BIOS—Basic Input/Output System—which will be tailorable to any kind of operating environment that you want." The BIOS became the customized portion that people would modify themselves to make their disk drive work with their computer system, and that's what made CP/M more universal. Though there were other operating systems that could work on more than one computer, thanks to the BIOS feature CP/M was easy to adapt. After the IMSAI purchase, orders rolled in. Kildall stopped counting CP/M sales after the first million. He estimates that over 200 million copies now exist. By the mid-1980s it was running on 300 computer models, and there were 3,000 software programs available for CP/M machines.

In 1980 IBM decided to get into the personal computer business. For its planned 16-bit personal computer, it needed an operating program, and it somehow got the impression that CP/M was owned by Microsoft, not Digital Research. Hoping to build an Apple-like computer, with small (5¼-inch) disk drives and software similar to Apple's, IBM turned to Microsoft to purchase CP/M. Bill Gates, chairman of Microsoft, could not, of course, sell CP/M to IBM. So the day after their visit to the Seattle headquarters of Microsoft, the IBM representatives were in Monterey to see Kildall.

He says he had no forewarning. Some reports have it that Kildall, who enjoys flying planes, was up in the clouds the day the IBM people arrived. But Kildall insists this is far from the truth: he was away on business until the afternoon of that day, and the IBM people met Dorothy McEwen, who handled contacts for Digital Research. IBM, according to Kildall, "threw a nondisclosure agreement at her, which is a typical IBM thing which basically scares . . . everybody." Kildall says IBM wanted to have in writing that it could use any ideas it heard from Digital. When Kildall, returning from his trip, discovered that IBM and his wife were held up on the nondisclosure accord, he decided that negotiations should be adjourned until the two Kildalls returned from a planned week's cruise in the Caribbean—although he favored signing the agreement. In the end, the deal was scratched. Kildall suspects that Gates "made what he considered a very good business decision."

In 1981 IBM introduced its first PC, with PC-DOS (its proprietary version of Microsoft's MS-DOS). When Kildall saw it, "I was totally amazed at the similarity between PC-DOS and CP/M. In fact, it was so similar that the system calls were the same. I got very livid about it with IBM and with Microsoft. Here we were, in good faith, in negotiations with IBM and they came in with a complete ripoff. There was absolutely no question that to anyone in the industry who looked at it, all the way down to the command lines [it was the same]. I sat down and used it with absolutely no documentation whatsoever. It was just an incredible thing for me to see happen."

Kildall spoke to the IBM people, informing them that he had seen the product and it was simply "a CP/M interface externally and internally." Calling it unfair, he told them, "I don't know how you can go out and take someone else's invention and just basically copy it." Though he was aware, he said, that the giant-sized IBM "can probably blow me over any way you want," he still failed to understand how IBM had done such a thing. IBM's response, according to Kildall, was that its people did not realize that the operating system was so close to CP/M. (Seeking a response from IBM to Kildall's assertions, the author was told in a letter from IBM's John H. Mihalec, Program Administrator, Information Services, in March 1987, "Any suggestion that IBM acted in an illegal, unethical, or improper manner in acquiring the rights to the operating system software for the IBM PC is absolutely false.")

Kildall decided against taking any legal measures. Digital Research, then earning $5 million a year, was not about to sue IBM. "That's the last thing you want to do," says Kildall. Rather than seek compensation from IBM, Kildall asked for a chance to introduce his new 16-bit operating system, CP/M 86, into IBM's software library. IBM was happy to oblige. A problem arose, however: when CP/M 86 was put on the market in the fall of 1981, it was priced at $250, while PC-DOS sold for $25. So, as Kildall says, "CP/M 86 basically died on the vine."

The penetration of IBM into the personal computer market affected Digital's approach to operating software. Digital introduced Concurrent CP/M in early 1983, with its advantage that a computer user could do several things at once. For instance, he could write a letter while the computer was printing out a tax return. It sold well because IBM at that time did not have a multitask operating system. Without PC-DOS compatibility, however, sales grew only to a certain point. Then, according to Kildall, a crucial decision was reached: "We said, 'Well, we'll go along with this if that's what people want. . . . PC-DOS was modeled after CP/M in the first place. Why not just go back there and make CP/M completely compatible with PC-DOS?" Thus was born Concurrent PC-DOS, a multitask conversion of Concurrent CP/M. The product was a big success when it came out in 1984.

Kildall works mainly at home ("it's just a little calmer atmosphere"), going to the office for meetings. His former wife Dorothy McEwen says of him: "He's a technical person, not a business person. He gets all encompassed by the project he's working on and he's quite good at it. If he has to stay up all night to work on a project, fine. He'll work 100 hours a week or whatever, because he's so involved in it, he's enthusiastic about it."

By the mid-1980s, Kildall, always looking for a new barrier to break in technology, saw a future in the connection betwen personal computers and videodisk players. Vidlink, Kildall's new product, links videodisk players, color television, and personal computers, offering a remarkably large storage capacity. One disk alone can hold 180 rolls of microfilm or 54,000 still video images. Another new product, KnowledgeDisc, is a videodisk intended to work on a remote-control unit or a videodisk player. Kildall has also been working with optical storage on CD ROMs—Compact-Disk Read-Only Memories—with the goal of storing ten encyclopedias on a single disk. "That's fun," he notes. In 1985 Kildall's firm Activenture announced that it planned to publish *Grolier's Encyclopedia* in a CD ROM format. One of Kildall's dreams was about to come true.

William Gates

Engine of the Small Computer Revolution

24

A magazine article was the catalyst. But the goal had long been there: to make computers accessible to everyone. The article appeared in January 1975—a date imprinted in computer buffs' memories as the dawning of the age of the personal computer. The cover story in that month's *Popular Electronics* introduced the very first personal computer. But a personal computer without a user-friendly programming language was machinery that few would want to touch. Whoever could come up with such a language for use with these new toys would push the revolution forward by a huge leap. Into that role stepped a young Harvard student named Bill Gates.

He was nineteen years old when, with the help of partner Paul Allen, he adapted BASIC for use in personal computers. Accordingly, as much as anyone else, he made the small computer revolution possible. He enabled the personal computer industry to reach millions of offices and homes—overnight. His effort made his own Microsoft BASIC the lingua franca for computer users. The secret of Gates's success has been an ability to write bug-free computer programs—slick, tight code, in Gates's terse phrase. In 1984 his operating software was being used by two million computers, making it the effective industry standard. Gates's MS-DOS replaced Gary Kildall's CP/M as the most popular operating system.

Microsoft, the company Gates built from scratch, was the first personal computer software firm. It helped to establish the microcomputer software industry. Gates says he loves being at the center of things, and that is precisely where this software genius has been. He may look like a graduate student in need of a square meal, with his sweater patched at the elbows, scuffed shoes, and ginger hair hanging over his steel-rimmed glasses, but he is the tycoon of American software. Microsoft doubled in size every year during its first nine years. With forty percent of his company's shares, Gates was said to be worth $390 million after Microsoft went public in the spring of 1986. Nearly every major computer manufacturer employs him. In January 1984 Microsoft was providing its operating system to more than ninety percent of the IBM personal computers and IBM-compatible equipment—or forty-five percent of the business microcomputers made in the United States. Located in Seattle, Washington, the firm had gone from $4 million in software sales in 1980 to $162.6 million in 1985.

Bill Gates's father is a prominent Seattle lawyer; his mother has served on numerous corporate, charitable, and civil boards. Gates was born in Seattle on October 28, 1955. He taught himself programming at age thirteen, having taken up computers in 1967 as a seventh-grader at the private Lakeside School in Seattle. His school's Mothers' Club had bought computer time on a time-sharing computer. Gates and a ninth-grader named Paul Allen became entranced. Gates set up a class-scheduling program to make sure that he took courses with the prettiest girls; a Lakeside math teacher would later recall that Bill had the ability to see shortcuts. For a summer's work of devising schedules he earned $4,200.

In the late 1960s Gates and some other Seattle teenagers would ride their bicycles each afternoon to the Computer Center Corporation office, where they searched for errors in the programming being run on the center's computer. They produced a 300-page tome called *The Problem Report Book* and eventually went on the firm's payroll. Gates had a mischievous side. He figured out how to cause an operating system to crash, and got into trouble when he caused the crash of Control Data Corporation's CYBERNET computer system. After a CDC reprimand he decided to give up computers, and he did so for a year. Working at computers, he recalls, "was not a mainstream thing. I couldn't imagine spending the rest of my life at it. I didn't see myself as a hacker forever."

The youngster could not stay aloof from computers for long. He and Allen put their talents to work for the public welfare. They were asked to analyze electrical power requirements around the Northwest and Canada. To do this they computerized the electricity grid for the Bonneville Power Administration. Gates recalls gleefully that no one knew then that he and Allen were only in high school. Still a fifteen-year-old, Gates, along with Allen, founded a small firm called Traf-O-Data that was to study the traffic patterns for the small communities around Seattle. They used Intel's 8008 chip. Though the firm had earned $20,000 by the time Gates reached tenth grade, business dropped off, apparently because engineers were reluctant to buy the services of someone so youthful.

The next venture brought better luck. Having heard of their skills, a large software firm, TRW, in Vancouver, Washington, offered Gates and Allen $20,000 a year each to work in a software development group. Gates took a year-long leave from high school during his senior year to go to work for TRW. When work diminished, he entered Harvard—to do "normal stuff," in Gates's words. He was planning to stay away from computers. Allen went to work as a systems programmer for Honeywell, near Boston.

After Gates entered Harvard in the fall of 1973, Allen challenged him to develop a BASIC interpreter for the Intel 8008, but Gates soon decided that the 8008 instruction set was not powerful enough for BASIC. Allen next urged that they start a microcomputer firm. The two had already spent $360 to purchase one of the very first microcomputer chips.

The turning point in their young careers came when they read the January 1975 issue of *Popular Electronics*. The Altair microcomputer, based on the 8080 chip, made by an Albuquerque, New Mexico, firm called MITS, and selling for $350, appeared on the cover. Allen was the first to see the article. He noticed a copy of the magazine at a newsstand and hastily tracked down Gates. Here was the first truly cheap computer! Allen ran through Harvard Square waving the article in front of Gates, issuing a friendly warning that the train was leaving, and if the two of them didn't get to work, they would not be aboard.

Gates's problem was whether to stick to his present studies in pursuit of the legal career his parents wished for him, or give full attention to computers. The latter won out; the two young men wanted to make sure they wouldn't miss what was happening. "We realized," Gates recalls, "that the revolution might happen without us. After we saw that article, there was no question of where our life would focus." To anyone who knew computers then, it was instantly clear that the Altair required more than anything else a BASIC interpreter, to permit users to write programs in a high-level language rather than in machine code. Allen proposed to Gates that the two try to write a BASIC—the simple, high-level computer programming language—for the Altair. At least one minicomputer firm had insisted that it was impossible to write a high-level language that would run on a personal computer. But the two young men wanted to give it a try. They informed MITS of their plan.

Allen and Gates spent February and March of 1975 working in Gates's small dormitory room at Harvard. Speed was of the essence, for MITS had warned the pair that others were also seeking to adapt BASIC to microcomputers. Because at that time memory was very expensive, they decided to develop a BASIC that would run in less than 4K of memory. The two young men didn't have a microcomputer, so they wrote their own simulator 8080 software on a PDP-10 at the Harvard Computer Center. Gates then worked on an 8080 BASIC interpreter that would run on the simulator.

They had never seen an 8080 chip. Gates and Allen called MITS to say they had nearly completed a BASIC for the Altair. Playing with the truth, they claimed they had already adapted the language to microcomputers. Ed Roberts, the MITS founder who had built the Altair, challenged Gates and Allen to demonstrate their wares: When could they come to Albuquerque to show their BASIC off? Gates took a look at Allen and said with great nonchalance, Oh, two or three weeks. They rushed out and obtained the Intel instruction book. For the next few weeks Gates and Allen spent every day and many sleepless nights working on the program. Sometimes they would doze at the terminal. They had still not actually seen an Altair computer.

Gates wanted to create what he called a "fail-safe BASIC," one that would always indicate a user error—and not simply crash or come up with the wrong result. The software would be put in ROM (read-only memory), which meant it could not be updated. Hence Gates and Allen had to be extra careful that the program did not contain hard-to-detect bugs. The main worry, of course, was that the simulator—the 8080 software written for the PDP-10— might not be correct.

One problem the two young men had was, how did the Altair process characters typed on a keyboard? They had no solution except to ask the Altair people. When they inquired, the Altair personnel, concluding that the two must be serious—no one else had come to them with that question—quickly supplied the answer. Allen arranged to fly to Albuquerque with a paper tape to load into the Altair. But during the journey he realized he had no bootstrap routine to do the loading. So he quickly found some scrap paper and wrote the loader program while the plane was descending.

Gates, waiting back in Cambridge, was nervous. He and Allen had spent weeks planning for this one moment. If Allen failed, a second opportunity might never come. Something inside him told him that it wouldn't work, that something would in the end go wrong. But he was mistaken: BASIC ran on the first try. Allen phoned to tell him. Gates saw clearly, even then, that computers would soon catch on in schools and elsewhere because of his breakthrough. In writing BASIC for the Altair, Gates and Allen were creating an industry standard, one that would hold the field for the next six years.

Allen was the first one to move to Albuquerque, becoming software director at MITS. Though he would never become a MITS employee, Gates spent much of his time there as well, working in a hotel across the street from the company offices. Roberts signed a royalty arrangement with the two young men for their BASIC. But Gates and Allen looked for other customers as well.

Gates dropped out of Harvard at the end of his sophomore year in 1975, despite objections from his parents. He actually took a leave of absence, but it seemed clear that if things worked out, the leave would become permanent. It was then that Gates and Allen formed Microsoft. Within eighteen months the two had made a few hundred thousand dollars for their new firm. They were writing programs for Apple and Commodore. During the first year Gates and Allen expanded BASIC so that it would run on other microcomputers. Their first release was called 4K BASIC: it allowed the user to run a 50-line BASIC program using four of MITS's 1K memory boards. The interpreter occupied about 3.2K and did full floating-point arithmetic. A family of four upwardly compatible BASICs developed, including Disk Extended BASIC, with an operating system that permitted the use of disk input/output either from programs or from BASIC's command mode. There were other Microsoft innovations, including peek and poke, and paint.

Not everything went smoothly. Gates discovered that some people objected to paying $200 for his BASIC. They figured out how to pirate it through paper tape copies. Because of that, Gates complained, his royalties had diminished to the point where he was making only $2 an hour. Gates became the first programmer to draw attention to the problem of piracy. He did so in his "Open Letter to Hobbyists," published in the January 1976 *Homebrew Computer Club Newsletter*.

By the end of 1976 MITS appeared increasingly unattractive. Gates and MITS got into a legal controversy over who owned Gates's BASIC. Roberts contended that he had paid Gates and Allen $200,000 for the software, but Gates disagreed. He and Allen prevailed in arbitration. In 1978 Microsoft moved from Albuquerque to Bellevue, a small town across Lake Washington from Seattle. It grew and grew. The original BASIC written for the Altair remained its most popular product, but Microsoft also sold FORTRAN and COBOL for personal computers.

Then in July 1980 came another key moment in the story of Bill Gates. IBM, planning its own personal computer, was on the phone to him, asking if it could send some researchers from its Boca Raton, Florida, office to talk about Microsoft. Gates happily agreed. Dressed in three-piece suits, the two IBM employees appeared at his Bellevue office. For the occasion Gates had even put on a coat and tie. He hoped the IBM representatives were interested in his BASIC, but nothing fruitful came out of that first meeting. In August the IBM people called to request another meeting. Gates suggested a time in the following week. But there was an urgency in their voices: they said they would have their men on a plane in two hours. When they arrived, the IBM representatives told him of the highly secret plans for Project Chess, the IBM personal computer. Something positive did come out of that second meeting. Gates became a consultant to IBM. He was to file a report on the design of a microcomputer to work with Microsoft software.

The IBM representatives wanted to acquire an operating system. Mistakenly believing that Gates owned CP/M—Gary Kildall's operating system, which had become the industry standard—they wanted to know if Gates would sell it to them. Gates said he didn't own CP/M and sent them to Kildall. When IBM and Kildall failed to reach agreement, IBM returned to Gates.

IBM asked Gates to design the operating system for the new machine—what would become the incredibly popular PC. The IBM PC was going to be not 8-bit but 16-bit; since there was no 16-bit software available, it made sense to design a brand-new operating system. Gates went to work on what would become MS-DOS—Microsoft Disk Operating System. He filed his report personally in Boca Raton in September, and in November he got the contract. No outsider had worked so closely with IBM on a computer. IBM began by pledging Gates to secrecy. He was given a deadline of March 1981, IBM personnel anguishing over the fact that the project was already three months behind schedule.

IBM wanted no leaks on Project Chess. Gates chose a small room in the middle of Microsoft's offices in the old National Bank building in Bellevue, and got to work. The room had no windows and no ventilation, and sometimes the temperature would rise to 100 degrees. For Gates the experience was trying. He flew back and forth frequently between Seattle and Boca Raton with no real guarantee against IBM's canceling the project at any minute. Despite the intense time pressure, and to Gates's considerable annoyance, some members of his team insisted on taking time off to watch some space shuttle launches in Florida.

The project was a success. Gates had managed to perfect the operating system that would control the IBM PC. He persuaded IBM to give up its secret design specifications: it agreed to use an open system for the PC, with the result that others, knowing how the operating system functioned, could build software for it much more easily. Some hundred firms, eager to be IBM compatible, obtained licenses for MS-DOS, and it very quickly became the major operating system for personal computers in the United States. Over two million copies of MS-DOS had been sold as of the spring of 1984, six times as many as CP/M.

Others turned to Gates as well. Apple asked him to develop software for its Macintosh. He helped design the Radio Shack Model 100. In Japan he introduced the MSX (for Microsoft Extended Basic) design, a way of standardizing the building of low-end home computers. Gates hoped that MSX might become the standard for the $2.8-billion-a-year home computer market. What was different about MSX was that the basic computer remained the same, and so software programs and peripherals designed for one brand would work with any other brand. In early 1983 Microsoft was approached by NEC, Matsushita, and Sony to write and license unique versions of Microsoft BASIC that would run on their new home computers. In turn, Gates asked the three firms to accept one set of software and hardware specifications. Within four months a total of eighteen of the big Japanese consumer electronics firms—all the major companies except NEC and Sharp—had agreed. Still, there was some question whether the MSX computers would be considered of high enough quality to compete successfully in the American home computer market. And indeed, when the home computer market nosedived in 1984 it no longer appeared realistic for the Japanese to export MSX computers to the United States. Beginning in the mid-1980s Microsoft has gone in for applications software, including Flight Simulator, which permits someone to sit at a computer and simulate the piloting of a plane; Multiplan, a spreadsheet program; and Microsoft Word, for word processing.

What is Bill Gates like? He reportedly has a temper, and he is fiercely competitive. He knew a dozen years ago that microcomputers would be a big hit on the market—and, just as significantly, that software would be the main part of microcomputers. Gates has driven himself hard. Between 1978 and 1984 he took only fifteen days' vacation—four of them at a Phoenix tennis ranch in 1982. Gates and Allen, the two Microsoft cofounders, managed to agree on nearly everything but prices: Allen wanted to charge what the market would bear, while Gates preferred a low price. Gates has usually got his way. Allen, in fact, has recently left the firm. One drawback of Gates's success: it leaves him no time for programming. He has to deal with the business.

The average age of Microsoft employees is twenty-six. The firm's goal, according to one vice-president, is to be to software what IBM has been to hardware. Bill Gates has come close. In fact, some would say he is already there. Gates has marked out for himself those areas of Microsoft for which he will have responsibility: strategy, software development, handling important manufacturers, motivating people, and Japan.

For some time Gates has been a leader in the research into CD (compact disk) technology for computers. In March 1987 Microsoft introduced on the market a $295 CD called Bookshelf, which contains digitized versions of ten basic reference volumes, including *Bartlett's Familiar Quotations, Roget's Thesaurus,* the *World Almanac,* and the *U.S. Zip Code Directory*. Bookshelf, together with a special disk drive and a personal computer, affords a writer immediate access to a treasure trove of information without having to interrupt word processing. A single CD delivers to the computer screen as much material as can be stored on 1,500 floppy disks.

The man who has put all this together is still in his early thirties. His peers call him brilliant, his dominance of the software field is a fact of life that few question. Now that Bill Gates has played such a major role in revolutionizing the computer industry, the question remains: What will he come up with next?

Dennis Ritchie   Kenneth Thompson

Dennis Ritchie and Kenneth Thompson

Creators of UNIX

25

"Our intent was to create a pleasant computing environment for ourselves, and our hope was that others liked it." Thus spoke Dennis Ritchie when he and Ken Thompson were presented with the 1983 Turing Award for developing and implementing the UNIX operating system.

UNIX. An awkward sort of name, not the kind Ritchie or Thompson would have chosen had they been interested in marketing their operating system to the widest possible audience. The name was actually a play on that of an earlier operating system called Multics, which the two men had used during their first years as researchers at Bell Laboratories in the 1960s. It was as a replacement for Multics—as an aid in their own work—that Ritchie and Thompson devised UNIX. Marketing it was far from their minds; they were simply trying to make life easier for themselves. But others eventually realized that the Ritchie-Thompson operating system could make computing more pleasant for them as well. As a result, beginning in the mid-1970s, when it was first given public exposure, UNIX inched its way toward a success that would rock the computer industry. It became one of the most popular operating systems for computers, particularly large and middle-sized ones, and had a major impact on the engineering and academic community. While there was doubt that it would ever replace Bill Gates's MS-DOS as the standard for personal computers, UNIX had by 1982 become, by Dennis Ritchie's estimate, the most widely transported operating system. Among the computers using it by the mid-1980s were the DEC VAX minicomputer, the 68000 and 8086 microprocessors, two versions of the IBM 370 mainframe, and the CRAY–2. UNIX offers so many advantages as an operating system that it has been called the Swiss army knife of software.

One of UNIX's main features is that it is multitasking and multiuser—a number of users can work on the machine on different tasks at the same time. In 1985 some 277,000 computer systems in the United States were using UNIX, according to Bruce Kin Huie, senior industry analyst at International Data Corporation, in Framingham, Massachusetts. He projected that figure would grow to nearly 2.1 million in 1990. The estimated total number of software packages available for UNIX was 2,000 by early 1987, as compared to the 300 available two years before.

UNIX caught on for a number of reasons. One was simply that it was, in Dennis Ritchie's words, "the crystallization of the main development of the traditional time-sharing ideas that came out of the sixties. It captured those ideas in a fairly usable way. And it had a number of actually interesting technical ideas." Another crucial reason for its success was its portability. UNIX was portable in the sense that it could be adapted to run on any computer, from a micro to a supercomputer. Most of the other operating systems had been written in an assembly language for a particular machine, making the task of reimplementation for another computer possible, but difficult and costly. UNIX skipped over such problems, and because it did, applications software could be written for UNIX and then used on all sorts of computers from desktops to mainframes, easing the financial and technical burden. In contrast, Gary Kildall's CP/M, the industry standard for personal computers in the 1970s, was tied to a certain chip and so could run only on computers containing that chip.

UNIX appeared at the right time. People were searching for alternatives to the large, centrally administered computer centers, which were remote and difficult to access. Moreover, the advent of the smaller computers, the minis—especially the PDP-11—had spawned a whole new group of computer users who were disappointed with existing operating software. They were ready for UNIX. Most of UNIX was not new, but rather what Ritchie calls "a good engineering application of ideas that had been around in some form and [were now] made convenient to use." Ken Thomp-

---

son estimates that rather than spending ninety percent of his time engaged in non-programming details, thanks to UNIX he spends only forty to fifty percent that way.

When they began their work in 1969, Ritchie and Thompson were not looking to set the computer world on fire. Indeed, nothing of their project was published until 1974. They were surprised at the interest shown in UNIX when it did come into public view, interest that was remarkably high considering that the product was not being marketed aggressively by AT&T at that time. A source license for UNIX, used by firms for high-level programming, cost $43,000, while universities became licensees free of charge, greatly aiding in the popularization of the Ritchie-Thompson invention.

Though Bell had hardly encouraged Ritchie and Thompson to develop UNIX, when the operating system became popular and Bell realized it had a gem, it was glad to have UNIX as one of its trademarks. One Bell executive has pronounced UNIX Bell's second most important invention after the transistor. When asked if he agrees with that assessment, Dennis Ritchie answers modestly, "In terms of work that has received public exposure, even publicity and so forth, it does seem that UNIX is quite an important development."

It all began back in the 1960s when the two men were placed in one of the great research facilities in the world, Bell Laboratories, and given a task so broad in scope, so vague in definition, that it would confound most others. They were simply told to think, specifically to think about problems in computer science. Those were the days of batch processing, when a computer programmer was forced to use mainframe computers that were slow, awkward, and inefficient. Bell Labs in the late 1960s began experimenting with a new computer system that had some distinct advantages over its predecessors. That new system was a multiuser time-sharing system called Multics (for multiplexed information and computing service), developed by General Electric and MIT to run on Honeywell mainframes. It had become a joint project of GE, MIT, and Bell Labs. Bell, however, withdrew from the project when it became too expensive. "Multics," observed Dennis Ritchie a few years ago, "turned into an expensive morass for the labs, because it was sold as an answer to real computing needs, not as just a research project."

Thompson and Ritchie were upset at Bell's decision to end the

Multics project, even though time sharing, as offered by Multics, was still inefficient and software for it not yet available. The post-Multics world at Bell would comprise computers and operating systems that belonged to the old batch-processing culture for the most part—an unfortunate step backward, in the two men's estimation. As Ritchie put it in 1980, "What we wanted to preserve was not just a good environment in which to do programming, but a system around which a fellowship could form. We knew from experience that the essence of communal computing, as supplied by remote-access, time-shared machines, is not just to type programs into a terminal instead of a keypunch, but to encourage close communication."

Multics, though providing an opportunity to use a time-sharing system, was, like the other operating systems around at the time, extremely complicated. It just seemed, says Ritchie, that there was more going on in the systems than was necessary. Nonetheless, Ritchie and Thompson had been spoiled by Multics, and they found the computing environment without it "painful." Says Ritchie, "We had become used to interactive environments where you could actually type things on the machine and get instant responses. It is just more satisfying to work that way. This is as opposed to taking our deck of cards and handing it over a counter, and coming back in an hour, and getting a big pile of listings." UNIX was their response to this situation.

Dennis Ritchie was born on September 9, 1941, in Mount Vernon New York. At age nine he moved to Summit, New Jersey. His father was director of Bell Laboratories' Switching Systems Engineering Laboratory. Ritchie majored in physics at Harvard, graduating in 1963. For the next five years he pursued a doctorate at the same school in applied mathematics, completing a thesis on recursive functions, which, as Ritchie describes it, was "sort of the mathematics of computation, the theory of what machines can possibly do." During his college and graduate years he became interested in computers, but his academic studies led him more toward theory than practical applications. It was while he was in graduate school that Ritchie became involved in Multics; he also worked part-time for Project MAC, the MIT computer time-sharing project, which got off the ground in the 1960s. He never received his doctorate, though he did complete the thesis. His explanation: "I was so bored, I never turned it in." In 1968 Ritchie went to work for Bell Laboratories, where he has been ever since; he and Thompson became attached to the Computer Science Research Department. Their mandate was ambitious, if vague: to investigate interesting problems in computer science.

Ken Thompson was born in New Orleans on February 4, 1943, the son of a navy man who did a lot of traveling. By age two Ken had lived in San Diego, Seattle, San Francisco, Indianapolis, and Kingsville, Texas. As a youngster he hung around a Kingsville radio shop, learning a great deal about electricity and ham radios. The transistor, then a relatively new item, sold for $10 apiece. Thompson, who had been saving up his money to send away for one, was delighted one day to find someone at the radio shop selling them for $1.50 each. He suspected that his father, wishing to forward his son's interests, had paid the man at the radio shop the other $8.50 for each transistor. But he never found out.

Kingsville was a town centered on the oil industry and the King Ranch. There were no telephones, only short-wave radios for the cars going to the oil rigs. The radio shop serviced the radios. Thompson would join the radio shop workers in their visits to the oil rigs and climb up the rigs to get to the radios in need of repair. Another hobby he pursued intensely as a boy was chess; years later, in the 1970s, he would create a piece of chess-playing computer software that became a three-time American champion.

Enrolling in 1960 at the University of California, Berkeley, Thompson majored in electrical engineering. He found work in a computer center in 1962. His job was to write progams as well as to help out when someone had a problem with a program. He worked for two half-year periods in 1963 and 1964 in a work-study program at General Dynamics in San Diego. He graduated from Berkeley in 1965 and received a master's degree in electrical engineering from the same school a year later. But he never used it afterward: "I used to be an avid hacker in an electrical sense, building things. And ever since computers, I find it very similar. Computing is an addiction. Electronics is a similar addiction but not as clean. Much dirtier. Things burn out."

Thompson went to work at Bell Laboratories in 1966. When it became clear that Bell was phasing out Multics, Ritchie and Thompson decided that they would build an operating system themselves. Thompson turned in some proposals to his superiors, but in the light of Bell's disappointing experience with Multics, they were hardly in a sympathetic mood. He was turned down. Determined to go ahead with the project, Thompson scrounged around, coming up with a discarded, obsolete computer, a DEC PDP-7. A fancy graphics terminal, it had been used to connect to one of the mainframe machines in the labs. It had a very fast disk and two terminals—a graphics display and a Teletype machine.

In creating an operating system, Ritchie and Thompson decided the place to start was with the question of how to store data in the machine—that is, the structure of the filing system. "We wrote the code for the manipulations that would run this file system," recalls Ritchie. "In the process it became evident that you needed various commands and software to test out the file system. You can't just sit there, you've got to make files and copy them. And so we wrote a small command interpreter that would be things that you typed to the keyboard, a command to copy files and delete them, do the various operations that you need to work on files. That is the essentials of an operating system: something to read the commands, something to hold the data." At the outset their operating system could not support itself. Notes Ritchie, "We started completely from scratch. There was no software on the machine at all. And the way the programs were written was by having a cross-assembler on the large GE machine. We'd write programs on the GE machine and assemble them, turn them into real, object programs there and punch them out on paper tape, and carry them down to the PDP-7 and load the paper tape in." Looking back on the process, Ritchie calls it "horrible"—"but it worked." Thompson wrote a little assembler on the GE that was actually an assembler for the PDP-7. The two men also wrote a small editor. With these programs in hand, the computer could support itself.

The actual creation of the UNIX system was Thompson's. One of Ritchie's main contributions was the suggestion that devices (such as terminals and tape drives) appear in the file system as files with the same kind of names as other items had. Ritchie notes that while this wasn't new, "it was a little bit novel." Though primitive in comparison with later versions, it was a complete program. After two years of work, the PDP-7 had worn out its usefulness; Thompson had his eye on a larger computer, the PDP-11, one of DEC's most impressive machines.

Ritchie and Thompson knew it was unlikely that their work would be usable by others as long as it ran only on an antiquated computer of which only a few existed. But for Thompson to tell his superiors that he wanted a new machine so that he could build a new operating system or get involved in a time-sharing project would be inopportune, given Bell's recent experience with Multics. So Thompson and his colleagues, learning that the labs' patent department was hunting for a word-processing system, penned a proposal for what amounted to an office automation system, though at the time no one called it that. Thompson called it an editing system for office tasks, and though the proposal first met with a negative reaction, it was eventually approved in May 1970. The new PDP-11 arrived toward the end of the summer. It was of little use, though. Its disk did not come until December, and the computer had no software. In time the patent department took over the PDP-11, and Thompson was able to purchase a larger one and a PDP-10 memory management unit. That provided the real launch for UNIX.

By the end of 1971 UNIX had been sufficiently developed that Ritchie and Thompson could test it with its first true users: three typists entering patent applications. The experiment was a success, and the Bell patent department adopted UNIX, becoming the first of many groups at the labs to give backing to the work of the two researchers. Part of the initial popularity of UNIX at Bell was due, in all fairness, to the PDP-11. The need for computer applications at Bell increased at this time, record keeping and trouble reports accounting for most of it and requiring multiprogramming or time sharing. The PDP-11 was selected to perform many of these tasks, because, as Thompson notes, "it had lots of good peripherals and was reliable, small, and cheap—a typical hardware kind of decision. When they couldn't make it go with the DEC software, they'd look around, hear about UNIX, and invariably adopt it."

UNIX grew slowly but steadily, both within and outside of Bell Laboratories. A development group was set up to support projects inside Bell, and several research versions were licensed for use on the outside. Thus UNIX was one of those rare products that were not rushed into the marketplace. Because of its unusually long gestation period, lasting essentially a decade, from 1969 to 1979, it came to users as a product that had been used, had been improved upon by its developers, and had the stamp of approval of a large number of users at Bell Laboratories and in most prominent computer science departments. When Ritchie and Thompson had completed the initial project, UNIX had no immediate impact. Few people outside Bell Labs knew of its existence until 1973. It was only in October of that year that UNIX was first publicly described at the Symposium on Operating Systems Principles held at IBM in Yorktown Heights.

The achievement of portability came even later—not until 1977. It meant a big step forward, and many at Bell had been interested in it. Ritchie and Thompson, in trying to move programs from a UNIX-operated computer to other computers, had discovered that there were more problems with the operating systems than with the programs themselves. They concluded that it was better not to worry about dealing with the differences in the software environment but simply to transport the whole environment. They went into the UNIX kernel, that part of the operating system which controls the computer and its peripherals, and they searched for places where it was dependent on the PDP-11. Finding those places, they rewrote them to make them machine-independent. This turned out to involve only ten percent of the system. Fully ninety percent—the file system, the queuing in the disk drives, memory allocation—could be expressed independently of the machine.

UNIX had been written originally in assembly language, however, and thus was still not portable. But writing an operating system in a high-level language for mainframe as well as small computers was considered extremely inefficient and impractical. One supposedly needed the efficiency of an assembly language. So Ritchie and Thompson came up with a new high-level language they called C. It possessed features of both high- and low-level languages and was therefore quite versatile for system programmers, who could address memory as input/output channels directly without assembler code. C combined powerful logical instruction with an ability to manipulate individual bits and characters, and it was significantly easier for a programmer to use than assembly language. Only when UNIX was rewritten in C did it become truly portable. C became popular as an implementation language or systems programming language in large measure because it was the language in which UNIX had been written.

It was in this machine independence that UNIX differed importantly from CP/M, the industry standard for personal computers in the 1970s. With UNIX, moving most programs was a matter of recompiling them for the new machine, a completely mechanical process carried out by the computer itself. Although some details, especially within the operating system, had to be done by hand and thus could lead to problems, it was generally possible to transport the operating system and all the other software to a new machine with a few months of human effort. CP/M, on the other hand, had been written in the machine language of a particular processor chip, the Intel 8080. Various manufacturers use this chip so they can offer CP/M.

Precisely what is UNIX like? It has a simple, structured architecture and permits users to process multiple tasks at once. One of UNIX's most radical departures is the fact that files are simply sequences of bytes. There is no interpretation of the data inside the files by the system, and there is no inherent structure of records. Files of text, for example, are simply characters with new-line characters separating the lines. They are not of fixed length. UNIX also offers stream processing, through an innovation called software pipes, which turn a program's output into another program's input without intermediate work files. One command can be connected to another, enabling the user to come up with new application programs by stringing together UNIX "words" into "sentences." UNIX employs more than 200 programmed commands and, unlike its more rigid predecessors, allows a user to combine commands with great flexibility. The programmed commands enable the sorting of data, text manipulation, and information searching. The system kernel of UNIX is very small, only 8,000 lines of code, of which only 800 are in assembly language. One of the virtues of UNIX is its economy. A few taps on the keyboard bring a great deal of action from the computer. A program that might otherwise take 100 to 1,000 lines of code can be written, with UNIX, in under ten commands.

UNIX has changed Ken Thompson's career, and turned a free life into a freer one. He has always done pretty much what he wanted at Bell Labs, but "the success of UNIX has helped in that no one cares now what I do." Does he ever have second thoughts about staying within a research environment, forgoing the chance to make a lot of money on the outside? "I think you care about money if you don't have enough," he replies. "And I certainly have enough for what I need to do." As for those who have capitalized on their inventions and developments, who have built large companies, "They're doing something that doesn't motivate me. I'm happy doing what I do."

Ritchie has lately been helping to produce the eighth edition of UNIX. "I've never been too far away from working on UNIX or related things." But he is ready to move on to other subjects—"I'm getting to the point where it's fairly obvious I would do well to find something different." He acknowledges that he has no other hobbies, that "most of the interest or energy is devoted in one form or another to playing around with the machine."

When the selection committee for the Turing Award, given by the Association for Computing Machinery, presented its prize in 1983 to Dennis Ritchie and Kenneth Thompson, its citation read in part, "The success of the UNIX system stems from its tasteful selection of a few key ideas and their elegant implementation. The model of the UNIX system has led a generation of software designers to new ways of thinking about programming. The genius of the UNIX system is its framework, which enables programmers to stand on the work of others."

UNIX had by the mid-1980s come to be regarded as a major standard of the computer industry, owing largely to the interest shown by the scientific and engineering communities. A large number of manufacturers were offering it. *Fortune,* on September 17, 1984, said that some 750 universities around the world and about eighty percent of those with computer science departments are UNIX licensees. Anyone graduating with a computer science major these days—and hence many of America's future programmers—will almost certainly have been exposed to UNIX.

Considering that Ritchie and Thompson were simply trying to create a more convenient environment for themselves, they certainly achieved more than they intended. Dennis Ritchie is uncertain about UNIX's future, however: "Given the unconventional way that UNIX spread, it was inevitable that different varieties should arise. Moreover, it is by no means certain, despite my strong advocacy of portability, that the same system will serve both the most advanced supercomputer like the CRAY-2 and an under-$1,000 Christmas toy. I have no doubt that UNIX will become more standardized. The efforts of AT&T and the national standards-making bodies are both pushing that way. I do doubt that it will become the universal operating system and push all others aside."

Daniel Bricklin

The Spreadsheet Pioneer Who Invented VisiCalc

26

It happened because of Dan Bricklin's daydreaming in school. There had to be, he said to himself, an easier, more efficient way for business students and businessmen to recalculate numbers. As a result he gave the world a piece of software called VisiCalc, which in time would turn the whole computer industry upside down. A presidential budget adviser used it. So did the space shuttle people. So did Mr. Average American Businessman, Big and Small. Five years after he had helped to create the software industry for personal computers, Dan Bricklin could happily say, "If I had a nickel for every dollar of productivity I helped the country with, it would be real nice."

Of course he will never know just how much productivity he nurtured with VisiCalc. But it is clear that once this magical piece of software came along, with its capacity to let businessmen calculate and recalculate numbers in minutes rather than hours, it had a major influence on the daily routine of American business. Mainframes and minicomputers had been around for some time, and their uses were well known; but no one quite knew what to make of the personal computer, which until VisiCalc was a product in search of a purpose. Bricklin's invention became the most popular personal-computer business program of its time, with over 800,000 copies sold by early 1985. It has been adapted for most major personal computers.

In the same way that word processing has helped writers, VisiCalc helped businessmen. Suddenly it became obvious to businessmen that they had to have a personal computer: VisiCalc made it feasible to use one. No prior technical training was needed to use the spreadsheet program. Once, both hardware and software were for hobbyists, the personal computer a mysterious toy, used if anything for playing games. But after VisiCalc the computer was recognized as a crucial tool.

VisiCalc helped the businessman do his job better. The faster he could calculate what a change in labor costs would do to his business, the faster he could react—and the better his chances of making speedy, correct decisions would be. VisiCalc permitted businessmen for the first time to do financial forecasting, analysis, and planning automatically. Those calculations and recalculations of rows and columns of numbers could now be done on a personal computer, without programming. VisiCalc took away the drudgery of the constant "what if" analysis that was part and parcel of any businessman's routine: "What if office boys demand a five-percent raise?" VisiCalc could tell you in seconds how costs, profits, and dividends would be affected.

VisiCalc author Daniel Bricklin was born in Philadelphia on July 16, 1951. He grew up there, attending the Solomon Schechter Day School. In 1969 he enrolled at MIT and began studying mathematics, switching in the middle of his junior year to computer science. At the Laboratory for Computer Science, which was then occupied with the time-sharing experiment called Project MAC, he helped design an on-line calculator, worked on the command environment, and was one of two programmers to implement the APL language—popular among engineers and others. At the end of his senior year Bricklin became project leader of a second implementation of the APL language. He worked a great deal with another programmer named Bob Frankston, then a graduate student: the two agreed they would go into business together one day. Bricklin graduated from MIT in 1973 with a bachelor of science degree in electrical engineering and computer science. He applied only to top graduate schools—Carnegie, Stanford, and MIT—but his grade average, though high, did not meet their standards.

Bricklin wanted to stay close to computers, so in the fall of 1973 he took a job at Digital Equipment Corporation, just outside Boston. His first task there was to program a wire-service interface to a newspaper typesetting system. He then did some designing of video terminals and typesetting systems. His most important job at DEC was as project leader of the company's first word-processing system, WPS-8, one of the earliest word-processing programs. Bricklin wrote one-fourth of the program's code, as well as the functional specification.

After a few years DEC insisted that he move to one of the firm's units in New Hampshire, a proposition that Bricklin greeted coolly. This seemed like a good time to pursue a graduate program in business administration, something he had thought of doing for some time. While he waited to hear from graduate school, he wound up taking a job in, of all places, New Hampshire! In the end he did not regret working there at all. In 1976 he became a senior systems programmer for FasFax, manufacturers of electronic cash registers. He had a chance to learn something about running a small business, and he profited from working closely with the firm's hardware designers. He left there in 1977 and that fall entered the Harvard Business School in pursuit of a master's degree in business administration.

There was lots of time to daydream in his classes, and in Finance and Production especially a certain constellation of thoughts began to swirl in his mind. The business school, famous for its case approach to business administration, required its students to sit and play company president, accountant, prophet. The mock organizations that the students had to help run were supposedly similar to ones in the real world. It was an intriguing exercise, but at times a slow one, given that all the students had to work with were pencil, paper, and a calculator. Numbers would be thrown on the blackboard by a professor; calculations had to be made, and then if a change was made in one number all the others had to be recalculated. Bricklin would pray that he had not made one tiny error. Otherwise he would have to start from scratch. Wasn't there an easier way to do this? Maybe he could think of a way to manipulate, not words this time, but numbers: "Sitting in class, I started to imagine the electronic calculator, the word processor that would work with numbers." Couldn't a personal computer speed up the calculations? He was a programmer, could he not apply his programming skills to creating a kind of electronic blackboard that would perform all these tedious steps automatically? If he could turn that idea into an actual program, businessmen might go for it in a big way, and then maybe he and Bob Frankston could start up that partnership they had been thinking about.

When he told some of his classmates about his idea, they were uniformly encouraging. It was all very amorphous at the start, though: while Bricklin could envision the keyboard and the calculator, putting the whole thing together would be a big task. He then did what any sensible student would do: he asked his professors what they thought of the idea. He wanted to begin with his finance professor, but not finding him around he turned to his production and operations management professor, who liked the notion, as did his cost-accounting professor. When Bricklin managed to track down his finance professor he got a response that made him wish he hadn't: Financial forecasting systems already existed, said the professor; the market was saturated. If you want proof, said he, why not get in touch with Dan Fylstra? Fylstra, an ex-student of his, had set up a software publishing firm and knew the market pretty well. Bricklin and Fylstra did eventually chat, but not about the new program. It was only later that the pair would team up.

Summer was approaching, and this would give Bricklin an opportunity to get cracking on what was still basically only an idea. He decided one day while taking a long bicycle ride on Martha's Vineyard that he would devote the next part of his career to implementing that idea. He put down on paper that fall a program that would do the job. "Because I was competing with the back of an envelope, this had to be faster to use than doing it by hand. You had to have a certain speed and ease of use: every keystroke could make a difference." Borrowing from a trial version he had written on a time-sharing system of Harvard, he created a prototype of an electronic spreadsheet, written in BASIC for an Apple II computer. Although it was only a few hundred lines of code, it took over twenty seconds to recalculate its 100 cells and couldn't scroll. Still, it was the first electronic spreadsheet.

Bricklin was now ready to produce the final, commercially viable, version. For a machine as limited as the Apple II it had to be written in machine code. In his second year of the Harvard MBA program, Bricklin lacked the needed time to complete the product. He agreed with Frankston that they would develop it jointly: Frankston would write the code, Bricklin would handle the functional design and initial documentation. It happened that Bricklin had already put Frankston on to Dan Fylstra's small software publishing firm, recommending his friend as an author to convert a bridge game program from the TRS-80 personal computer to the Apple II computer. Frankston told Fylstra about Bricklin's idea of an electronic spreadsheet, and the reception was quite positive. In October 1978 Bricklin and Frankston had dinner with Fylstra, and the three of them worked out an arrangement by which Bricklin and Frankston would write the program and Fylstra's firm would do the marketing. They signed a contract the following April. The real writing of the program began that winter; Fylstra loaned them an Apple II, the machine that he felt would be best for the first implementation (to be followed by versions for other popular computers).

Meanwhile Bricklin and Frankston went ahead and set up Software Arts, Incorporated, working at first out of Frankston's attic office in Arlington, Massachusetts. The company was officially formed in January 1979, with Frankston as president and Bricklin as chairman. Now the work on VisiCalc accelerated. In his final semester of business school that winter and spring, Bricklin attended classes during the day while Frankston slept. They would meet in the evenings to talk about the program. Rather than buy their own small development system, they chose to work on a time-sharing computer that was more sophisticated than anything they could have afforded to purchase; they rented time late at night because it was cheaper. Bricklin rented a Selectric typewriter to write the manual specification. At this stage one main concern was how to add replication. Another was the issue of relative and absolute cells. At some point, they knew, they would have to decide just how many features to include in the program. Reflecting their determination to keep it short and efficient, the final form of VisiCalc was only 25K long.

Somewhere in the midst of all that work Frankston and Fylstra took time out for a very early breakfast meeting at a Cambridge restaurant. Among other things, they talked about what to name the product. Calculature? Electropage? Electronic Blackboard? Electric Paper? Everyone agreed the name wasn't all that important, but at least it should be pronounceable. Later, at a meeting with various wives, business associates, and girlfriends, all the proposed names were gone over, and VisiCalc was chosen. Early in its development

Fylstra took a copy of the program out to the West Coast and showed it to people at Apple and Atari. Apple exhibited little interest, and Atari did not have its machines ready.

Slowly the program took shape. At first it only worked with integers. Then full floating-point was added, but the program could only add and subtract. Then came multiplication. Replication, that important feature that enables one to say, "Make the next ten columns similar to the first," was also introduced. Bricklin had not done well in a recent exam in a production class, having been up the entire previous night working on his program. He later brought the professor over to Software Arts' attic to see the program, and happily the professor was impressed. "So," observes Bricklin. "I resurrected myself in his eyes."

At one point during that spring Bricklin was working on one of those famous Harvard Business School cases for his consumer marketing class. After keying in the numbers on VisiCalc for a variety of scenarios, he copied down the results (outputing to a printer was not yet in the program) and set off to school. That day he raised his hand in class and got called on. He described his investigation of the various scenarios, each projected out for three, four, five years, and so on, noting how changes here and there would affect the overall situation. This would normally have been the result of hours and hours of work with a pencil, paper, and calculator. An astonished professor asked what method Bricklin had used, and he explained how he had performed a series of additions, subtractions, and multiplications to arrive at the answer, never mentioning that he had relied upon a computer and a special new program to do all of the tedious work in a fraction of the time they thought he had spent. Bricklin could have used division to do a simple ratio, the professor explained: it wouldn't be as accurate as actually doing the additions and multiplications, as he had done, but it would have taken less time. He had wanted to be more precise, Bricklin said, not letting on that Bob Frankston hadn't finished the VisiCalc division code yet.

In April Software Arts signed with Fylstra's Personal Software. The latter would market and distribute VisiCalc, with Software Arts getting 35.7 cent for every dollar of revenue. For copies sold in quantity, Software Arts would get 50 cents. In May an early version of VisiCalc was shown to computer dealers at the West Coast Computer Faire, to a mixed reaction. In June Personal Software showed VisiCalc publicly for the first time, at the National Computer Conference in New York City, hoping to make waves. Frankston had prepared a paper on VisiCalc that garnered an audience of only twenty people, most of whom were family or friends, and the paper didn't even make it into the proceedings. Also that June, Bricklin graduated from business school.

There was still work to be done on the program. Bricklin and Frankston decided the time had come for them to purchase a time-sharing computer of their own; this would spare them those late-night hours. They put together $20,000 in cash from savings and relatives and took out a bank loan for $65,000. In July they purchased a Prime 550 minicomputer and continued work. That summer another employee was hired, Steve Lawrence, and the team moved into new offices in Cambridge. By fall they had finished the original Apple II version of VisiCalc, had hired another employee, Seth Steinberg, and had started making additional versions of VisiCalc for other popular personal computers, such as the TRS-80, PET, and Atari. A major boost came from one of the personal computer industry's most respected analysts, Benjamin Rosen, who wrote in his widely read *Electronic Letter*, "VisiCalc could someday be the software tail that wags (and sells) the personal computer dog."

VisiCalc was finally offered commercially in October 1979, at a retail price of $100. The initial reception was lukewarm, but over the next year the product slowly gained a word-of-mouth acceptance. Accordingly the price was raised to $150. It sold 500 to 1,000 copies a month at first. Bricklin would help teach local computer stores what the product was all about. The real proof of VisiCalc's popularity came when customers walked into a computer store to buy an Apple computer just so they could use the spreadsheet program.

Allen Sneider, a partner at the accounting firm of Laventhol and Horwath in Boston, was the first commercial user of VisiCalc. He had bought an Apple computer in 1978 and was trying without much success to run financial models on it. A friend showed him a test copy of VisiCalc at the local computer store, and Sneider knew that this was the tool he had been looking for. He wrote a check on the spot. The more he used the program, the more impressed he became. He asked senior management to introduce more Apples and VisiCalc, putting the computers and programs to work in different departments. The time it took to run applications on a time-sharing system was thereby cut by eighty percent. The spreadsheet revolution was on its way. For the first year VisiCalc ran only on Apple, but then Hewlett-Packard, TRS-80, Commodore, PET, and Atari 800 were added. By 1981 VisiCalc was selling 12,000 units a month. With the addition of the IBM PC late in 1981 that figure would jump to 30,000 for some months. Revenues for both Software Arts and Personal Software grew. Within two years 200,000 copies of VisiCalc would be sold. In due time the imitations hit the market, and they were promptly dubbed VisiClones or Calcalikes.

Spreadsheets had put the personal computer on the corporate map. Some 2.7 million personal computers were bought in 1985; that same year 2 million spreadsheet programs were purchased. In fact, spreadsheet programs have been the leading software category since 1980—and VisiCalc has much to do with that. Some 7.1 million copies of spreadsheet programs were in users' hands as of the fall of 1986.

Enhancements to VisiCalc eventually appeared, one important one being DIF, a file format introduced in 1980. It permitted VisiCalc to interact with other programs on mainframes and minicomputers, as well as personal computers. An advanced version of VisiCalc was announced at the 1982 National Computer Conference, permitting easier implementation of prewritten VisiCalc forms for the new computer user. At Software Arts, Bricklin, though involving himself in program design to some extent, would mainly handle business details, while Frankston would deal with the technical side. For Bricklin the Harvard Business School grad, it was as if he had been given a laboratory in which to test out all that he had just learned—though he soon turned over the day-to-day running of the company to a management team headed by Julian Lange and Tracy Licklider.

At first Bricklin was reluctant to market a second product, lest it not be as well-received as VisiCalc. In November 1981 he was given the Grace Murray Hopper Award by the Association for Computing Machinery, for significant accomplishment in computers by people under thirty. After receiving the award he was reminded of Andy Warhol's comment that everyone would be famous for fifteen minutes. Bricklin had had his fifteen minutes, and now, he said to himself, he could go back to work.

It was time to look beyond VisiCalc. And this time he would not only design the product but market it as well. And so in February 1983 Software Arts hit the market with TK!Solver (TK is the proofreader's abbreviation for "to come"), the first equation-processing program developed for personal computers. Bricklin hoped it would do for business and scientific models what VisiCalc did for spreadsheets. The initial reception was most gratifying: it sold in the tens of thousands. In September 1984 Software Arts marketed another new product called Spotlight, described by Bricklin as a speedy, functional desktop manager and one of the first to employ the pop-up window.

Relations between Bricklin's firm and Fylstra's deteriorated, culminating in an unpleasant lawsuit over the right to market VisiCalc. In September 1983 VisiCorp—Fylstra had renamed his company in early 1982—sued Bricklin's Software Arts for $60 million, claiming that Software Arts had failed to enhance VisiCalc and come out with a promised new version. Countersuing in February 1984, Software Arts charged that VisiCorp had favored its own Visi-On product rather than doing its best to continue to market VisiCalc. VisiCorp had demanded that Software Arts stop selling VisiCalc, but a Boston district judge would not agree. The case was settled out of court in the fall of 1984, with Software Arts getting the right to VisiCalc; VisiCorp paid Software Arts $500,000 as part of the settlement and was thus released from Software Arts' counterclaims.

In time VisiCalc was replaced in popularity by the Lotus 1-2-3 program, developed by Mitch Kapor and Jonathan Sachs. This was the first piece of software to offer not only an electronic spreadsheet but also data management and graphics applications, all in one program. VisiCalc sales dropped from 20,000 a month in early 1983 to only 2,500 a month by the summer of 1984. In the spring of 1985 the products and many other assets of Software Arts were purchased by Kapor's Lotus firm for a reportedly low figure. Had Software Arts concluded such a deal a few years earlier, it was said, the shareholders might have received $50 million for the firm. But Software Arts had been forced to wait until the lawsuit ended, and by that time it was far in debt and the market for software firms had soured considerably.

Freed by the purchase from what had become an onerous responsibility, Bricklin planned henceforth to concentrate on designing programs—which is what he has found he is best at. "I'll probably spend the next thirty years doing computer tools. That's what I do." He began by designing a new product called Dan Bricklin's Demo Program, which enables other designers to create new programs faster and more easily. In the fall of 1985 he set up a mail-order business, Software Garden, Inc., in his Newton, Massachusetts, home, selling Demo Program for $75.

Bricklin's program does far more than simply create demonstrations of existing programs. It helps developers set up storyboard demonstrations that show potential customers what a program can do—before the design has been completed. Individual images or "slides" depict each step in the operation of a new program. For each slide, one can define the appropriate response to any keystroke. Hundreds of slides can be chained together to form what seems to be a fully functional program but is in fact a screen show. Using this program, a graphic artist can design a new interface for a program without having to depend upon a programmer. *PC Week* has called the program a "gem," and by November 1986 Bricklin had sold 8,000 copies. Running a very small company—Software Garden has two employees, including himself—appeals to Bricklin. He especially enjoys being allowed to concentrate on one product. Yet, though he may now be cultivating a garden rather than presiding over a huge enterprise, it must be remembered that he is one of the major pioneers of the computer industry. "I'm not rich because I invented VisiCalc," Bricklin said in November 1985. "But I feel that I've made a change in the world. That's a satisfaction money can't buy."

Bringing the Computer to the Masses

Nolan Bushnell

Captain Pong, Leader of
the Video Game Revolution

27

A white blip moves back and forth across a television screen. Two children sit before it, plastic joysticks in their hands, guiding their electronic "paddles" and slapping the phosphorescent dot—the ball—over the net. This was Pong, the first major electronic video game; it had converted the TV screen into an electronic ping-pong table. It arrived on the scene in 1972 and in time would spawn the $5-billion-a-year video game industry that in turn helped launch the personal computer. Through Pong, millions of average Americans would have their first contact with a computer. These were not, of course, general-purpose computers, and many considered them just another passing fad. But Pong and the entire video game industry represented a dramatic turning point. The man responsible for this revolution was Nolan Bushnell, inventor of Pong, founder of Atari, and one of Silicon Valley's great success stories. He is a unique mixture of technological whiz and entrepreneur. Although he is known as Silicon Valley's philosopher king, he prefers being thought of as a fourteen-year-old mind locked inside an adult's body.

Bringing Pong to the public was no easy matter. Silicon Valley in the early 1970s was not churning out consumer products, and the public had a most grudging show-me attitude toward any consumer product that was new and technologically oriented. Bushnell's Atari cautiously predicted that 50,000 Pong home games would be bought in its first year. By Christmas of 1973, however, double that number had been sold.

Success was a great joy to Nolan Bushnell. But then nearly everything in life seems to be joyful for him. Now in his forties, he retains a child's love of games and fantasy. That Bushnell loves games is one of the great givens of Silicon Valley, that he makes millions of dollars from his games is another. He is a big man—six feet four—with an easygoing disposition. There are no stories of him suddenly losing his temper, storming out of a meeting. Almost every photo of him shows him puffing thoughtfully on a pipe. To know what makes Nolan Bushnell tick, one must only figure out what is his biggest enemy: boredom. He is, in a sense, still the youngster trying to make sure that every moment is filled.

Bushnell came along at a time when Americans were searching eagerly for new forms of entertainment—and, of course, new gadgets. Bushnell's genius has been that he reads the market so well. Of all the young entrepreneurs who have left their imprint on Silicon Valley, none seems to have the respect and admiration of so many people. Bushnell is decidedly unconventional, but then who among the success stories in the highly competitive computer industry isn't?

He was born on February 5, 1943, in Clearfield, Utah, near the shores of the Great Salt Lake. The very beginning of his fascination with electronics was a third-grade science project. Assigned the unit on electricity, Bushnell made electromagnets and batteries to show the class. He then went home and searched out flashlights, light switches, and wires; placing them on a card table in his room, he tried to duplicate what he had just demonstrated to the class. At ten, the proud owner of a ham radio license, he looked for jobs to pay for the radio parts. Bushnell was not the easiest child to have around the house: his idea of fun seemed to be trying to blow things up. The garage was turned into a laboratory; his bedroom was a place for experimentation as well—his mother eschewed setting foot in it for fear of being electrocuted. Bushnell was not altogether successful in building a liquid-fuel rocket engine, which he strapped to a roller-skate: he almost burned down the garage. At least he was frightened by the incident.

Electronics was less important to him in high school than other pursuits. He played basketball and was on the debating team. His interests drifted to automobiles and skiing: "I knew I was coming of age when I traded one of my pieces of communication gear for a pair of skis." His zest for electrical foolery had not been entirely quenched, however: one evening he attached a 100-watt light to a large kite and tried to persuade the populace that Utah had come under alien attack.

In the fall of 1961 Bushnell entered Utah State College, in Logan, Utah; he transferred after a few years to the University of Utah in Salt Lake City. An engineering major, he also studied economics, philosophy, mathematics, and business. One of the great stimulants to Bushnell's eventual career was the course in computer graphics given by David C. Evans and Ivan E. Sutherland. Bushnell became entranced with computers, and especially with the video games, then very primitive, that the experts were playing. The most popular one was Spacewar. He was an avid player, and early on he began to wonder whether it would be possible to convert this game, written only for a mainframe computer, to a system that would be accessible to consumers. He envisioned an add-on coin-input system that would entice large numbers of youngsters to play for pay.

Bushnell founded his own business during his college years. Called the Campus Company, it produced, three times a year for each of four universities, a blotter with the school calendar of events printed in the center and advertising around the border. Bushnell gave the blotters away free; selling $3,000 worth of advertising for each edition, he would pocket all but the $500 production cost. His Campus Company work one summer led to a second occupation, of a very different kind. "I was selling advertising during the day, and I always felt the best way to keep from spending money, which I had a penchant for, was to have another job." So on summer nights he worked at an amusement park, guessing people's weights and ages. He was later put in charge of the park's games department. Probably the most important benefit from the job was the knowledge Bushnell acquired about the workings of the coin-operated game field. He studied people's spending habits and their preferences. The parkgoers, Bushnell realized, didn't want anything too cerebral— they liked a game that tested their manual dexterity and whose rules were simple. The idea was to let the parents go off for a while without the children.

He thought of coupling his findings with the magic that was occurring at the university computer lab. All games fascinated him, and he knew already that business was the ultimate game: one kept score with money, won or lost, and maybe got a little smarter after a defeat. At the University of Utah he learned how to play the ancient Chinese game Go. An expression traditionally used by players of the game is "Atari," meaning "Watch out or I'm going to get you on your next move"—a polite warning to an opponent that he is in peril. Later Bushnell would find another use for the term.

After graduating from college in 1968, he tried to get a job with Walt Disney but was turned down. He had married in 1966; he and his wife now moved to Santa Clara, California, where he worked two years for the advanced technology division of Ampex Corporation, a tape recording pioneer. At Ampex Bushnell was always dreaming of get-rich-quick ventures. When he announced that he was leaving Ampex to go into the coin-operated game business, his friends thought he was crazy, exchanging a good job for participation in a nonserious enterprise reputedly run by organized crime.

Still, it had been Bushnell's dream to develop computer video games and sell them to the public. He had once thought of using a $10,000 PDP-11 computer but realized it was too expensive for a quarter-a-game operation. The real breakthrough came with the invention of the integrated circuit and, most important, the invention in 1970 of the microprocessor, permitting a game manufacturer to use a hundred chips—at a cost of fifty cents a chip—and still produce a game cheaply enough to sell on a large scale. Thanks to Ted Hoff's computer on a chip, a machine could be found that was small enough to permit a coin-input system. The electronic game could go public.

It is no surprise that the people Nolan Bushnell admires most are Robert Noyce and Walt Disney: Noyce because he helped to bring cost down and reliability up in electronics, to a point where Bushnell's ideas began to look feasible; Disney because of his wizardry in the creative uses of technology, the nonscientific, nonmilitary side of technology. Bushnell has always taken Walt Disney and Disneyland seriously. Of Disneyland he says, "Although it was a place devoted to fun and frivolity, it was really on the cutting edge of technology. People don't realize that frivolity is the gateway to the future, in that most future products don't start as necessities but as toys."

Bushnell spent his spare time in a makeshift lab in his daughter's bedroom, rounding up $500 and developing Computer Space, a spinoff of Spacewar and the first commercially oriented computer game. Meanwhile, he and a former Ampex associate had built up a coin-operated game route, placing pinball machines in bars and taverns and collecting the proceeds each night. When a firm called Nutting Associates—a small arcade-game manufacturer—agreed to produce Computer Space, Bushnell came aboard as product engineer to help in marketing his game. By late 1971 he had become convinced that he could run the business better than it was being run. On offering to straighten out the firm for a twenty-percent part of the ownership, Bushnell was promptly told by President Bill Nutting that he should stay in engineering. The revenues from the pinball route plus the $500 he had earned in royalties from Computer Space permitted Bushnell to quit his job at Nutting and start Syzygy, the firm that would become Atari. The name Syzygy—meaning an alignment of celestial bodies—fell by the wayside when Bushnell learned that another firm had already registered it.

If Computer Space had not been a big winner, that was not enough to make Bushnell throw in the towel. He felt that Computer Space was too complicated—and not enough fun. He would try for something simpler, yet more realistic. Maybe in designing the first game he had had the computer hackers too much in mind. He would shoot for Mr. Average American. He hired another Ampex veteran, Al Alcorn, and at first thought of devising a car-driving game. But Bushnell realized he would be pushing his new employee too far, too fast: the game would have to be very complicated and hence not feasible within a reasonable cost. Just a simple game, a moving spot, two patterns on the sides—he explained it to Al and asked him to build the thing. In an interesting twist of the truth, Bushnell told Alcorn that he had a contract with General Electric to do a consumer product: a letter had come from GE, but it was simply a request for Bushnell to submit a proposal for a game. While Alcorn worked on the game, it never occurred to him to ask why the GE people had opted for such a low profile. Bushnell did not have the heart to tell him that there was no prearranged buyer for their product, for fear Alcorn would drop out. In only three months the game was complete. To Bushnell it seemed like great fun. Only it was economically unsound to market, costing far more than the $100 they would have to charge.

Alcorn was depressed. Bushnell was philosophical. He asked Nutting to look at the product but got a cool reception from his former boss. Wherever Bushnell turned, doors would slam. If he could not get someone to market the game for him, he would recast his old company and do the marketing himself. Thus Atari was born. Bushnell and Alcorn put together a small table-top model, added a coin box on the side, and plugged it into an old Hitachi TV. As an experiment, it was placed on the bar of Andy Capp's in Sunnyvale, California. In a short time people were coming to the bar not to buy beer but to play the game. They had a product! They called it Pong. The first Pong games were shipped in November 1972.

Pong was used first as a coin-operated arcade game. Video games had been on the market since 1962, but until Pong came along no one had manufactured coin-operated versions and put them in the arcades to compete with pinball machines. For a few months in 1973, it was a huge seller. Bushnell was now working on a home version that could be hooked up to the television set. When Sears Roebuck learned about the home version, it bought out the entire Atari inventory before the machine hit the market. By 1974 Pong was on the shelves of Sears Roebuck. All was not well, however. Sales eventually dropped off, presumably because kids eventually got bored with the game. But Pong had been a phenomenal success, creating an entire industry. In fiscal 1973 Atari had $3.2 million in sales.

After Pong, distributors went back to pinballs, still not convinced that video games were here to stay. Pong was quickly imitated, however: even Bushnell's Atari came out with new programmed cartridges that altered Pong into other games—Race track, Poker, Hangman, and Scrabble. A new game called Gran Trak came out in late 1974, beginning a run of Atari triumphs. Then in 1975 a new home version of Pong scored a big success.

There was an Atari culture as well, a frivolity that seemed to match the product line. Employees would walk into the Los Gatos, California, headquarters at any hour of the morning, dressed in blue jeans and T-shirts, creating an impression of casualness bordering on chaos. Admitting that he was a "bizarre manager," Bushnell installed hot tubs to be used as think tanks for his engineers. "It was a company run by a lot of green guys with a product line that a lot of people didn't understand. But it was very easy for people to confuse foolishness of product with foolishness of company." It seemed a funny way to do business, but the money kept rolling in, and somewhere someone was obviously doing something right.

Successful though it clearly was, Atari had yet to get its hands on big money. Venture capital would not have been hard to find, but Bushnell had no appetite for turning the company over to non-Atari types, diminishing his own role and degree of ownership. He had built Atari, and he wanted to keep it: it was his toy. Who would want to let it go? By 1976, Atari was a $40-million company. Yet, faced with the need for millions of dollars in cash in order to sell to the broad consumer market, Bushnell overcame his reluctance and sought a buyer. Video games might well be a passing fad; it seemed too risky to be out there on his own, especially when the other big firms, Texas Instruments for instance, were threatening to give Atari new competition. Bushnell projected that Atari would need $80 million to stay in the video game business. "It was time for a deep pockets investor, I was tired of chasing the cash, and I was naive enough to think that I wouldn't mind working for a big company. It seemed like a good chance to cash out, to consolidate some of my win."

His first choice was the company founded by his hero, Walt Disney. How wonderful if Disney Productions would wave its magic wand over this new industry. It considered the idea but in the end said no. Bushnell looked around some more and finally found a willing buyer in Warner Communications. It bought Atari for $28 million in August 1976. Bushnell himself got half that amount and remained as chairman. He thought his share was adequate: "I felt $14 million is all the money you need in the world."

As part of the takeover agreement, Warner required Bushnell to promise not to compete with Atari for the next seven years—until October 1, 1983. It was an arrangement under which Bushnell would predictably chafe, his creative urge imprisoned by a piece of paper. Bushnell had given Warner one idea that he would ultimately buy back for a half-million dollars. It was Pizza Time Theatre, a collection of pizza parlors offering video games and performing robots while customers waited for their orders. He had noted that there was a consistent twenty-minute wait for pizza and asked himself, why not let kids fill that time up by spending their money on video games? The first Pizza Time Theatre opened in May 1977.

Bushnell remained at Atari as chairman for two years after the Warner takeover. He was there to preside over Atari's launching of its Video Computer System, the cartridge-programmable home game machine, and its 400/800 personal computer system. When consumers failed to go for the $180 VCS machine, Warner blamed Bushnell. The conflict ended in Bushnell's resignation in January 1979.

Now it was time for Nolan Bushnell the entrepreneur to spread his wings again. He would not concentrate on just one enterprise, but—as Walt Disney had done—would spread his wealth, his energy, and his imagination around, like a bee spreading pollen. This business strategy seemed to accord with Bushnell's assessment of his own strengths as a businessman: "I've always said that in order to be really successful in life you need to be better than most people in two different fields. I'm not the best engineer around, I'm not the best marketeer, I'm not the best financial strategist. But I think I'm better than anyone at all three of those at the same time."

And so he played the game of business, the game he loved the most. At first Bushnell put his all into building up Pizza Time Theatre; again, he seemed to have a magic touch, for the chain grew from seven restaurants in 1979 to eighty-eight in 1981—to over two hundred in 1982. Having done so well in business, he thought he ought to give politics a try. In 1980 he put a campaign together in anticipation of his taking part in the Republican primary for the Fourteenth Congressional District in California; he even purchased a home in Georgetown. Bushnell thought he could win easily, but at some point he realized that he was not truly suited to the life of a politician; the job would lose its interest for him over the long run.

In late 1981 Bushnell took on the role of venture capitalist with a passion. He formed a holding company called Catalyst Technologies; he liked to call it an incubator for new ideas. It would provide the capital, would make it easy for the inventor or the pioneer to market his new idea. Bushnell remembered the problems he himself had encountered in running Atari—it would have been wonderful to spend his time being creative, but running the business had used up that time. Catalyst was the answer to a genius's prayers: it would provide the infrastructure, take care of the setting up of the business, manage the store. Eventually, the analysts would call it one of Silicon Valley's most innovative business ideas. It served as an umbrella for at least twelve independent corporations, beginning with Androbot, a robot manufacturer and the first company to sell a true automaton as a consumer item. One of its products, a robot called Bob that sold for $2,500, would patrol a house and call the police when its heat sensor sniffed an intruder. It could also clean. Perhaps its best trick was to look a human up and down and then say, "What strange-looking creatures. Where are your wheels?" Robots, Nolan Bushnell believed earnestly, would be the product that would bring high tech to the average American household.

There were other companies, one trying to improve the resolution of color televisions, another running a computer camp, a third supplying an electronic shopping service. In late 1983 Bushnell's luck soured. Pizza Time went into heavy debt, Bushnell resigned as chairman at the turn of the year, and by March the company had filed for reorganization under the federal bankruptcy laws, owing its creditors some $100 million. Bushnell considered this his first real failure. By 1986 most of Catalyst's firms no longer existed, and in the process Bushnell had used up several million dollars of his personal funds. The most successful surviving company was Etak, Inc., which made computerized maps for cars.

Ever optimistic, Bushnell was not put off by these setbacks. He saw them as part of a larger scheme. Such , after all, is the nature of venture capitalism. Bushnell is highly critical of other venture capitalists: "They put money in the wrong places. That is not being conservative, it's simply foolish. Putting your money on a company that is between fifth and one-hundredth in the industry, which is what these people do, is a significantly higher risk than trying to pioneer in the industry."

Having begun the home computer industry via Atari, is Nolan Bushnell satisfied with the shape of things a decade later? No, he is not. "I think the industry has committed suicide. It would be hard to imagine how any industry could be more mismanaged. The lack of change has been phenomenal. They have still not definitely shown why you need the damn things in your home. It's a solution in search of a problem. They really should have gone towards integrated systems in which the system is really the centerpiece of the home entertainment center." Bushnell loves the role of futurist. He has been right so often when others have scoffed at his ideas. What then of the future? "Don't even think of computers, think more in terms of functional blocks in which everything has intelligence. Start thinking of anticipatory functions in which you don't have to push buttons, but you have a building block of functionality and it knows what it's supposed to do and it does it a lot better than you."

Bushnell likes to live well. He owns a condominium in Aspen, a home in Georgetown, a palace in Paris next to the Eiffel Tower, and the old Folger mansion, south of San Francisco. He owns a restaurant in Silicon Valley called the Lion and Compass—he started it because he was tired of not having a place to go for a good meal in the area. In early 1985 one of Bushnell's dreams appeared to be coming true. He began his own toy and game manufacturing company, Axlon. He planned to push products such as trivia card games, talking stuffed animals, and programmable robots.

A major recent development has been the merger of Bushnell's talents with those of another Silicon Valley genius, Apple computer developer Steve Wozniak, who resigned from Apple in early 1985. Their plan was hatched in the spring of 1986 at a family barbecue in the backyard of Bushnell's Woodside, California, home. Wozniak watched in fascination as his two children played with some of Axlon's robot toys; later he and Bushnell decided they would build their own toy, code-named NEMO (for Never Ever Mentioned Outside). The toy was in fact to be a pair of robots that could be steered by remote control or—and this was the unique part—directed by audio signals encoded in the sound tracks of television programs or video cassettes. A child could pit his own robot against one that was responding to TV signals. Bushnell describes these as "video games that spill off the screen and run around your feet." The Bushnell-Wozniak team plans to sell its tiny warriors for between $150 and $200 a pair. It is by no means a drawback to the project that Wozniak is worth a reported $40 to $50 million, the fortune he acquired from starting Apple.

Nolan Bushnell is a man who must always have something interesting to work on. He is always looking beyond, eager to figure out a way to hit the world with something new. When you ask him what his favorite among his many creations is, he hardly knows how to answer. He never looks back. His favorite project? The next one, of course.

Steven Jobs

Cofounder of Apple

28

His aim was to make computers easy to use, attractive to look at. Before Steve Jobs got into the business of selling computers, it would take someone twenty to thirty hours to learn how to get one of the fancy machines to behave. Before he founded Apple, a name that would become almost synonymous with the personal computer revolution, computers were science-fiction monsters approachable only by a priestly caste. Jobs was born seven years after the transistor was invented. He was a teenager when the microprocessor was invented. It was left to him to take those inventions and put them to practical use.

He was no inventor, no technical genius. He was instead a businessman, a youngster after the big buck, an evangelist in the world of commerce with a big idea to peddle. And he peddled it well. He has called his success an accident, noting that he should have been one of those semitalented poets who drift off to Paris. He got sidetracked into building computers. Sidetracked, and phenomenally rich.

In allowing the average individual to acquire a computer, Jobs made his firm a household word. The company began, in true American-dream fashion, in a garage in 1977. In six short years Apple had made the *Fortune* 500 roster, becoming the youngest firm to be on that exalted list. Its sales in 1983 totaled $983 million. Apple was in short the success story of the personal computer industry. By the mid-1980s over two million Apple computers were in use.

Apple's 1984 sales reached $1.5 billion. Jobs has boasted that Apple created over a hundred millionaires—he of course being one of them. By 1984 his personal worth came to $200 million. According to *Forbes Magazine,* he was the youngest of the four hundred richest people in America in 1984. At the end of 1982, in fact, Jobs had been worth $450 million; but when Apple's stock fell in 1983 he had lost on paper $250 million. He joked that being in such reduced circumstances was character-building.

Steve Jobs did not invent the original Apple computer. That was the work of Steve Wozniak. Steve the inventor and Steve the entrepreneur together built Apple, going from the garage to the corporate boardroom like a meteor. Wozniak had no real interest in starting a company, but Jobs did. Because of Steve Jobs the world has the Apple II, a computer that dominated the personal computer market for five years; after it came the Apple III, Lisa, Macintosh, and Macintosh Plus.

He was not born to this business, young Steve Jobs, not in the way one could say John von Neumann was, figures rolling around in his head, not in the way John Atanasoff was, taking his father's slide rule over from him at an early age. Computers didn't enter Jobs's mind until relatively late in the game. He was an orphan, born on February 24, 1955, raised by adoptive parents, Paul and Clara Jobs. When he was five months old, the family moved from the outskirts of San Francisco to south San Francisco. Steve's adopted father was a machinist at Spectra-Physics. When the boy was five, he moved with his parents to Palo Alto, because his father had been transferred. It was from his father that Steve acquired his first interest in mechanical things and electronics.

Jobs did not take to school. His mother had taught him to read before he entered elementary school, so he found the first years boring. He was a self-admitted "little terror" until fourth grade, when he came under the influence of a teacher who instilled in him a desire to learn. He was twelve when he saw his first computer, a desktop at Hewlett-Packard. The company had invited a group of schoolchildren to the plant for lectures and some hands-on practice. The experience left Jobs in awe of the device. He wanted one of his own. Some months after that, he phoned directly to William Hewlett, cofounder of Hewlett-Packard, to ask for some help in building a frequency counter—a device used to measure the speed of electronic impulses—for a school project. After a twenty-minute chat, Hewlett provided the youngster with some parts. He also offered him a job for the summer after his high-school freshman year, putting screws in frequency counters at Hewlett-Packard. Despite the menial nature of the work, Jobs was enthralled.

Jobs was thirteen when he met his eventual business partner, Steve Wozniak, then eighteen. Jobs later said that Wozniak was the first person he had met who knew more about electronics than he did. Both had a gift for putting technology to lighthearted uses. One Jobs-Wozniak idea that they marketed was a "blue box" that permitted the making of free long-distance telephone calls. Some two hundred were sold; many more might have been, but the young entrepreneurs were advised by friends to drop the idea, for it bordered on the illegal. On another occasion they designed a mechanical sign that had a large hand making a common, rude gesture. Jobs further developed his business skills in high school, fixing stereos and selling them to classmates.

Jobs graduated from Homestead High School in Los Altos in 1972 and that fall went off to Reed College in Portland, Oregon. This was the beginning of an unfocused, experimental period in his life that continued for two years. He remained a student at Reed only one semester but stayed around the campus for another year, immersing himself in whatever the counterculture had to offer, whether the *I Ching,* meditation, or LSD. He gave up meat and began visiting the Hare Krishna sect's house in Portland. Jobs left Reed for good in early 1974. At that time he answered a help wanted ad ("Have fun and make money") placed by Atari and became the fledgling video game company's fortieth employee, working in video design. After working on a basketball game that proved unsuccessful, he volunteered to travel to Europe to do repair work on Atari games. While there he got Atari's approval to take a leave of absence, winding up in New Delhi. Jobs, now nineteen, and a friend searched for Neem Karoli, the well-known spiritual leader, moving around India for several months. Back home in the fall of 1974, he returned to Atari as a consultant.

The turning point in Jobs's young life came when he began dropping by the Homebrew Computer Club, an organization of computer enthusiasts. Wozniak, a founding member of Homebrew, had been designing calculators at Hewlett-Packard during this time.

In the beginning there was Steve Wozniak's technical genius. And there was a streak of perseverance in the two young men. But there was no financial acumen. "Woz" didn't even want to market their first product. They bought a $25 microprocessor and decided to try to put together a computer. As a workshop they used the living room of Jobs's parents' house in Palo Alto.

Each machine they put together took sixty hours to complete. They had to assemble and wire each computer from scratch. Soon they created a printed circuit board, which simplified the job. If they were going to mass-produce the little machine, they had to cut corners—and hours. They did. Wozniak built, but built for himself. Jobs looked at his machine and said, "Let's market it." Jobs sensed that the market for personal computers was there.

What the two men planned to sell was not the personal computer as we have come to know it. Their product was just a printed circuit board without a keyboard, case, memory, or power supply. It could, however, be used for developing programs, playing games, and running BASIC. If the Apple I lacked some important ingredients, it was nevertheless pathbreaking. While other small computers required add-on boards, the Apple I had only one board with sixty-two chips, half the number of chips other computers used. It was easy to work, and it didn't break down often—one of its biggest advantages, for home computers at that time were most unreliable.

The product and the company the two Steves would found needed a catchy name. Jobs, according to the unofficial version, thought of a summer he had spent picking fruit off the trees in Oregon. The official version: The founders were looking for a name that represented the simplicity they were trying to achieve in the design and use of the computer—hence Apple.

Jobs and Wozniak raised $1,300 as investment capital. To do so, Jobs sold his Volkswagen van and Wozniak his Hewlett-Packard programmable calculator. The formal introduction of the Apple I came in April 1976 before the Homebrew crowd. Then in July Jobs showed computer retailer Paul Terrell the machine at a Homebrew meeting, and Terrell said he thought it looked promising and that Jobs should stay in touch. The very next day, Jobs walked barefoot into Terrell's Byte Shop in Mountain View, California—one of the country's first computer stores—and told the proprietor, "I'm keeping in touch."

Terrell placed an order for fifty Apples—but he had to have them in thirty days. Twenty-nine days later he received them. Eventually, the two young men sold 150, at $666 each, some in the San Francisco Bay area, some by mail. The firm, now operating out of Jobs's garage, made $95,000. The Apple I left hobbyists and computer dealers with a feeling that the computer was reliable, and that was a lot for a machine that cost under $1,000. When Jobs and Wozniak got around to planning their next product—what would become the best-selling Apple II—they had an easier time. For one thing, finding investors was suddenly less difficult. A. C. "Mike" Markkula, then the marketing manager at Intel, liked what he saw and put up $91,000; he found another $600,000 through other venture capitalists. In May 1977 Markkula became Apple's chairman of the board. Michael Scott, taking a fifty-percent drop in salary, left National Semiconductor to become Apple's first president. Apple was in business.

What was missing in the Apple I—keyboard, power supply, video terminal, and memory—would be found in the new model. The Apple II would be elegant-looking, a new idea in selling computers for which Jobs could take the credit. The Apple II would have a sleek, lightweight, beige plastic case; the keyboard and computer would merge in a modular design. The Apple II was introduced in 1977. In February Apple Computer had its first genuine office—two large rooms in Cupertino, just a few miles from Homestead High School. Wozniak the pessimist thought no more than a thousand Apple IIs would be sold. Jobs the evangelist hoped to put a computer in everyone's home. He had one purpose in mind, selling Apple II, and so he lobbied Wozniak's friends to urge a reluctant Woz to quit his job at Hewlett-Packard and go full-time with Apple. The lobbying worked.

The $1,350 Apple II weighed twelve pounds and was easy to use. It became known as the Volkswagen of computers. It was the first finished product, the first computer that one could buy ready-made—no longer did one have to buy a kit and put the computer together. But what made Apple II such a huge success was its "open system," which enabled users to acquire add-on features for numerous applications. Seven internal expansion slots were put inside the machine for third-party developers, who went ahead and made such add-ons as voice and music synthesizers, digitizers, enhanced graphics generators, internal modems, bubble memory cards, clock cards, process control devices, and burglar alarm controllers. Computers that ran CP/M still had more programs available, but with its color and graphics, and in particular its educational software, the Apple II became the most popular.

Two milestones in Apple history are especially noteworthy. One was the announcement in the summer of 1978 of the availability of a disk drive, which provided faster, more efficient access to the computer's memory than the previous method used by the Apple II: tape cassettes. The second milestone was the arrival of the spreadsheet program called VisiCalc. It was at first available exclusively on Apples, beginning in October 1979, and sold for only $100. The impact of both these developments on Apple sales was great, especially in the second case: Apple executives estimate that of the 130,000 computers sold by September 1980, fully 25,000 were bought for the sake of VisiCalc.

The rise of Apple Computer was truly remarkable. Sales reached $117 million in 1980, $335 million in 1981, $583 million in 1982, $985 million in 1983. Apple went public in 1980 in one of the most successful high-tech stock offerings ever; Jobs's block of stock was worth $165 million at the time, Wozniak's $88 million.

What makes Steve Jobs tick? For one thing, he has been willing to take large risks—gambling $15 million in advertising on the Macintosh, for example. Certainly in the early years he derived great pleasure from beating the adult world at its own game, the game of work and money and power. His appearance in those early years—scraggly beard, shoulder-length hair, blue jeans—was enough to frighten off financiers. But he developed a way with people. He managed to lure Pepsi-Cola president John Sculley over to Apple in 1983 by telling him that if he stayed on at Pepsi, in five years he would have accomplished nothing more than getting kids to drink a lot more Pepsi. Whereas, if he came over to Apple, he could—in Jobs's hyperbolic phrase—change the world. The personal side of Steve Jobs has been difficult to uncover—so much of his life has been caught up in the Apple success story. Some of his heroes are Polaroid camera inventor Edwin Land, Chrysler chairman Lee

Iacocca, and William Hewlett, cofounder of Hewlett-Packard. Jobs contends that he is not political or party oriented. On the subject of romance, he describes the kind of women he likes as "young, super-intelligent, artistic." They are to be found in New York, not Silicon Valley.

Between 1977 and 1982 Apple dominated the personal computer market. But that dominance was shaken when IBM entered the field in 1981. Two years after the introduction of its PC, IBM had captured 28 percent of the market. Steve Jobs had his back to the wall. He had to fight for Apple's survival. His response was the introduction of a pair of new computers, the Apple IIe and the Lisa. (The Apple III, available since November 1980, had been promoted as a significant improvement over the II, with larger memory capacity, a built-in disk drive, and a better operating system. But it had never achieved any popularity, and only 90,000 were sold. Some called it a lemon: some 14,000 machines had to be called in and repaired.) Their arrival was announced in January 1983.

Years before, in late 1979, Jobs had latched onto the idea of that electronic rodent, the mouse—a pad with a rolling ball that permitted one to move the cursor on the monitor without using the keyboard. And thus began Lisa (for Local Integrated Software Architecture). With great fanfare, the $50-million gamble that was Lisa was introduced to 1,200 Apple stockholders in Cupertino, California. "The personal computer was created by a hardware revolution of the 1970s," Jobs said at the meeting. "The next dramatic change will come from a software revolution, which Apple is introducing here today." Lisa was meant to herald the second generation of personal computers: it was supposed to change the way people communicated with their machines. Instead of the twenty hours it took to learn how to use the Apple II, with Lisa it would take only twenty to forty minutes. This was supposed to be the ultimate in user-friendly machinery. Jobs predicted that Lisa would dominate the market for the next decade: the forecast was that 50,000 would be sold in the first year. But at $10,000 it was priced too high for the personal computer buyer. Further, Apple was late in getting software for the new product. It did not live up to expectations: 20,000 were actually sold by the mid-1980s.

Though Apple still had 21 percent of the personal computer market in 1983, IBM had 30 percent. If IBM did not actually want to wipe Apple off the face of the earth, as Jobs contended, it was certainly making its presence felt. In November 1984 IBM had 35 percent of the personal computer market to Apple's 19 percent. Jobs continued to fight back, launching the Macintosh in January 1984. Similar to the Lisa in many ways, it was more attractively priced, at $2,495. *Time* magazine thought the Macintosh looked "like an offspring of E.T. and R2-D2 that might start walking." It had a white screen, small pictures representing choices of programs and a mouse. It was billed as the first moderately priced computer that was simple to use. It had a memory (128K) that was too small to run complicated programs, and it had no business software; but it was still a gem. Using the Motorola 68000 microprocessor, a 32-bit one, the Mac had ten times the power of the Apple II while employing half as many chips.

The history of the Macintosh began back in 1979 when Jobs was given responsibility for the Mac project as compensation for not running the more important Lisa project; others in the firm had convinced him he was too inexperienced for the Lisa job. Jobs reluctantly agreed but bet the head of the Lisa division $5,000 that the Mac would be out first. Jobs lost the bet, but in the end the Mac far outsold the Lisa.

The Macintosh was Steve Jobs's electronic baby. He shaped it, nourished it, pampered it into life. To say that he put his everything into it is an understatement. Working on the Macintosh project was the most exciting and absorbing thing Jobs had ever done. The project took on do-or-die proportions: the Mac would be the best that Jobs and his team could possibly make it, and if it failed, well, said Jobs, then Apple deserved to fail. Employees of the Mac project had to endure Jobs's endless string of get-the-work-done-quickly demands. He seemed a cross between football coach and Chairman Mao. He held parties, gave out medals, and offered Apple stock for programmers and engineers who did well. He also delivered quotes from "Chairman Jobs," among them "It's more fun to be a pirate than to join the navy" and "True artists ship." Mac project members retaliated by wearing T-shirts that read, "Working ninety hours a week and loving every minute of it." One participant compared the project to an endless cocktail party with chips and software in place of drinks. Though Jobs had sworn his team to secrecy, he himself was so excited about the project that he showed an advance model of the Mac to folk singer Joan Baez.

The Mac was indeed an original. When pressure grew to make it IBM-compatible, Jobs resisted, saying that he wanted to create a second industry standard, that he wanted to sell five million Macs a year. Becoming IBM compatible simply wasn't the path to take. By early 1985, however, he had changed his mind, in order to make the Mac more attractive to businesses that were already dependent on IBM mainframes. He was asked if he had consulted the public for advice on how the new computer should be built. His reply: "Did Alexander Graham Bell do any market research before he invented the telephone?" He did, however, model some of the features of the Mac after work done at Xerox Corporation, expecially the mouse and the graphics capabilities.

Sales of the Mac started well. It sold 70,000 in the first hundred days, 20,000 above its goal. By the end of the Mac's first year 250,000 computers had been sold, half to businesses, making it the most successful personal computer kickoff to date. The figure had reached 400,000 by June 1985, and a half-million by the start of 1986. In 1986 some 405,000 Macs were sold, and the forecast for 1987 was that another 600,000 would be purchased. But Jobs was still not satisfied: to be truly successful the Macintosh would have to break IBM's stranglehold on the business world. So in January 1985 he announced the Macintosh Office, centered around AppleTalk, a system that would permit businesses to connect as many as thirty-two Macintosh computers, at just $50 a hookup, into an office network. Mac was no longer a stand-alone computer and would thus appeal to businesses. Meanwhile, in April 1984 Apple had introduced the 7½ pound Apple IIc portable computer, priced at $1,300.

By the mid-1980s the Apple strategy was to try to focus public attention on the Macintosh, the super-fancy electronic whiz that dominated nearly every interview Steve Jobs would give. Some found this counterproductive—for in November 1984 the two millionth Apple II had been sold, making it the most widely used computer of its kind. And in September 1984 more Apple IIs—both the IIe and the IIc—were bought than at any time in its eight-year history. The Apple II was a survivor. Jobs had ballyhooed the Lisa and the Macintosh as the computers of the future; but Lisa was proving a major disappointment, and Macintosh, despite its spectacular start-up, had fewer buyers in all of 1984 than the Apple IIs had in the fourth quarter alone. Apple IIs accounted for 75 percent of Apple's sales in that year.

The explanation of course lay in the Apple II. No computer is as flexible. When Apple boasts that there are more people doing more things with Apple IIs than with any other computer, they are more than likely correct. The Apple II can run over 10,000 software programs. The Macintosh, however, was sealed, with no chance for physical expansion. Jobs has an answer for that one: In the old days—way back in the late 1970s—hardware expansion was the only way to customize computers to meet the needs of the user. Now, however, Apple knows more or less what its buyers want, and whatever customization is necessary can be done via software. Nevertheless, the public is still voting for the old-new Apple IIs.

Still, one day Jobs's prediction may come true—Macintosh may indeed become the industry's biggest-selling product. Jobs had announced that this would happen within a year and a half of the appearance of the Macintosh on the market. Clearly it's going to take quite a bit longer than that.

The year 1985 was not a good one for Apple or for Steve Jobs. IBM was becoming increasingly dominant in the personal computer field, and even a giant like Apple had trouble competing. In April, Apple announced that it was stopping as of that summer the production of its top-of-the-line business computer, the $3,995 Macintosh XL, formerly the Lisa. This came just four months after the Lisa was renamed. Its primary market, the large corporations, had preferred IBM machines. Apple's transition from marketer of computers for the school and the individual to marketer for business was just not working.

In early June of that year a major reorganization of Apple occurred, with Jobs yielding his control over the Macintosh division. He retained the title of chairman of Apple. Jobs then held 11.3 percent—or seven million—of the company's sixty million common shares, worth in early 1983 $400 million but in June 1985 about $120 million. Apple spokesmen explained that Jobs planned to "take a more global role in new production innovations and [would] continue to be a creator of powerful ideas and the champion of Apple's spirit." Press reports, however, indicated that he had been stripped of day-to-day operational responsibility after a falling-out between the Apple II division and his own Macintosh division. The Apple II employees complained, according to the reports, that Apple had treated them like second-class citizens, giving more attention to Macintosh than to their product. In the course of this corporate shake-up, Steve Wozniak departed.

Jobs's decision to bring John Sculley into the Apple family had backfired when, in the spring of 1985, Sculley had come to the conclusion that Jobs was a drag on the firm and had begun to ease him out of his direct supervisory role. With Apple not doing well, Jobs became the scapegoat: he had put all of Apple's marbles into the Macintosh; he was not aware enough of the customer's needs; he was too preoccupied with elegant technology. Whether Sculley was right or not, the statistics told of Apple going downhill. And that of course had an impact on how others thought of Jobs. In 1985 Apple posted earnings of $61.2 million—down 4 percent from 1984—on revenue of a record $1.92 billion. Revenue was up 26 percent over 1984, but that hardly mattered.

As the founder and guiding force of Apple from its inception, Jobs was not likely to take such treatment from Sculley lightly. Throughout that summer he sulked in a new office in an auxiliary building—an office he nicknamed Siberia. With little to do, he took long walks on the Stanford University campus. One day in late August he lunched with Paul Berg, a Nobel Prize–winning geneticist at the school. They talked about how wonderful it would be if Berg's expensive experiments could be distributed for teaching purposes via computer simulations. Berg complained that universities didn't have the computers or the software. That switched on a light in Jobs's mind. Here was a new challenge, here perhaps was a project that would get his restless brain busy again.

Meeting soon thereafter with a few close associates from Apple, Jobs decided to tell the Apple board, meeting on September 12, what was jelling in his mind. At first Sculley and the other board members seemed sympathetic to the idea; they even mentioned that Apple might share in the new Jobs project, purchasing as much as ten percent of it. Such talk, hardly anything Jobs would consider seriously—he wanted to be rid of Apple—at least rekindled in him some of the old, warm feelings he had once had for Sculley.

Those warm feelings didn't last long. The trouble began, so Sculley notes, when Jobs handed him a list of the names of those who would be leaving Apple to go with his new venture. Though Jobs had promised to take only low-level people, the list contained, in Sculley's view, five key employees. This amounted to deception on Jobs's part and the ugly word *lawsuit* was spoken.

Lawsuit or not, Jobs was on his way out of Apple. He resigned as chairman on September 17, 1985, remaining the largest shareholder, with some 5.5 million shares, or 9 percent of the stock. A week later, Apple announced that it was suing Jobs for "secretly scheming" to exploit company research for a new venture and for deceiving Apple about his plans. In reply, Jobs insisted that he had never planned to steal any of his old firm's technology.

Meanwhile he established his new firm, called Next. His plan, he said, was to market a sophisticated "scholar's workstation" for under $10,000 to universities and colleges. It would be the equal of existing machines that cost $20,000 to $35,000. Jobs turned down all offers of venture capital: this time he would keep majority control. Financing for Next came from the roughly $100 million worth of Apple stock Jobs sold in 1985 and early 1986.

Having spent.many hours with lawyers, having worried for months whether the suit would hinder his moving on to the next phase of his career, Jobs was delighted when in January of 1986 the ordeal with Apple came to an end. Announcement was made then of an out-of-court settlement that in some ways tied Jobs's hands but, most significantly, did not prevent him from going to market with the educational computers he planned. Under the terms of the settlement, Jobs agreed to submit a prototype of his firm's new computer to Apple. Apple would have thirty days to inspect the machine to see if any of its proprietary technology had been used. Limiting the period to just thirty days meant that there would be no foot-dragging on Apple's part: Jobs was pleased with that part of the settlement. The settlement further stipulated that the Next computer must be more powerful than any of Apple's and must have a different operating system and different software. It was not permitted on the market until July 1, 1987. Jobs also promised that he would not do any raiding of Apple employees for six months.

With lots of spare cash and a fresh start on life, Jobs was able to breathe a bit easier. He wasn't eager to tie himself down to one project. He went on the prowl that winter of 1986, acquiring an enterprise that had long appealed to him, Pixar. Pixar had once been the computer graphics division of Lucasfilm, the maker of Star Wars and other fantasy films, and a pioneer in the use of computer graphics for moviemaking wizardry. Jobs, putting in one day a week as the new chairman of the board of Pixar, planned to take the computer graphics division, all forty-three people, and stretch it to its limits, to go beyond the film business.

As for Next, Jobs told a group of education officials in Pittsburgh in November 1986 that its first advanced workstation for universities would be announced in 1987. He also showed a film of software running on the $100,000 graphics workstation made by Pixar. The first program displayed a three-dimensional, rotating simulated human pelvis, built by processing small amounts of CAT-scan data with complex classification algorithms. Said Jobs, "It has never before been possible to see this without surgery." Five years from now, he asserted, "I want to be able to do this on a $5,000 workstation."

Reversing his earlier decision to avoid venture capital in order to preserve his independence, Jobs took on a surprising "angel" in Ross Perot in the winter of 1987. With funds running low, Jobs had actively sought venture capitalists, and Perot came knocking, putting up $20 million for a 16-percent stake and a seat on the Next board. Jobs was jubilant, observing that Perot had told him that he thought the new team would "hit one out of the ball park." Perot too was excited: "In terms of a start-up company, it's one that carries the least risk of any I've seen in 25 years in the computer industry."

Whether Jobs will turn Next and Pixar into a great success is unclear. What is quite clear, however, is that Steve Jobs, the kid who puttered around the garage in the mid-1970s and brought off a computer revolution, is not down and out. He is, after all, only thirty-two years old.

Adam Osborne

He Made the Computer Portable

29

He wanted a computer that would fit under an airplane seat, that could be dropped (and still work), that would come with lots of software. He wanted a computer that would be easy to make. And so Adam Osborne gave the world the Osborne I in April 1981. It was the first commercially successful portable computer with accompanying software. Nothing like it existed before. "I saw an opportunity. It seemed like an obvious thing to do . . . to focus on the things that people really needed—and to get prices down. That's all."

When he was on the rise, and his computer was the hit of the industry, people asked for Osborne's autograph. He was sitting on a gold mine. For the year ending in May 1983, its best year, Osborne Computer Corporation earned $100 million. It was one of the fastest-growing companies in the short history of Silicon Valley. By 1984 some 100,000 people would buy the Osborne I.

But no sooner had Osborne's star ascended than it fell. His descent into bankruptcy in September 1983 was observed by those in the computer world with at least as much fascination as his rise had been, for it signaled some of the unforeseen pitfalls that might await others.

Adam Osborne was born to British parents in Bangkok, Thailand, on March 6, 1939. His father taught history at the University of Bangkok. During World War II Adam and his mother lived in a village in South India near Madras; his father was stranded in Bangkok, unable to leave until the war was over. As a young child

Osborne was sent to a Catholic boarding school run by nuns who, as he recalls, "tended to be very nasty women." They were especially nasty to the non-Catholic children, so Osborne became a Catholic largely in self-protection. He abandoned that faith at age seventeen and became what he calls a theist ("I believe in God and that's it").

He went to England at the age of eleven and attended schools in Warwickshire. In 1961 he graduated from Birmingham University as a chemical engineer. A girlfriend, not the lure of big money, was the inspiration for his move to the United States in July 1961.

Osborne first held a job with M. W. Kellogg in New York, as a chemical design engineer. Sensing that he was not cut out for the corporate world, and with some strong encouragement from his wife, he decided to advance his education. So he enrolled in graduate school at the University of Delaware. The meager scholarship on which he had to live was a strong incentive to finish his doctoral work expeditiously: he selected a thesis that would allow him to employ computers, because he had seen how long it took others to do their theses without them—two years to collect data, another three to analyze it. Osborne received a doctorate in chemical engineering in 1968.

He began working for Shell Oil in Emeryville, California (across San Francisco Bay), in 1968, doing mathematical modeling on computers. Three years later he was fired after a series of conflicts with the bosses: he was, in his own view, an extremely aggressive, frustrated overachiever. He then formed his own company, Osborne and Associates. In 1972 a Southern California minicomputer firm named General Automation hired Osborne's firm to write manuals in simple language. Within two years he had fifteen people working under him, but a management change at General Automation left him jobless. During this period he had written a small book entitled *The Value of Power,* which was given away to clients. Osborne renamed an expanded version *An Introduction to Microcomputers* and offered it to a publisher, who rejected it. He then published it himself. It was one of the first books about personal computers and sold 300,000 copies. Without seeing it in advance, thirteen universities bought it as soon as the first copy was printed. It has since been used as a textbook in hundreds of universities. Osborne's publishing house put out forty books on computers in the next five years; he himself wrote twelve of them. Then in 1979 McGraw-Hill bought him out. The purchase price was never revealed, but reports vary between $3 million and $10 million.

In 1975 Osborne had begun writing a magazine column about computers called "From the Fountainhead," first for *Interface Age* and later for *InfoWorld*. The idea was to inform consumers of the shortcomings of computers, and at first Osborne did just that. But he eventually turned to muckraking pieces, alleging that some computer firms were manipulating customers. He condemned the common policy of announcing equipment before it was ready and financing its development with the funds that came from advance orders. (Following his bankruptcy, some of Osborne's critics noted with irony that his company's downfall had apparently been at least partly due to its announcing the Executive computer too early.)

Osborne was especially critical of "the smaller, 'schlock' outfits who were foisting a product [on the public] that didn't work, charging them, then not giving them their money back." One charge Osborne leveled at microcomputer producers was that they offered frills and add-ons instead of simple, inexpensive machinery. He was in fact providing the rationale for the Osborne I. After a few years Osborne got the feeling that no one out there was listening; he stopped writing the column in March 1981. And by that date, of course, he had a new business to run.

A year earlier he had decided that he would start up a company and build a portable computer himself. Osborne believed strongly that computers should go portable. He couldn't understand why the Silicon Valley firms had failed to take that step. Of course small computers had been around for a while, but these were largely used by professionals. Osborne planned to bring small computers to the people. "I wanted to make something people could really use. I knew that people would be very happy to move a computer from one desk to another without getting a hernia, or without having pieces falling all over the place, having to unplug everything and plug it up again." Unlike the prevailing situation, with hardware and software sellers working separately, Osborne planned to offer "bundled software," some $2,000 worth (Wordstar, Supercalc, CBASIC, MBASIC), with the machine—free of charge. That would make potential buyers pay attention.

At the West Coast Computer Faire in San Francisco, Osborne

found the man to build the machine—Lee Felsenstein, whom he had known from the Homebrew Computer Club. Osborne gave Felsenstein some specifications: the computer had to be sturdy, and small enough for travel. It also had to be easy to make. The machine Felsenstein would design would have only forty screws and would take sixty-eight minutes for assembly. Osborne wanted a forty-column display (in fact, he got fifty-two), and he wanted the computer to be cheap. At $1,795, the Osborne I was indeed forty to sixty percent cheaper than other comparable equipment on the market. Had it been up to Osborne, the price would have been below $1,000, but colleagues convinced him this was unreasonable.

Most of the design for the computer was worked out in a large room in a Berkeley building. The prototype took four months to build, at a cost of $28,000. In January 1981 Osborne took office space in Hayward, California. The Osborne I was introduced at the West Coast Computer Faire in April. It was the smash of the computer show. Weighing only 24 pounds, and truly a portable computer, it was the computer industry's best bargain—at $1,795, including all that software. One joke making the rounds was that Osborne was really selling the software, and giving the computer away for free. Critics looked at the new Osborne I and disparagingly said it resembled a World War II field radio, with all its dials and wires in the front. Yet it was a computer: it had a detachable keyboard, a 5-inch screen, 64K of memory, and two built-in disk drives. And one could take it from home to office—and back home again!

In July 1981 the first computers were shipped. Osborne had market projections that showed sales reaching 10,000 a month within the first year. Some predicted he wouldn't even come close to that. But, Osborne said later with great pride, we got there. In fact Adam Osborne had created his own niche in the computer business, and it would be some time before rivals could catch up. He had found a market and had exploited it quickly and successfully. In September 1981 Osborne Computer Corporation (OCC) had its first $1-million month in revenues. At the peak, some 10,000 Osborne I's would be sold a month.

Between August and December 1981—the first calendar year of the new product—the Osborne I had $6 million in sales. In the second year it reached $70 million. That first year was not perfect by

---

any means: in August 1981 the IBM PC reached the market. Then too, during the first six months after their appearance some ten to fifteen percent of the Osborne I's required service during their ninety-day warranty period. In August 1982 Osborne came to realize that OCC required professional management: he had five hundred employees and was doing $10 million a month of business. He chose Robert Jaunich, president of Consolidated Foods of Chicago, to take over the firm.

The following November two new Osborne computers were being planned. One was the Executive, which was to have more memory than the Osborne I, a 7-inch screen, and a price of $1,995; the other was the Vixen, with a 5-inch screen priced at $1,495. Both were to be introduced by February 1983.

Then the trouble began. "I and most of the other people in this industry were incredibly naive," Osborne reflected two years later. "We were not businessmen. We were having fun, and what really happened is [that] the moment we started to do really well, the vultures started to come in, the three-piece-pin-stripe-suited vultures all started to come in. And they started to rape the initial entrepreneurs one at a time. I got raped, very simply, but I also got a hell of a good education in the process, and it won't happen again." The well-dressed vultures were big businessmen, who, Osborne claims, seized the opportunity to make a good deal of money by taking over new computer firms on the rise. It would appear that Osborne had his own experience with Jaunich in mind when he accused the "three-piece-pin-stripe-suited vultures" of raping early entrepreneurs like himself.

Difficulties attended the arrival of the Executive. First, Osborne and Jaunich disagreed over the price: Osborne favored a low $1,995, but Jaunich had his way and the machine was priced at $2,495. The Executive was announced with a flourish during the early part of 1983. March sales of the Osborne I dropped, dealers eagerly awaiting the arrival of the Executive. Later, Adam Osborne would recall in frustration that he had warned others in the company that such a drop-off would inevitably occur with the announcement of the Executive, but no one had listened. In addition, word spread that shipments were being delayed. Osborne contended that this was a false rumor, but nevertheless dealers were becoming uneasy about OCC.

Though Osborne had insisted to dealers that the Executive would not compete with the Osborne I, many orders for the Osborne I were canceled. From the 10,000 sold in February 1983, sales dropped to only 100 in April. Shipments of the Executive did not start until May. Some 20,000 Osborne I's were waiting to be sold when the announcement of the Executive came. The Vixen was never introduced.

That summer, creditors were not paid on time. Employees were laid off. On July 27, 1983, the price of the Osborne I was cut from $1,995 to $1,295; some stores sold it for as little as $800. On September 13 Adam Osborne's miracle company went bankrupt. OCC had $45 million in liabilities and six hundred creditors waiting. It was a shock to the industry.

OCC executives had had trouble controlling the company's extremely rapid growth. Though Adam Osborne had acknowledged that the company would be better off with businessmen than with computer experts running it, the switch to Jaunich had not made the necessary difference. Industry people quipped that Osborne had gone from the Second Coming to the first going. Adam Osborne did not find the joke amusing.

After the bankruptcy Osborne and John Dvorak, a writer on the computer industry, coauthored *Hypergrowth,* Osborne's version of what happened at OCC. After two publishers turned them down, Osborne published it himself. In the book Osborne placed much of the blame for OCC's downfall on Jaunich; Jaunich called the book the work of a third-rate novelist.

By the spring of 1984 Osborne had formed a new firm, Paperback Software International. Getting the cash to start the firm was no easy matter for Osborne, who found that venture capitalists were perfectly willing to meet him—after all, he was a combination of media star and industry curiosity—but not prepared to turn over their money. He did obtain $200,000 from an electronics distributor in Menlo Park, California, and used $150,000 of his own funds. In January 1985 Osborne took Paperback Software on the penny stock market and sold six million shares at ten cents apiece. The offer was sold out, raising $540,000.

OCC received some loans to help it buy time and handle its debts. By the summer of 1984 a federal bankruptcy court in San Francisco had accepted a reorganization plan. In July Adam Osborne resigned as chairman at OCC. He had still, however, to deal with investor lawsuits related to the bankruptcy.

Osborne's new workplace was the guest house of his Berkeley Hills estate above San Francisco Bay. Just as he had succeeded in creating inexpensive hardware, he hoped now to duplicate the feat by selling inexpensive software. Others might have left the computer business after an experience like Osborne's; might, at least, have feared so quick a return. But not Adam Osborne. He plunged right in with another daring idea. His popularity did not suffer at all from the bankruptcy. He was in demand as a speaker but limited himself to just two lectures a month, in order to ensure that he would have enough time for his new business.

Osborne is convinced that the price of software can and must come down radically. Programs now selling for over $500 could be marketed for as little as $50 to $100, he believes, without sacrificing a great deal of quality. What is more, the software vendor would be the main beneficiary, for many more people would buy software. Once the price drops to $20 to $30 a program—and Osborne thinks this will happen in time—people will buy software the way they buy hardcover books.

He intends to act as the distributor and packager for small software firms that cannot individually afford to do what he will do. He plans to sell, through bookstores, data-management and electronic spreadsheet programs for under $100—four or five times less than what they have been selling for. In the spring of 1985 Paperback Software launched a $50,000 advertising campaign, which featured full-page color photographs of Osborne—an attempt to exploit his wide public recognition. Osborne thinks he deserves that recognition. After all, he is the father of the portable computer.

Adam Osborne has proved himself one of the real survivors of the computer industry. In the winter of 1987 he remained committed to selling software at reasonable prices. It was too early to say whether Paperback Software would put Osborne back on top again. But Osborne, at least, was giving it a try.

William Millard

The Man Who Built ComputerLand

30

Once the computer had become a mass-produced commodity, the question was how it would be marketed—in big department stores, in office-supply stores, in radio and TV stores? With the emergence of a retail chain called ComputerLand, a new answer was clear. There were 820 ComputerLand stores as of early 1986—making it the world's largest computer retailer.

The man who founded this $1.5-billion business is William Millard. In 1975 he was broke. Ten years later he was one of America's wealthiest businessmen. (Millard was number 31 on *Forbes*'s list of the 400 richest Americans in 1984.) He got that way by peddling computers. "I hear numbers that indicate that by the end of this century, the computer industry may be the largest single industry on the planet," says Bill Millard. "Well, we have an opportunity, at least, to become the largest retailer of the largest segment of the largest industry on the planet."

Millard spearheaded the drive that would put personal computers into the offices and homes of millions. He was one of the first to recognize the potential of the microprocessor for personal computer applications: his IMSAI 8080, marketed in 1975, has been called the first commercial-grade personal computer.

William Millard was born on June 2, 1932, in Denver, Colorado. In 1936 his parents left Denver and found work in East Oakland, California, his father as a clerk with the Southern Pacific Railroad and his mother as a secretary in the Oakland Montgomery Ward store. It was the Depression, and Millard's father set great value on holding onto a job—something the boy had trouble understanding at the time. The family did not starve, but there weren't too many extras other than the free railway pass that allowed them to visit family in Denver each Christmas. Until the age of ten, Bill was an only child. Over the next eighteen years his five sisters were born.

As a small child he supplemented the family income by raising chickens and selling the eggs. At the age of nine he went door to door selling magazines. He then took on a newspaper route, selling the Oakland *Tribune,* though he was below the legal minimum age. Millard worked at that 365 days a year, until his junior year at St. Elizabeth's High School in Oakland. He had no time for sports or any other recreation. After he graduated, he had neither the cash nor the inclination to attend college. For the next three years he worked as a conductor and switchman for the railroad.

The start of the Korean War found Millard digging ditches and shoveling gravel into a cement mixer in a munitions depot. After that he worked as a truckdriver, a welder's helper, an accounting clerk. He entered the University of San Francisco in the spring of 1952, remaining only three semesters. There he took philosophy and premedical courses but had a hard time deciding on a career, as every subject he studied appealed to him. Homework, however, did not appeal—understandable under the circumstances: he was combining college with outside work, collecting fares on the Berkeley area train, working at a bank, adding a 45-hour work week to his studies. One favorite recreation—when he had time—was taking apart car engines. School at last proved just too expensive, and Millard dropped out.

In 1954 he began working in the Oakland branch office of a consumer finance firm, Pacific Finance Corporation. He started in the lowest job, field representative—essentially a bill collector going door to door. His youthful looks—he was twenty-one but appeared fourteen—didn't help in bill collection, but he was persistent. From there he became a credit interviewer and then a collection manager. Thinking nothing of putting in a 70-hour week, Millard was determined to win promotion. And he did. In 1956, at age twenty-three, he was named Pacific Finance's Oakland branch manager—the youngest ever. In that year too he married Pat Nolder, whom he had met at Pacific Finance.

Millard's entry into the computer world came in 1958. Pacific Finance decided to set up a data-processing facility employing mainframes. Though he was one of three hundred branch managers and lacked a college degree, Millard did well enough on tests and his work record was strong enough that he was chosen one of three people to work in the new central data-processing operation. He had to move to Los Angeles, and there he went to work on the twenty-sixth UNIVAC computer ever built. Gazing at the magical piece of equipment, Millard felt that he was a member of a privileged class. He remained at that job for three years. Futurist technology intrigued him, and he stayed abreast by reading *Scientific American*. Senior people in the firm wanted to make him general auditor, but without that college degree they could not do it.

Then Millard responded to an ad that was to take him a notch higher. In 1961 he became the first chief of data processing for Alameda County. He enjoyed this job enormously—he traveled throughout the county, talking to county officials, explaining to them how computers could make their jobs and life easier. In 1963 he directed the design of a county wide police information system. It employed remote computer terminals that accessed a central computer via telephone lines and was the first of its type in the world. Millard acquired a national, even an international, reputation. In 1965 he worked as a consultant to IBM on state and local government. In the wake of his Alameda County success, the city of San Francisco took him on to perform the same miracle.

It was time for Bill Millard to set off on his own. He wanted to run his own business. He was now a leading figure in the data-processing field and hoped to capitalize on that fact. In 1969 he and Pat formed Systems Dynamics, a firm specializing in telecommunications software. Selling software was new, and Millard hoped to outpace IBM. Things didn't work out; Bill and Pat Millard worried constantly about how to meet the payroll, and they accumulated large debts. Finally, they closed the firm in May 1972, a painful decision. Millard had optimistically believed he had the experience to become a businessman, but now he acknowledged that he had been confusing being a manager with being a businessman. It was a valuable lesson. Setting up Systems Dynamics, he would say later, was like entering the stock market in 1929. He felt lonely, lost, uncertain about the future. He was no longer in demand, and it frightened him.

It was in 1975 that he formed Information Management Sciences—IMS—a small firm that built prototype computer products. He operated the business out of the basement of his home in San Leandro, California. His original purpose was not at all to build a computer. In fact, he wanted to stay in data processing, figuring out what kinds of computers a business should use and then helping it to use those computers. He actually formed IMS as a vehicle for landing a contract to design and implement an on-line information retrieval system for the Los Angeles Sheriff's Department. IMS survived over the next three years; but working as he did on a contract basis, first in software and then in hardware, Millard had to endure the frustration of starting from scratch after each contract was completed.

He built a computer almost as an aside. In early 1975 a New Mexico car dealer asked Millard to help him locate a computer that would ease his accounting tasks. Millard planned to buy a computer and add on whatever the dealer required. First he thought of a DEC minicomputer, for which he would design special peripheral controllers; but that didn't work out. He turned to other brands of minicomputers, but like the DEC they proved too expensive. After spending half the money available for the entire contract, Millard realized he was only one-third of the way through the project; he desperately sought a solution. It was then that he decided to design a commercial-grade computer system based upon an Intel 8080 microprocessor silicon chip. It dawned on him that if he could build a computer complete with programs, he might be able to turn a profit after all by selling it as a general-purpose computer in markets outside the auto dealer industry.

Millard knew all about the newest chips, the 8008 and the 8080, but even the people who had produced them at Intel weren't positive that one could perform standard data-processing operations with them—reading a file, outputting it to a printer, and the rest. Of course they were good for automating washing machines and cars, and maybe even for performing as "intelligent" computer terminals; but that was all. Millard thought differently.

In January of that year a technician had showed Millard the current issue of *Popular Science,* which featured the MITS Altair, the kit computer based on the 8080 chip. Millard's interest was piqued: could he go one better, could he build a computer sophisticated enough to do industrial and commercial work? It all seemed to come down to adapting the Altair's bus structure—what would become the S100. Then IMS would be better able to do other jobs for other customers: after one contract was finished, they could build on what they had done to engineer other products.

Millard, his wife, and their three daughters sat around the kitchen table, on which sat muffin tins filled with parts. Each Millard would hand-sort parts from the tins into plastic bags, then toss in instructions. What they were assembling was the IMSAI 8080 computer kit, for which hobbyists would pay $399—eventually $499. Once they had acquired the parts, buyers would still have to solder them together. The new computer was similar to the Altair but incorporated a variety of new and upgraded features and components that Millard considered necessary for a commercial-grade machine.

For several months after the IMSAI 8080 design was completed, buyers could obtain the product only through the mail. Remarkably, the new gadget evoked enormous interest. A small ad in *Popular Electronics* produced 3,500 replies. Some people even sent in checks before receiving the product. Millard's sales pitch was appropriately hyperbolic: typewriters would grow obsolete, the personal computer revolution was under way. Not quite yet. For one thing, weighing in at eighty pounds this was not exactly a handy item to have on your desk, or to carry around. Then too, no software had been written for it. Programming it was left to the professionals, since it could be programmed only in machine language. Still, the IMSAI 8080 represented a major step forward, providing so much computer power at so low a price.

In 1976 IMS decided to sell the 8080 computer as a finished product, seeking to capitalize on the sudden development of a personal computer market. For a brief time Millard was the leader of the personal computer revolution. But problems arose with the quality of subsequent versions of his computer, and soon more advanced products hit the market, especially the Apple II in 1977. Meanwhile, IMS began to move in a different direction. The firm began getting requests for dealerships—these were in fact the very first retail computer stores. IMS quickly grew to some two hundred domestic and international dealers, with almost all sales stemming from these dealer stores and systems houses.

Despite the revolutionary IMSAI computer, Millard's IMS firm very soon collapsed. In 1978 he filed for bankruptcy. By that time, however, he was already well under way in getting ComputerLand started, so the fall of IMS was cushioned. Millard's intuition about the future of computer stores was right on the mark. Before the advent of ComputerLand stores, places that sold computers were often unpleasant, evincing few signs of stability, as reflected in the unattractive handwritten wall posters that passed for advertising. Expecting the public's appetite for computers soon to be voracious, Millard became convinced that there was great potential for a "professionally designed," well-run retail computer store chain. Though it sold hamburgers and not computers, MacDonald's was a favorite model for Bill Millard. He admired the way it grew without sacrificing standards—the hamburgers were always edible and the restaurants were always spotless.

ComputerLand began on September 21, 1976, with Millard as chairman of the board. Edward Faber, Millard's sales manager at IMS, became ComputerLand's first president. A pilot store was opened in Hayward, California, in November 1976, and the first franchise store opened in Morristown, New Jersey, in February 1977. Millard believed in the franchise approach. That way the ownership did not need to worry each day whether a store would open on time. With hundreds of stores, Millard figured he would have needed district, regional, area, county, even hemisphere managers. Each one would have a car, an office, a secretary, a personal computer, an expense account, personnel problems, communications problems, health problems. At first the firm was called Computer Shack. Millard thought this was a wonderful name, but Radio Shack did not. Certain that he had right on his side, Millard also knew that Radio Shack had time and money on its side. So he backed down, removed the signs on all the stores—and came up with ComputerLand.

Millard sensed early that computers would be sold far more to businesses than to homes. Experience supported this feeling: In 1976 he had offered an IMSAI machine, at $1,500, that could be programmed to control many of the functions of a home—run a sprinkling system, turn lights on and off, regulate the heat, handle the fire and burglar alarms. But he had sold only two of the machines.

By the end of 1977 there were 24 ComputerLand stores in thirteen states; the number grew to 50 by September 1978, 100 by November 1979, and 500 by August 1983. The first store overseas was opened in Sydney, Australia, in January 1978. By 1983 ComputerLand was doing $983 million in sales, the sixth straight year it had doubled sales. On September 14, 1984, the 700th store opened. ComputerLand Corporate had 1,300 employees, the franchises another 15,000. Until July 1982 the stores had been handling Apple products, but at that time they stopped after Apple demanded the right to approve store locations. Apple soon afterward returned to the fold, without getting a veto over store sites. When the IBM PC came out, ComputerLand had (along with Sears Roebuck) the exclusive right to sell it for about six months.

By the mid-1980s ComputerLand stores were doing eighty-five percent of their sales with the business and professional community. People were still not buying computers for home use in large numbers. ComputerLand stores, which average $2 million a year in sales, are free to choose their own products, within certain standards of quality. These usually fall in the $2,000 to $5,000 range. After shipping hardware and software to the franchises at cost, ComputerLand Corporate takes eight percent of the franchisees' sales revenues off the top, in addition to one percent for advertising; ComputerLand Corporate does not dictate price to franchises. The stores are not obliged to buy products from ComputerLand Corporate, but it has proved economical to do so because of bulk purchasing; they may, however, buy from whomever they want. ComputerLand Corporate will not commit itself to buying very large amounts of computers from a company. If the product doesn't sell, Corporate doesn't want useless inventory. Store design, fixtures, and furniture are customized. ComputerLand gets a hundred new products a week to evaluate, and only three or four will be approved for sale in ComputerLand stores (if the franchisees want to carry them). Millard has been careful never to say which are his favorites among the product lines his stores carry.

For quite some time Millard kept out of the public eye. He was a wealthy man but felt no need for attention. He liked being able to come and go as he pleased and where he pleased. This made him one of the computer industry's great men of mystery. Then, in the late summer of 1983, Millard underwent a change of mind. Perhaps he sensed that his invisibility was causing many franchises to feel isolated. He decided to acquire a public face, and to do so in a big way. In August he attended his first ComputerLand annual conference. If he harbored any second thoughts about stepping into the glare of publicity, they were made moot when in October 1983 *Forbes* magazine put him on its list of the nation's 400 wealthiest people for the first time. And in its December 5, 1983, issue the magazine ran a story about him headlined "The Instant Billionaire." Millard soon concluded that being a public figure wasn't all bad: he decided to become the company's chief spokesman.

Millard completed a course in Werner Erhard's EST training, a self-help program that seeks to develop clarified and enhanced personal goals and capabilities. Keeping one's agreements and being honest and straightforward with people are also aims of EST, and Millard declares these to be fundamental principles of his company. Given Millard's adherence to EST, it became popular among ComputerLand employees to fall in step with the Erhard approach.

At least until the mid-1980s, Millard had the reputation of being able to keep situations from falling apart. His forte was not so much the daily management of the firm—that he left to family members and some other trusted executives. Instead he focused his efforts and attention on initiating, guiding, and monitoring the company's general direction. His coup in getting ComputerLand into China—a deal completed in May 1984—was perhaps the best example of that.

He wanted his firm to be wildly successful. The way to achieve that, he thought, was by making sure that both sides of every business deal triumphed. He called it his "win-win" approach; ComputerLand employees lived and breathed the slogan. Within the first few sentences of every conversation with ComputerLand people in the winter of 1985, one heard that slogan. Millard's employees talked about his round-the-clock work habits, and especially his intensity. They spoke with awe of the way he would concentrate on one thing to the exclusion of all else. They liked to recall the day in October 1984 when he was talking to ComputerLand employees in Tokyo, and his interpreter suddenly stopped translating and began trembling. Why had he stopped? Millard asked. The translator told him there had been an earthquake.

Until very recently, ComputerLand the corporation truly *was* Bill Millard. He refused to have the company go public. He owned ninety-five percent of ComputerLand, and his family played a significant role in the company: his daughter Barbara was president of the corporate affairs division; his daughter Anne was a personal assistant to her father; the youngest daughter, Elizabeth, the computer specialist in the family, also worked in the corporate affairs division, managing the Millard Family Foundation, a philanthropic concern aiding organizations in San Francisco and elsewhere. Millard's wife, Pat, was a company director and a member of the corporate management committee. Barbara's husband, Jon Noellert, was a corporate officer.

Millard suffered a major setback in mid–March of 1985 when an Alameda County jury ordered him to honor a nine-year-old note held by an investor group called Micro/Vest. In 1976 he had been trying to keep IMS going and had borrowed $250,000 from a Boston-area investment company named Marriner, which had subsequently sold the note to Micro/Vest. The note was convertible into twenty percent of the stock in Millard's firm.

ComputerLand contested the order. By August company officials were saying that ComputerLand might be forced to enter into bankruptcy in order to continue its legal fight. That fight was eased considerably that month when the California Court of Appeals permitted ComputerLand to post a $25-million cash bond rather than the $283 million usually required. By the end of September Millard and his daughter Barbara had agreed to yield control of the company in order to prevent a threatened revolt by franchisees, who claimed that their royalty fees had become too much of a strain given the slump in computer sales, and that ComputerLand had not provided them with sufficient aid.

On December 12, 1985, ComputerLand and Micro/Vest announced that they had settled some of their differences. The settlement released ComputerLand from paying $141.5 million in damages or posting the $25-million bond to file an appeal. It also called for the company to go public within two years.

Little was heard from Millard for the next six months, but by July 1986 he and his family had moved to a South Pacific island, the 47-square-mile Saipan, one of the Northern Marianas, about 200 miles northwest of Guam. Newspaper articles at the time noted that the island was considered a tax shelter for American citizens. Millard himself insisted that he had moved there because of its beauty and proximity to expanding Pacific markets. He said he planned to become a Saipan entrepreneur and toward that end had already formed a firm, Commonwealth Utilities Corporation, which would look into the privatization of the government-run utility system. ComputerLand officials passed word during the summer of 1986 that Millard intended to sell his ninety-five percent share of the business. Were that to happen, it would mean the sad and disappointing end of a major chapter in Bill Millard's life. During the winter of 1986 he made clear that he had no intention of retiring. No matter what he does in the future, Bill Millard's name will always be linked with ComputerLand, an institution that had much to do with the spread of computers to the public at large.

Computer Science Pioneer

Donald Knuth

The Preeminent Scholar of Computer Science

31

When you read the name Donald Knuth, it is almost always followed by the phrase, "the most important computer science scholar in the world." A second or third name is not mentioned. It is as if Knuth's preeminence precludes others. Though Knuth (the *K* is sounded) is certainly the classic professor, toiling in a crowded, tiny office, what astonishes one is what else he is: gifted writer, composer of music, expert on typography. From the incongruous fact that his very first publication was in *Mad* magazine to the discovery that he once wrote a novella in six days, an image emerges of a most unconventional figure. He is known above all else for his pathbreaking series of books called *The Art of Computer Programming,* widely regarded as the bible of computer science. One reviewer has said that this series is as important a work for computer science as Euclid's was for geometry.

As of the mid-1980s, Knuth was only about midway through the vast project, having published (in 1968, 1969, and 1973) three of the planned seven books. To the probable chagrin of his publishers, he had taken a nine-year detour from the enterprise in order to undertake a new, unexpected challenge: the computerization of typesetting. Knuth's work during this period has revolutionized the field of typography.

Donald Knuth was born on January 10, 1938, in Milwaukee, Wisconsin. His father taught bookkeeping to high-school students and had a printing business at home in the basement. As a child Knuth enjoyed playing with his father's Remington Rand calculator, which could multiply a ten-digit number by a ten-digit number—but took ten to twenty seconds to print the answer. Knuth recalls trying to find the square root of ten with the calculator, by trial and error. Discovering that the answer lay somewhere between 3.16 and 3.17, he concluded that this interesting number must also be the true value of pi—not 3.14, as his schoolbook said. He learned soon enough that his conclusion was nonsense.

If numbers intrigued him, so, equally, did words. During the seventh and eighth grades he spent much time diagramming sentences: the ones in English prose came easy, but sentences in the hymnal seemed impossible. When a Milwaukee candy company ran a contest asking entrants to find how many words could be made out of the letters in "Zeigler's Giant Bar," Knuth feigned a stomachache, remained at home for two weeks, and, using an unabridged dictionary, came up with 4,500 words. This was 2,500 more than the judges had found. Later he realized he could have constructed even more words had he not forgotten to use the apostrophe! The prize was a toboggan for Knuth, a TV for his classroom, and a Zeigler's Giant Bar for everyone in the class.

Knuth's love of mathematics was heightened during his freshman year in high school: he became obsessed with the graphing of algebraic functions—a realm of infinite possibilities. He worked out a system whereby anyone who gave him a pattern of connected straight lines could soon find an equation for that pattern. Knuth traces METAFONT, his system of computer-assisted typography, back to his childhood fondness for graphing.

Physics appealed to him too, and he was torn between that subject and music—a serious piano student, he had also written some orchestrations. Knuth acknowledges having an inferiority complex. That explains, he says, why he has always worked so hard. As a senior at Milwaukee Lutheran High School he worried that low scores in mathematics might keep him from getting into college, an incredible concern considering that he wound up with the all-time record for grades—a 97.5-percent average.

In 1956 he enrolled at Case Institute of Technology in Cleveland, Ohio, as a physics major. It was in his freshman calculus class that he was first exposed to higher mathematics. Again out of fear that he would not do well, Knuth put in extra hours feverishly studying calculus and analytic geometry. He published his first article that freshman year, in, of all places, the June 1957 issue of *Mad* magazine. The title of the piece was, "The Potrzebie System of Weights and Measures." The *Mad* weights and measures provide an alternative to the metric system in which, for example, a million potrzebies is a "furshlugginer potrzebie" and one-millionth of a potrzebie is a "farshimmelt potrzebie." The system was so complete that it included a new calendar based on 100 clarkes (days) per cowznofski.

During the summer between his freshman and sophomore years in college, Knuth encountered a computer for the first time. He had a summer job drawing graphs for statisticians at Case. In the next room there was a new machine, an IBM 650. So infatuated with it was Knuth that he dedicated *The Art of Computer Programming* "to the Type 650 computer once installed at Case Institute of Technology, in remembrance of many pleasant evenings." Some of his teachers advised him to stay away from computers, claiming they would lead him nowhere. But his curiosity was aroused. Once someone had explained to Knuth how the 650 worked, he was spending marathon night-long sessions at the console, excited particularly by its flashing lights.

In the fall of 1957 he took an especially engrossing course in abstract mathematics. The professor gave his students a special problem, not revealing whether a solution was possible; doing the problem was optional, but anyone who did solve it was promised an automatic A in the course. No one in the class saw any hope in attacking the seemingly impossible challenge. But one Saturday, having missed the bus for the marching band, of which he was a member, the nineteen-year-old Knuth found himself with nothing to do and so decided to kill some time by trying to work out the problem. He figured it out, turned in the answer the next Monday, and was immediately awarded an A for the course. Though he felt guilty doing so, he cut class the rest of the term. Over the years, Knuth would send new solutions to the problem to his old professor.

Knuth easily abandoned physics. His lab experiments never seemed to work, he dropped items on the floor, he was often the last to finish. Welding proved a catastrophe: at six feet four inches he was too tall for the welding tables, and he had trouble seeing because his eyeglasses didn't fit under his goggles. He was also scared stiff of getting an electric shock. He dropped physics at the end of his sophomore year and became a mathematics major.

Knuth succeeded in putting his computer expertise to use in the service of no less illustrious an institution than the Case basketball team, of which he was the manager. He worked out a complicated formula for rating each player, resulting in a number that indicated how much of a contribution the player had made to a game, not just the total number of points he had scored. Knuth would sit at the IBM 650 and input the game statistics, with the coach standing nearby. Using the Donald Knuth program, the coach could tell who were truly the most valuable players and could use them accordingly. The program seemed also to have the effect of spurring the players to try harder. In 1960 Case won the league championship, and Knuth's "magic formula" received some unexpected publicity from Walter Cronkite's Sunday news program and from *Newsweek*.

Knuth received a bachelor of science degree in mathematics, summa cum laude, from Case in 1960. He was so impressive a student that the faculty took the unprecedented step of voting him a master's degree at the same time. During the summer of 1960 he worked for the Pasadena office of Burroughs, the office machine firm newly involved in computers; he wrote software and analyzed hardware. For an ALGOL compiler he wrote, Knuth was paid $5,500. Later he would learn how much he had undersold himself: software firms were paying other programmers several times that amount.

He began his doctoral studies in the fall of 1960 at the California Institute of Technology. Word was out that this graduate student knew how to write compilers. And so in January 1962 the publisher Addison-Wesley suggested that he write a book on the subject. Knuth liked the idea. He sketched out twelve chapter topics; the notes he would use in teaching a course at Cal Tech that fall could become the first three chapters.

Cal Tech awarded Knuth a doctorate in mathematics in June 1963. He then joined the school's faculty as an assistant professor. Soon thereafter he began working on a chapter about sorting for his book, although he knew virtually nothing about the subject. Still in its infancy, computer science suffered from a literature that was at best spotty. (Computer science, Knuth liked to say, was nothing more than the study of patterns of 0s and 1s.) When Knuth went to survey the field, he found many of the published articles simply wrong. Thousands of programmers were developing new algorithms all the time for the big mainframes. But if a good idea came along, it would more often than not get lost in a low-circulation journal or technical report. Many programs simply went unread. One result was that people would rediscover techniques and methods that had already been pioneered but were too buried in the literature to have gained any notice. It occurred to Knuth that it would be useful to have a summary of those parts of the literature that were of value. Those who had previously tried summarizing computer programming had been biased by their own theories on the subject, he found. Not having developed any new ideas, yet confident that he was a good writer, Knuth felt he was the right person for the job.

Knuth's aim in this monumental work was to be an adequate spokesman for everyone who had invented computer programming techniques—and to put the existing knowledge in the field into a coherent pattern. His major contribution was to be his organization of the material and his analysis of the methods. He would attempt to develop the most appropriate theories for the various methods and to fill in the gaps in those theories—gaps that he was often the first person to perceive, being the first to put this unorganized material together. With luck, the gap wouldn't be hard to fill, and he would have fun getting first crack at it. If he found a problem intractable, he could state it as a research problem.

At first Knuth believed he would write only one book on compilers. Ater drafting some chapters, however, he felt the book would have to be much larger in scope than first thought. Given the green light by his publisher, he wrote, and wrote, and wrote. By June 1965 he had completed a first draft of twelve chapters. It was 3,000 hand-written pages long! In October he sent off the first chapter to Addison-Wesley, whose editors estimated that, based on the length of that chapter, the book would contain 2,000 printed pages. Addison-Wesley proposed that the twelve chapters be published as seven separate books, containing just one or two chapters each.

Knuth had some fun with the writing. The reader who looks up circular reasoning in the index to volume 1 will be told to "See Reasoning, circular." Turning to "Reasoning, circular," he will be directed to "*See* Circular reasoning." It was Knuth's way of illustrating one of computer software's biggest headaches, the infinite loop.

Chapter 1 became half of volume 1. Volume 2 turned out to be a combination of Knuth's first idea of chapter 2, on random numbers, and chapter 6, originally entitled "Miscellaneous Utility Routines." His excitement in writing volume 2 led him to devote days and nights to the project, prompting a serious ulcer attack in the summer of 1967. He remembers the time well: he was in the middle of Euclid's algorithm—what is now page 333 of volume 2.

The series has turned out to be one of Addison-Wesley's major sellers. In the mid-1980s two thousand copies of each of the three books were still selling each month, a figure that has been constant since the mid-1970s. The work has been translated into Chinese, Rumanian, Japanese, Spanish, and Russian, with Portuguese and Hungarian versions planned. When the Association for Computing Machinery gave Knuth the Turing Award in 1974, it noted that "his series of books have done the most to transfer the whole set of erstwhile esoteric ideas into the standard practices of computer scientists of today. The collections of techniques, algorithms, and relevant theorems in these books have served as the nucleus for developing curricula and as an organizing influence on computer science." More kudos flowed Knuth's way: in 1979, at age forty-one, he was awarded the National Medal of Science by President Jimmy Carter for his work on algorithms.

With his huge size, Donald Knuth is quite a presence. He talks quickly, his hands constantly moving. Among his interests is music. He designed a baroque-style pipe organ with some 1,000 pipes for the Bethany Lutheran Church in Menlo Park, California, and built a slightly smaller version for his home. Since 1968 he has been a member of the Stanford University faculty, as professor of computer science.

It may seem incongruous, but Donald Knuth is a writer of fiction as well. His novella *Surreal Numbers: How Two Ex-Students Turned On to Pure Mathematics and Found Total Happiness* was published by Addison-Wesley in 1974. Woven into the story is an exploration of a new number system invented by Cambridge University's John Horton Conway. Knuth learned of the system from Conway himself over lunch one day in 1972. Afterward, he awoke in the middle of the night and announced to his wife that he had this novella inside him that was eager to get out. She should not worry, however: unlike his computer programming series, this one would take only a week to finish. While on sabbatical in Norway in December 1972, Knuth took a hotel room in downtown Oslo, near where the great Henrik Ibsen had written his plays, and completed the novella in the allotted time. It has sold reasonably well and been translated into many languages. The story's two main characters explore and build Conway's number system, something Knuth was doing himself as he was writing. One reviewer noted that this was the first time a major mathematical discovery had been first published in a piece of fiction. Knuth wrote the book not to teach Conway's theory but to explain how one might craft such a theory.

In the spring of 1977, with no advance warning, Donald Knuth shifted careers in midstream. While looking at the galley proofs of the revised edition of the second volume of his computer programming series, he suddenly sensed that the typography of books was in need of massive overhaul. He wanted to tear the galleys up, they looked so bad. The spacing of the characters was awful, an especially acute problem in books that have both standard type and mathematical equations. Knuth wanted to find out why the printing job—which used photo reproductions of type—was so unattractive. He decided to invest a few months in trying to apply computer science and mathematics to the task of improving the appearance of books. The project ended up taking nine years!

Knuth invented TeX, the first standard language for computer typography, and METAFONT, a system that makes use of classical mathematics to design alphabets. TeX has been called one of the most important inventions in the history of typesetting. Some compare it in significance to the Gutenberg Bible; Knuth is embarrassed by such talk.

TeX allows typesetters to space letters and symbols on the page with a degree of flexibility and of aesthetic quality heretofore out of reach. In the Knuth system the original page is created electronically from a grid of black and white dots on a computer screen. In essence, the computer is instructed, using digital language, where to put the dots. Then the page is copied photographically to become a master plate for printing.

METAFONT permits a designer to create electronically an

entire type face, or font—complete with letters, numbers, and punctuation in a specific style. The font can be put on a video display terminal and immediately changed in all sorts of ways. In the past, type designers were forced to spend months, even years, to get a font perfect; they would often make dozens of drawings of each character. Each small change in a character meant changes in all the others, interrelated as they were in matters of shape, size, and spacing. With METAFONT, one command to the computer can achieve the same result.

Knuth put both programs in the public domain; neither he nor Stanford earned a penny from them. He wrote the programs, he says, out of love for books, and to give the field a necessary push. "I already had a claim to fame. My books were selling well. I didn't want proprietary rights to something I just loved to do. Besides, mathematicians aren't used to getting money for theorems."

When Knuth reset volume 2 of *The Art of Programming,* using METAFONT and TeX, the result was better but not perfect. The numbers were malformed. So he spent another five years working with leading graphic designers in order to refine the new systems and exploit their full potential. In the spring of 1986 his research on typography was concluded, and the five-volume *Computers and Typesetting* was published. The first volume is a user's guide for TeX; the second contains the complete source code listings for TeX; the third and fourth are, respectively, a user's guide for META-FONT and the complete source code listings for it; the fifth volume depicts over 500 examples of METAFONT programming.

Donald Knuth has done perhaps more than any other person to build computer science into an independent discipline. "What unites computer scientists," he has said, "is that we have an academic home where we can talk to people like ourselves. Now we have a name for what we can do well. In the old days some of us were called physicists or mathematicians; but we didn't really fit in any existing field. Today we are called computer scientists. Once we got together, we could exploit the power of computers."

Knuth is still thinking about volume 4 of *The Art of Computer Programming.* On that very first day in 1962 when he planned the project, he included a chapter entitled "Combinatorial Algorithms." What was then almost an afterthought to Knuth has become the most developed area of computer programming. He doubts whether he can cover the subject in just one volume. After he completes all seven volumes of his programming series, he wants to write music, a part of his life almost as important to him as computer science. As Peter Gordon, Knuth's editor at Addison-Wesley, observed at a reception honoring his author in May 1986, "If he has been compared to Euclid for his work on *The Art of Computer Programming* and to Gutenberg for his work on TeX, we can only wonder what the next comparison will be."

Knuth estimates that it might take another twenty years to write the remaining four books in the programming series. There is so much yet to do. However, he has already concluded just what computers are all about. He has an elegant formula for describing their nature and function: The difference between art and science is that science is what people understand well enough to explain to a computer. All else is art.

Notes

Charles Babbage

p. 7 "The whole of arithmetic now appeared. . . ." Quoted in Joel Shurkin, *Engines of the Mind* (New York: Norton, 1984), p. 47.

Alan Turing

p. 19 "I propose to consider. . . ." Quoted in Dirk Hanson, *The New Alchemists* (Boston: Little, Brown, 1982), p. 39.

John von Neumann

p. 27 "The conversation soon turned to my work." Herman H. Goldstine, *The Computer: From Pascal to von Neumann* (Princeton: Princeton University Press, 1972), p. 182.

p. 27 "The whole atmosphere of our conversation. . . ." Goldstine, *The Computer,* p. 182.

p. 29 "It is obvious. . . ." Goldstine, *The Computer,* pp. 197–198.

Claude Shannon

p. 34 "That's the story. . . ." Quotes from Claude Shannon are, except where otherwise indicated, taken from the author's interview with him on July 16, 1985.

Konrad Zuse

p. 47 "I wasn't a magician. . . ." All quotes from Konrad Zuse are taken from the author's interview with him on July 12, 1985.

John Atanasoff

p. 53 "After Babbage, I was the one. . . ." All quotes from John Atanasoff are taken from the author's interview with him on January 30, 1985.

p. 60 The source for the von Neumann report is *The Moore School Lectures,* edited by Martin Campbell-Kelly and Michael R. Williams (Cambridge, Mass.: MIT Press, 1985), p. 514.

p. 61 "J.V. was a most unusual. . . ." Robert Stewart, "On the Surface," Naval Surface Weapons Center, September 14, 1984, p. 7.

p. 61 "If you will help us. . . ." As related by Atanasoff in his interview with the author on January 30, 1985.

p. 62 "Eckert and Mauchly did not. . . ." Quoted in John V. Atanasoff, "Advent of Electronic Digital Computing," *Annals of the History of Computing,* July 1984, p. 27.

John Mauchly and J. Presper Eckert

p. 67 On December 4, 1940, Mauchly wrote. . . . Kathleen R. Mauchly, "John Mauchly's Early Years," *Annals of the History of Computing,* April 1984, p. 124.

p. 69 ". . . which are nothing like your machine. . . ." Quoted in Joel Shurkin, *Engines of the Mind* (New York: Norton, 1984), p. 100.

p. 73 "Watch this. . . ." Mrs. Kathleen Mauchly provided this account in an interview with the author on February 3, 1985.

Howard Aiken

p. 83 ". . . a switchboard. . . ." Quoted in the *Communication of the Association for Computing Machinery,* June 1962, p. 298.

p. 83 "Rather suddenly. . . ." Quoted in a Memorial Minute adopted by the Harvard Faculty of Arts and Sciences, May 21, 1974.

p. 85 "No one looking. . . ." Interview with the author on January 30, 1985.

p. 88 "Don't worry about people. . . ." Quoted by Kenneth E. Iverson at Glen Riddle, Pennsylvania, in April 1973.

p. 89 "[He was] at the height. . . ." Brooks was speaking at the American Federation of Information Processing Societies' Pioneer Day, 1983.

Jay Forrester

p. 95 "There it is. . . ." All quotes from Jay Forrester are taken from the author's interview with him on August 5, 1985.

Thomas Watson, Sr.

p. 108 "I wonder if I might. . . ." Quoted in Katharine Davis Fishman, *The Computer Establishment* (New York: Harper and Row, 1981), p. 43.

William Norris

p. 115 ". . . the dumbest thing he ever did. . . ." All quotes from William Norris are taken from the author's interview with him on January 28, 1985.

Ross Perot

p. 127 "A lot of guys. . . ." *Business Week,* October 6, 1986.

p. 129 ". . . had never been in anything. . . ." Quotes from Ross Perot are, except where otherwise indicated, taken from the author's interview with him on January 24, 1985.

p. 135 "It takes five years. . . ." *Wall Street Journal,* July 23, 1986.

William Shockley

p. 142 "I allowed myself to be stopped. . . ." Quoted in Shirley Thomas, *Men in Space* (Radnor, Pa.: Chilton Book Company, 1962), p. 176. Copyright with author; reprinted with permission of the publisher.

p. 143 "He said he was looking forward. . . ." Interview with the author on January 16, 1985.

p. 144 "The aim was a general one. . . ." Interview with the author, January 16, 1985.

p. 146 "The things you can do. . . ." Quoted in Thomas, *Men in Space,* p. 188.

p. 147 "I think there was an inevitability. . . ." Interview with the author, January 16, 1985.

p. 149 "A particular talent. . . ." Quoted in Thomas, *Men in Space,* p. 195.

p. 150 ". . . the brutal elimination mechanism. . . ." Quoted in *Discover,* April 1982.

Robert Noyce

p. 157 ". . . really more of a brute-force approach. . . ." Quotes from Robert Noyce are, except where otherwise indicated, taken from the author's interview with him on January 21, 1985.

p. 158 "It would be desirable. . . ." Quoted in T. R. Reid, *The Chip* (New York: Simon and Schuster, 1984).

p. 158 "We were really working. . . ." Quoted in Reid, *The Chip.*

Jack Kilby

p. 165 "If you want to be totally creative. . . ." All quotes from Jack Kilby are taken from the author's interview with him on January 25, 1985.

Ted Hoff

p. 175 ". . . that the computer, a little chunk of intelligence. . . ." All quotes from Ted Hoff are taken from the author's interview with him on January 18, 1985.

p. 177 "He had the uncanny. . . ." "The Man Who Launched the Computer Revolution," *at Rensselaer* (Rensselaer alumni bulletin), Winter 1983.

Gene Amdahl

p. 186 "So . . . I decided. . . ." All quotes from Gene Amdahl are taken from the author's interview with him on January 16, 1985.

Seymour Cray

p. 195 ". . . simple, dumb things." Quoted in *Update,* a publication for Friends of the University of Minnesota, Spring 1983, vol. 10, no. 2.

Gordon Bell

p. 212 "All that happens. . . ." All quotes from Gordon Bell are taken from the author's interview with him on February 9, 1986.

Grace Hopper

p. 220 "When I did geometry problems. . . ." All quotes from Grace Hopper are taken from the author's interview with her on January 30, 1985.

John Backus

p. 233 "Can a machine translate. . . ." Quoted in Richard L. Wexelblat, ed., *History of Programming Languages* (New York: Academic Press, 1981), p. 28.

p. 234 "Today . . . a programmer is often. . . ." John Backus, "Programming in America in the 1950s—Some Personal Impressions," in N. Metropolis, *A History of Computing in the Twentieth Century* (New York: Academic Press, 1980), p. 126.

p. 234 "They wanted to convince others. . . ." Backus, "Programming in America in the 1950s," pp. 126–127.

p. 238 "I worked very hard. . . ." From a talk to the Industrial Research Institute, San Francisco, November 8, 1983.

p. 239 "The functional approach. . . ." John Backus, "Function-Level Computing," *IEEE Spectrum,* August 1982, p. 22.

p. 239 "An alternative functional style. . . ." John Backus, "Can Programming Be Liberated from the von Neumann Style? A Functional Style and Its Algebra of Problems," *Communication of the Association for Computer Machinery,* August 1978, p. 613.

p. 239 "I'm in the business. . . ." Interview with the author on January 18, 1985.

John Kemeny and Thomas Kurtz

p. 242 "I occasionally kid Tom. . . ." All quotes from John Kemeny and Thomas Kurtz are taken from the author's interview with them on February 7, 1985.

Gary Kildall

p. 257 "There was never any thought. . . ." All quotes from Dorothy McEwen are taken from the author's interview with her on January 21, 1985.

p. 259 ". . . threw a nondisclosure agreement. . . ." All quotes from Gary Kildall are taken from the author's interview with him on January 21, 1985.

William Gates

p. 264 ". . . was not a mainstream thing. . . ." Quotes from William Gates are taken from the author's telephone interview with him on August 6, 1985.

Dennis Ritchie and Kenneth Thompson

p. 274 "The crystallization of the main development. . . ." Quotes from Dennis Ritchie and Kenneth Thompson are, except where otherwise indicated, taken from the author's interview with them on February 4, 1985.

p. 275 "Multics turned into. . . ." Quoted in Alfred Rosenfeld, "1982 Award for Achievement," *Electronics,* October 20, 1982, p. 5.

p. 276 "What we wanted to preserve. . . ." Dennis Ritchie, "The Evolution of the UNIX Time-Sharing System," in Jeffrey M. Tobias, ed., *Language Design and Programming Methodology* (Berlin, New York: Springer-Verlag, 1980), p. 1.

Daniel Bricklin

p. 285 "If I had a nickel. . . ." Quotes from Daniel Bricklin are, except where otherwise indicated, taken from the author's interview with him on February 6, 1985.

p. 291 "VisiCalc could someday. . . ." Quoted in *Inc.,* January 1982.

p. 294 "I'm not rich. . . ." Quoted in *Newsweek,* November 11, 1985.

Nolan Bushnell

p. 298 "I knew I was coming of age. . . ." Quotes from Nolan Bushnell are, except where otherwise indicated, taken from the author's interview with him on February 10, 1985.

p. 306 ". . . video games that spill. . . ." Quoted in *Newsweek,* May 5, 1986.

Steven Jobs

p. 321 "It has never before. . . ." Quoted in *InfoWorld*, November 17, 1986.

p. 321 ". . . hit one out of the ball park." Quoted in *Business Week*, February 9, 1987.

p. 321 "In terms of a start-up company. . . ." Quoted in the *New York Times*, February 2, 1987.

Adam Osborne

p. 323 "I saw an opportunity. . . ." All quotes from Adam Osborne are taken from the author's interview with him on January 17, 1985.

William Millard

p. 331 "I hear numbers. . . ." Quoted in the *San Jose Mercury News*, April 30, 1984.

Donald Knuth

p. 350 "I already had a claim. . . ." Quotes from Donald Knuth are taken from the author's interview with him on January 18, 1985.

p. 351 "If he has been compared. . . ." Quoted in *TUGboat*, vol. 7 (1986), no. 2, p. 95.

Bibliography

Asimov, Isaac. *Asimov's New Guide to Science* (New York: Basic Books, 1960).

Augarten, Stan. *Bit by Bit: An Illustrated History of Computers* (New York: Ticknor and Fields, 1984).

Bell, C. Gordon; Mudge, J. Craig; and McNamara, John E. *Computer Engineering: A DEC View of Hardware Systems Design* (Bedford, Massachusetts: Digital Press, 1978).

Braun, Ernest, and Macdonald, Stuart. *Revolution in Miniature: The History and Impact of Semiconductor Electronics* (Cambridge: Cambridge University Press, 1978).

Chandor, Anthony, with Graham, John, and Williamson, Robin. *The Penguin Dictionary of Computers* (Middlesex, England: Penguin Books, 1970).

Darcy, Laura, and Boston, Louise. *Webster's New World of Computer Terms* (New York: Simon and Schuster, 1983).

Ditlea, Steve, editor. *Digital Deli* (New York: Workman Publishing, 1984).

Drury, Donald William. *The Art of Computer Programming* (Blue Ridge Summit, Pennsylvania: TAB Books, 1983).

Feigenbaum, Edward A., and McCorduck, Pamela A. *The Fifth Generation: Artificial Intelligence and Japan's Computer Challenge to the World* (New York: Addison-Wesley, 1983).

Fishman, Katharine Davis. *The Computer Establishment* (New York: McGraw-Hill, 1981).

Follett, Ken. *On Wings of Eagles* (New York: New American Library, 1983).

Freiberger, Paul, and Swaine, Michael. *Fire in the Valley* (Berkeley, California: Osborne/McGraw-Hill, 1984).

Garr, Doug. *Woz: The Prodigal Son of Silicon Valley* (New York: Avon Books, 1984).

Goldstine, Herman H. *The Computer: From Pascal to von Neumann* (Princeton, New Jersey: Princeton University Press, 1972).

Hanson, Dirk. *The New Alchemists* (New York: Avon Books, 1982).

Heim, Steve J. *John von Neumann and Norbert Weiner: From Mathematics to the Technologies of Life and Death* (Cambridge, Massachusetts: MIT Press, 1980).

Hodges, Andrew. *Alan Turing: The Enigma* (New York: Simon and Schuster, 1983).

Hopper, Grace Murray, and Mandell, Steven L. *Understanding Computers* (St. Paul, Minnesota: West Publishing Company, 1984).

Hyman, Anthony. *Charles Babbage: Pioneer of the Computer* (Oxford: Oxford University Press, 1984).

Kidder, Tracy. *The Soul of a New Machine* (Boston: Little, Brown, 1981).

Levering, Robert; Katz, Michael; and Moskowitz, Milton. *The Computer Entrepreneurs: Who's Making It Big and How in America's Upstart Industry* (New York: New American Library, 1984).

Levy, Steven. *Hackers: Heroes of the Computer Revolution* (Garden City, New York: Doubleday, 1984).

McClellan, Stephen T. *The Coming Computer Industry Shakeout: Winners, Losers, and Survivors* (New York: John Wiley and Sons, 1984).

McCorduck, Pamela. *Machines Who Think* (New York: W. H. Freeman and Company, 1979).

Mahon, Thomas. *Charged Bodies: People, Power, and Paradox in Silicon Valley* (New York: American Library,1985).

Moritz, Michael. *The Little Kingdom: The Private Story of Apple Computer* (New York: William Morrow, 1984).

Norris, William C. *New Frontiers for Business Leadership* (Minneapolis: Dorn Books, 1983).

Osborne, Adam, and Dvorak, John. *Hypergrowth: The Rise and Fall of Osborne Computer Corporation* (Berkeley, California: Idthekkethan Publishing Co., 1984).

Peters, Thomas J., and Waterman, Robert H., Jr. *In Search of Excellence* (New York: Warner Books, 1984).

Reid, T. R. *The Chip: How Two Americans Invented the Microchip and Launched a Revolution* (New York: Simon and Schuster, 1984).

Rheingold, Howard. *Tools for Thought: The People and Ideas behind the Next Computer Revolution* (New York: Simon and Schuster, 1985).

Rogers, Everett M., and Larsen, Judith K. *Silicon Valley Fever: Growth of High-Technology Culture* (New York: Basic Books, 1984).

Shelley, John. *Microfuture* (London: Pitman Books, 1981).

Shurkin, Joel. *Engines of the Mind: A History of the Computer* (New York: W. W. Norton, 1984).

Sobel, Robert. *IBM: Colossus in Transition* (New York: Bantam Books, 1981).

Williams, Michael R. *A History of Computing Technology* (Englewood Cliffs, New Jersey: Prentice-Hall, 1985).

Zientara, Marguerite. *The History of Computing* (Framingham, Massachusetts: CW Communications, 1981).

Illustration Credits

Index